25 YEARS *of* FAVORITE BRAND NAME™ BAKING

Publications International, Ltd.

Favorite Brand Name Recipes at www.fbnr.com

Pictured on the front cover *(clockwise from top right):* Chocolate Chip & Macadamia Cookies *(page 152),* Chocolate Syrup Swirl Cake *(page 244),* Lollipop Cookies *(page 148)* and Aloha Bread *(page 80).*
Pictured on the back cover *(from left):* Strawberry Cinnamon French Toast *(page 58)* and Blueberry Yogurt Cake *(page 236).*

ISBN-13: 978-1-4127-2493-7
ISBN-10: 1-4127-2493-7

Library of Congress Control Number: 2006903674

Manufactured in China.

8 7 6 5 4 3 2 1

Microwave Cooking: Microwave ovens vary in wattage. Use the cooking times as guidelines and check for doneness before adding more time.

Preparation/Cooking Times: Preparation times are based on the approximate amount of time required to assemble the recipe before cooking, baking, chilling or serving. These times include preparation steps such as measuring, chopping and mixing. The fact that some preparations and cooking can be done simultaneously is taken into account. Preparation of optional ingredients and serving suggestions is not included.

Table of Contents

It's amazing to think how life has changed in the last 25 years, but the world of baking has hardly changed at all. Home-baked treats will always have that special touch that store-bought items will never quite capture. Maybe it's because of the thought and love that go into creating a sweet or savory creation right in your own kitchen. Whether you are an expert with cakes and pies or are turning on the oven for the first time, this collection of classic and contemporary baking recipes will be a treasured asset when you are ready to bake for any occasion. **25 Years of Favorite Brand Name™ Baking** is filled with recipes for timeless desserts, cakes and pies, adorable cookies and cupcakes, fabulous yeast and quick breads, as well as a variety of year-round holiday treats. In addition, make sure to take advantage of these baking techniques and tips to get you started.

Yeast Breads

Proofing the Yeast: This step ensures that the yeast is still alive before you move onto the next step in a recipe. Yeast that is not living can not make bread rise. To proof, sprinkle dry yeast and sugar over warm water (105° to 110°F), using the amounts specified in the recipe. Allow the mixture to stand 5 to 10 minutes or until bubbly. If the mixture does not bubble, it means that the yeast in inactive and should be thrown away. If this is the case, check the expiration date on the package or the temperature of the water—water that is too hot will kill the yeast.

Kneading the Dough: The way that ingredients are combined will affect the outcome of the recipe. After the ingredients are mixed together, either by hand or an electric mixer, it is time to get your hands dirty! Kneading the dough develops the gluten, the protein in flour, that will create the elasticity in bread dough. The elastic strands trap carbon dioxide, which makes the bread rise. To knead properly, place the dough on a floured surface.

Using lightly floured hands, bring a portion of the dough toward you, then push the dough away from you with the heel of your hand. Turn and repeat this technique until the dough is smooth and fairly elastic. Be careful not to overknead, because this will create a tough end product.

Fermentation: The time that yeast dough is left to rise is known as fermentation. Place the dough into a lightly oiled bowl, turn dough over to coat top with oil and cover the dough with a clean kitchen towel to prevent drying. Place the bowl in a warm, draft-free place (75° to 85°F) until the dough is doubled in size.

Punching Down the Dough: After fermentation, gently punch down the dough using your fingers. This is done to redistribute the gas throughout the dough and relax the gluten that has stretched during fermentation.

Portioning the Dough: After punching down the dough, it is now ready to be formed into loaves or other shapes. Cover the dough that you're not working with to prevent drying.

Proofing the Dough: This is the final rise of the dough before baking. Dough should be covered and left to rise in a warm, draft-free place. The dough is ready to bake when it has doubled in size and springs back when lightly touched.

Baking: Follow the recipe directions for specific baking times and temperature settings.

Storing Bread: Once the bread is completely cooled, wrap it in plastic wrap or place it in a resealable food storage bag. Bread should be kept at room temperature up to a week or frozen up to six months. Don't refrigerate bread, because it will become stale more quickly.

Cookie and Bar Cookie Tips

- Cookies that are uniform in size and shape will finish baking at the same time. To create uniform drop cookies, use a small ice cream scoop with a release bar. When slicing refrigerator cookies, use gentle pressure and a back-and-forth sawing motion. Rotating the roll between slices will keep the roll round.

- Unbaked dough can be refrigerated for up to two weeks and frozen for up to six weeks. Make sure to wrap it tightly to prevent drying.

- The best cookie sheets to use are those with little or no sides. They should be shiny rather than dark. Dark cookie sheets will result in cookies with dark bottoms.

- When making brownies or bar cookies, use the pan size called for in the recipe. Baking times must be adjusted if using another pan.

- Allow cookie sheets to cool between batches. Otherwise, the dough will spread too quickly if placed on a hot cookie sheet.

- Store soft cookies in airtight containers at room temperature. Keep crisp cookies in containers with loose-fitting lids. Bar cookies and brownies may be stored, covered, in their baking pans once they are completely cool.

- Freeze crisp cookies, buttery bar cookies and brownies in freezer bags up to six months. Allow them to thaw at room temperature. Fruit-filled, meringue-based and chocolate-dipped cookies don't freeze well.

Types of Cakes

Cakes are generally divided into 3 groups based on how they are leavened. Shortened cakes are chemically leavened, foam cakes are air leavened and chiffon cakes are a combination of both.

Shortened Cakes: This category includes pound cakes, most chocolate cakes and fruitcakes. They use baking powder or baking soda as the primary leavening agent. Shortened cakes contain fat in the form of butter, shortening, margarine or oil. Solid fats, such as butter, shortening and margarine need to be softened to room temperature before beating together with sugar for the method known as creaming. The fat-sugar mixture should be smooth, light and fluffy.

Foam Cakes: Angel food cakes, sponge cakes, genoise and flourless chocolate cakes fall into the foam cake category. These cakes rely only on air beaten into eggs or egg whites for leavening. They contain no baking powder or soda. Angel food cakes contain no fat because they are made using only egg whites. Sponge cake and genoise do contain some fat, because they are made using a combination of egg whites and yolks. Flourless chocolate cake is also leavened using eggs and some type of fat, usually butter.

Chiffon Cakes: This type of cake is a hybrid because it shares characteristics of both shortened and foam cakes. Chiffon cakes usually contain a combination of fat, eggs and a chemical leavening agent.

Understanding Techniques for Successful Cakes

Preparing the Batter: When mixing the batter for shortened cakes, softened butter or shortening should be creamed with sugar.

The eggs (or yolks, if the whites are beaten separately) should be at room temperature, added one at a time, and beaten thoroughly after each addition. Combined liquids and flavorings, such as buttermilk or vanilla, should be added alternately with dry ingredients. The liquid and flour mixtures are generally divided into halves or thirds before adding. As the flour is added, it is important not to overmix or the cake will be tough. If the egg whites are beaten separately, they should be gently folded into the batter with a rubber spatula as the final step. Throughout the mixing process, be sure to scrape the side and bottom of the bowl with a rubber spatula to ensure that all of the ingredients are well blended. The cake pans should always be greased and floured to ensure easy removal of the cakes.

Shortened cakes that use vegetable oil or melted fat are mixed differently. Combine all of the dry ingredients, such as flour, sugar, baking powder and spices, in a large mixing bowl. Add the wet ingredients, such as liquid, fat, eggs and flavorings, either gradually if combined, or one at a time and mix thoroughly after each addition.

When preparing most foam cakes, the following general recommendations are useful to remember. (Techniques for sponge and chiffon cakes may vary from these guidelines, so be sure to follow each recipe carefully.) The egg yolks should be separated from the egg whites, and the egg whites placed in a very large, perfectly clean bowl. (Any trace of fat will interfere with foaming and will prevent the whites from reaching their full volume.) With an electric mixer on low speed, mix the whites until they are foamy. Add a small amount of cream of tartar to stabilize the egg white foam. Increase the mixer speed to high and beat until soft peaks form. For angel food cake, some sugar should be beaten in, a little at a time, until the whites are thick and glossy and stiff peaks form. Very gently fold in the flour mixture.

(Cake flour is generally used in angel food cake; it should be sifted at least three times. In angel food and some chiffon cake recipes, part of the sugar is sifted with the flour.) Cake pans for foam cakes are not greased, as grease will prevent satisfactory rising.

Baking: After pouring batter into the cake pan, immediately place it in the center of a preheated oven. Cake batter should not sit before baking, because chemical leaveners begin working as soon as they are mixed with liquids and the air in foam batters will begin to dissipate. Oven racks may need to be set lower for cakes baked in tube pans. If two racks are used, arrange them so they divide the oven into thirds; stagger the pans so they are not directly over each other. Avoid opening the oven door during the first half of the baking time. The oven temperature must remain constant in order for the cake to rise properly. Most cakes are considered done when a toothpick inserted into the center comes out clean and the edges of the cake begin to pull away from the side of the pan.

Cooling: Many cakes can be removed from the pan after 10 to 15 minutes of cooling on a wire rack. Two important exceptions are angel food cakes and flourless cakes. Because they have a more delicate structure, they are cooled completely in the pan. Angel food cakes and

some chiffon cakes are cooled in the pan upside down. An angel food cake pan has three metal feet on which the inverted pan stands for cooling. If you use a tube pan instead, invert the pan on a funnel or narrow-necked bottle.

Before attempting to remove a cake from its pan, carefully run a table knife or narrow metal spatula around the outside of the cake to loosen it from the pan. Using oven mitts or hot pads (if the pan is hot), place a wire cooling rack on top of the cake and pan. Turn the cake over so that the wire rack is on the bottom. Gently tap the pan and lightly shake it to release the cake from the pan. Place the rack on a counter and remove the pan.

Frosting: Make sure the cake is completely cool and brush off any loose crumbs from the cake's surface before frosting it. To keep the cake plate clean, place small pieces of waxed paper under the edges of the cake; remove them after the cake has been frosted. For best results, use a flat metal spatula for applying frosting. To achieve a more professional look, first apply a thin layer of frosting on the cake as a base coat and place cake in the refrigerator for a few minutes to help seal in any remaining crumbs. Then apply the rest of the frosting and decorate as desired.

Weights and Measures

Dash = less than ⅛ teaspoon

½ tablespoon = 1½ teaspoons

1 tablespoon = 3 teaspoons

2 tablespoons = ⅛ cup

¼ cup = 4 tablespoons

⅓ cup = 5 tablespoons plus 1 teaspoon

½ cup = 8 tablespoons

⅔ cup = 10 tablespoons plus 2 teaspoons

¾ cup = 12 tablespoons

1 cup = 16 tablespoons

½ pint = 1 cup or 8 fluid ounces

1 pint = 2 cups or 16 fluid ounces

1 quart = 4 cups or 2 pints or 32 fluid ounces

1 gallon = 16 cups or 4 quarts

1 pound = 16 ounces

Perfect Pastry Crusts

For tender, flaky pie crusts, follow these basic guidelines:

- If you use butter in your pastry dough, it must be chilled. If the butter is soft, it can not be distributed evenly throughout the flour. Vegetable shortening and lard, although soft at room temperature, do not need to be chilled. Make sure that the added liquid is cold. The cold liquid helps to keep the fat solid.

- Blend the flour and salt together, then cut the fat in quickly with a pastry blender or two knives—or use your fingertips—until the fat particles are about the size of peas.

- Add cold water gradually, 1 tablespoon at a time, stirring lightly with a fork. Add just enough water so that the mixture holds together with slight pressure and can be gathered into a ball. Too little water produces a dry, crumbly pastry that will not hold together; too much water makes the dough sticky and develops the gluten.

- Do not overwork the dough. Wrap the ball of dough in plastic wrap and refrigerate it for at least 1 hour. Chilling the dough makes it easier to handle and helps prevent shrinkage during baking.

- Before rolling the dough, flour the rolling pin and work surface just enough to prevent sticking. Handle the dough quickly and lightly.

- Place the chilled dough on a lightly floured surface and flatten it into a ½-inch-thick circle. Roll the dough with a floured rolling pin, pressing out from the center to the edge using quick, short strokes. Continue rolling until the dough is ⅛ inch thick and 2 inches larger than the inverted pie pan.

- Loosely fold the dough into quarters and place the point of the folded dough into the center of the pie pan. Gently unfold the dough and ease it into the pan; do not stretch the dough or it will shrink during baking. For a single-crust pie, trim the dough and flute the edge.

Types of Baked Pies

A pie is a sweet or savory baked dish with a crust and a filling. Dessert pies may be baked or chilled. They are usually made in a pie pan. They feature a variety of crusts made from pastry dough, graham cracker or cookie crumbs.

Custard pies are single-crust baked pies with a sweet, rich custard filling made from eggs and milk. Fruit pies may have single or double crusts. They are filled with fresh, canned or frozen fruit and baked.

Single-Crust Pies: Some single-crust pies, like custard pies, are baked in an unbaked pastry shell. Others require the shell to be prebaked so

that it does not become soggy. If the pastry shell is to be "blind baked" (baked without the filling), prick the dough all over with a fork. Line the pastry shell with foil, waxed paper or parchment paper and spread dried beans or pie weights over the bottom. Weighing down the pastry prevents it from puffing up and losing its shape during baking. (The dried beans are not edible after baking, but they can be reused for blind baking.) The pastry can be fully or partially baked in this manner. Cool it completely before adding the filling.

Double-Crust Pies: These pies usually contain fruit between two unbaked layers of pastry. Spoon the filling into the prepared pastry shell and brush the rim of the shell with water. Roll out the top crust and place it over the filling. Press the pastry edges together to seal, then trim and flute. Cut a few slits or vents in the top crust to allow steam to escape. Before baking a double-crust pie, try glazing the top crust with milk or cream to promote browning. Brushing it with beaten egg will add color and shine; sprinkling it with granulated sugar will add a little sparkle. If the crust is browning too quickly, cover the pie loosely with foil and continue baking.

Fluting Pastry Crusts

Cutouts: Trim the edge of the bottom crust even with the pie plate. Re-roll dough scraps and cut out the shapes using a tiny cookie cutter. Moisten the pastry edge with beaten egg and place the cutouts on the pastry edge, overlapping slightly. Press into place. Brush with beaten egg or milk to add color and shine.

Fork Edge: Trim the edge of the bottom crust even with the pie plate. Press the crust to the rim of the pie plate using a four-tined fork. Leave about 1¼ inches between marks. Go around the crust edge again, filling in spaces with the fork held at an angle.

Pinwheel: Fold the overhang of the bottom crust under; press flat. Cut slits around the edge of the pastry the width of the pie plate rim, leaving about 1 inch between slits. Fold under on a diagonal to form pinwheel points.

Rope Edge: Fold the overhang of the bottom crust under and stand the edge up. Press your thumb into the pastry at an angle. Pinch the pastry between your thumb and the knuckle of your index finger, rolling your knuckle towards your thumb. Place your thumb in the groove left by your finger and continue around the edge.

Substitution List

IF YOU DON'T HAVE:	USE:
1 teaspoon baking powder	¼ teaspoon baking soda + ½ teaspoon cream of tartar
½ cup firmly packed brown sugar	½ cup granulated sugar mixed with 2 tablespoons molasses
1 cup buttermilk	1 tablespoon lemon juice or vinegar plus milk to equal 1 cup (Stir; let mixture stand 5 minutes.)
1 ounce (1 square) unsweetened baking chocolate	3 tablespoons unsweetened cocoa + 1 tablespoon shortening
3 ounces (3 squares) semisweet baking chocolate	3 ounces (½ cup) semisweet chocolate morsels
½ cup corn syrup	½ cup granulated sugar + 2 tablespoons liquid
1 cup honey	1¼ cups granulated sugar + ¼ cup water
1 teaspoon freshly grated orange peel	½ teaspoon dried peel or lemon peel
1 teaspoon pumpkin pie spice	Combine: ½ teaspoon ground cinnamon, ¼ teaspoon ground nutmeg and ⅛ teaspoon each ground allspice and cardamom

Marvelous Muffins & Scones

Confetti Scones

2 teaspoons olive oil
⅓ cup finely chopped red bell pepper
⅓ cup finely chopped green bell pepper
½ teaspoon dried thyme
1 cup all-purpose flour
¼ cup whole wheat flour
1½ teaspoons baking powder
½ teaspoon baking soda
½ teaspoon sugar
¼ teaspoon ground red pepper
⅛ teaspoon salt
⅓ cup sour cream
⅓ cup milk
2 tablespoons minced green onions
¼ cup grated Parmesan cheese
Nonstick cooking spray

1. Preheat oven to 400°F. Line baking sheets with parchment paper; set aside.

2. Heat oil in small skillet over medium heat. Add bell peppers and thyme; cook and stir 5 minutes or until tender. Set aside. Combine all-purpose flour, whole wheat flour, baking powder, baking soda, sugar, red pepper and salt in large bowl; mix well. Stir in sour cream, milk and green onions until sticky dough is formed. Stir in cheese and bell pepper mixture. Do not overmix.

3. Drop dough by rounded tablespoonfuls onto prepared baking sheets. Spray tops lightly with cooking spray. Place scones in oven; *immediately reduce oven temperature to 375°F.* Bake 13 to 15 minutes or until golden. Remove to wire rack to cool. *Makes 24 scones*

Blueberry White Chip Muffins

2 cups all-purpose flour
½ cup granulated sugar
¼ cup packed brown sugar
2½ teaspoons baking powder
½ teaspoon salt
¾ cup milk
1 large egg, lightly beaten
¼ cup butter or margarine, melted
½ teaspoon grated lemon peel
2 cups (12-ounce package) NESTLÉ® TOLL HOUSE® Premier White Morsels, *divided*
1½ cups fresh or frozen blueberries
Streusel Topping (recipe follows)

PREHEAT oven to 375°F. Paper-line 18 muffin cups.

COMBINE flour, granulated sugar, brown sugar, baking powder and salt in large bowl. Stir in milk, egg, butter and lemon peel. Stir in *1½ cups* morsels and blueberries. Spoon into prepared muffin cups, filling almost full. Sprinkle with Streusel Topping.

BAKE for 22 to 25 minutes or until wooden pick inserted into centers comes out clean. Cool in pans for 5 minutes; remove to wire racks to cool slightly.

PLACE *remaining* morsels in small, *heavy-duty* resealable plastic food storage bag. Microwave on MEDIUM-HIGH (70%) power for 30 seconds; knead. Microwave at additional 10- to 15-second intervals, kneading until smooth. Cut tiny corner from bag; squeeze to drizzle over muffins. Serve warm. *Makes 18 muffins*

Streusel Topping: COMBINE ⅓ cup granulated sugar, ¼ cup all-purpose flour and ¼ teaspoon ground cinnamon in small bowl. Cut in 3 tablespoons butter or margarine with pastry blender or two knives until mixture resembles coarse crumbs.

helpful hint:

Streusel, a word meaning "sprinkle" in German, is a crumbly mixture of flour, sugar, spices and sometimes nuts. This mixture is used to top coffeecakes, muffins, pies and tea breads before they are baked. This results in a crunchy, crumbly topping that adds both flavor and texture to baked goods.

Blueberry White Chip Muffins

Double Chocolate Zucchini Muffins

2⅓ cups all-purpose flour
1¼ cups sugar
⅓ cup unsweetened cocoa powder
2 teaspoons baking powder
1½ teaspoons ground cinnamon
1 teaspoon baking soda
½ teaspoon salt
1 cup sour cream
½ cup vegetable oil
2 eggs, beaten
¼ cup milk
1 cup milk chocolate chips
1 cup shredded zucchini

1. Preheat oven to 400°F. Grease 12 jumbo (3½-inch) muffin cups.

2. Combine flour, sugar, cocoa, baking powder, cinnamon, baking soda and salt in large bowl. Combine sour cream, oil, eggs and milk in small bowl until blended; stir into flour mixture just until moistened. Fold in chocolate chips and zucchini. Spoon into prepared muffin cups, filling half full.

3. Bake 25 to 30 minutes until toothpick inserted into centers comes out clean. Cool in pan on wire rack 5 minutes. Remove from pan. Cool completely on wire rack. Store tightly covered at room temperature. *Makes 12 jumbo muffins*

Orange-Currant Scones

1½ cups all-purpose flour
¼ cup plus 1 teaspoon sugar, divided
1 teaspoon baking powder
¼ teaspoon salt
¼ teaspoon baking soda
⅓ cup dried currants
1 tablespoon grated fresh orange peel
6 tablespoons (¾ stick) chilled butter, cut into small pieces
½ cup buttermilk, plain yogurt or sour cream

1. Preheat oven to 425°F. Lightly grease baking sheet. Combine flour, ¼ cup sugar, baking powder, salt and baking soda in large bowl. Stir in currants and orange peel.

2. Cut in butter with pastry blender or 2 knives until mixture resembles coarse crumbs. Stir in buttermilk until mixture forms soft dough that clings together. (Dough will be tacky.)

3. Lightly flour hands and shape dough into a ball. Pat dough into 8-inch round on prepared baking sheet. Cut dough into 8 wedges with floured chef's knife.

4. Sprinkle wedges with remaining 1 teaspoon sugar. Bake 18 to 20 minutes or until lightly browned. *Makes 8 scones*

Double Chocolate Zucchini Muffins

Miniature Fruit Muffins

    1 cup whole wheat flour
    ¾ cup all-purpose flour
    ½ cup packed dark brown sugar
    2 teaspoons baking powder
    ½ teaspoon baking soda
    ¼ teaspoon salt
    1 cup buttermilk, divided
    ¾ cup frozen blueberries
    1 small ripe banana, mashed
    ¼ teaspoon vanilla
    ⅓ cup unsweetened applesauce
    2 tablespoons raisins
    ½ teaspoon ground cinnamon

1. Preheat oven to 400°F. Spray 36 mini (1¾-inch) muffin cups with nonstick cooking spray; set aside.

2. Combine flours, sugar, baking powder, baking soda and salt in medium bowl. Place ⅔ cup dry ingredients in each of 3 small bowls.

3. To first bowl of flour mixture, add ⅓ cup buttermilk and blueberries. Stir just until blended; spoon into 12 prepared muffin cups. To second bowl, add ⅓ cup buttermilk, banana and vanilla. Stir just until blended; spoon into 12 more prepared muffin cups. To third bowl, add remaining ⅓ cup buttermilk, applesauce, raisins and cinnamon. Stir just until blended; spoon into remaining 12 prepared muffin cups.

4. Bake 18 minutes or until lightly browned and toothpick inserted into centers comes out clean. Remove from pan. Cool 10 minutes on wire racks. Serve warm or cool completely.

Makes 36 mini muffins

Ham and Cheese Corn Muffins

    1 package (about 8 ounces) corn muffin mix
    ½ cup chopped deli ham
    ½ cup (2 ounces) shredded Swiss cheese
    ⅓ cup milk
    1 egg
    1 tablespoon Dijon mustard

1. Preheat oven to 400°F. Line 9 standard (2½-inch) muffin cups with paper baking cups.

2. Combine muffin mix, ham and cheese in medium bowl. Beat milk, egg and mustard in small bowl. Stir milk mixture into dry ingredients; mix just until moistened.

3. Fill muffin cups two-thirds full with batter. Bake 18 to 20 minutes or until light golden brown. Remove muffin pan to cooling rack. Let stand 5 minutes. Serve warm.

Makes 9 muffins

Serving Suggestion: For added flavor, serve Ham and Cheese Corn Muffins with honey-flavored butter. To prepare, stir together equal amounts of honey and softened butter.

Miniature Fruit Muffins

Marmalade Muffins

2 cups all-purpose flour
2 teaspoons baking powder
¾ teaspoon salt
1 cup (2 sticks) unsalted butter, softened
1½ cups sugar
2 eggs
1½ teaspoons vanilla
1 cup orange marmalade
1 cup buttermilk
Additional orange marmalade

1. Preheat oven to 350°F. Line 18 standard (2½-inch) muffin cups with paper baking cups.

2. Sift flour, baking powder and salt in medium bowl; set aside.

3. Beat butter and sugar in large bowl with electric mixer at medium speed 5 minutes until light and fluffy. Add eggs, one at a time, beating until blended. Add vanilla; mix well. Fold in half the flour mixture just until moistened. Stir in 1 cup marmalade and remaining flour.

4. Stir in buttermilk. Do not overmix. Fill muffin cups three-fourths full. Bake 20 to 25 minutes or until edges are golden brown and toothpick inserted into centers comes out clean. Top with additional marmalade.   *Makes 18 muffins*

Fruited Oat Scones

1½ cups all-purpose flour
1¼ cups QUAKER® Oats (quick or old fashioned, uncooked)
¼ cup granulated sugar
1 tablespoon baking powder
¼ teaspoon salt (optional)
⅓ cup (5⅓ tablespoons) margarine
1⅓ cups (6-ounce package) diced dried mixed fruit
½ cup milk
1 egg, lightly beaten
1 teaspoon granulated sugar
⅛ teaspoon ground cinnamon

Preheat oven to 375°F. Combine flour, oats, ¼ cup sugar, baking powder and salt; mix well. Cut in margarine with pastry blender or two knives until mixture resembles coarse crumbs; stir in fruit. Add milk and egg, mixing just until dry ingredients are moistened. Shape dough into ball. Turn out onto floured surface; knead gently 6 times. On lightly greased cookie sheet, pat out dough to form 8-inch circle. With sharp knife, score round into 12 wedges; sprinkle with combined 1 teaspoon sugar and cinnamon. Bake about 30 minutes or until golden brown. Break apart; serve warm.   *Makes 1 dozen scones*

Marmalade Muffins

Cherries and Cream Muffins

2½ cups frozen unsweetened tart cherries, divided
1 cup granulated sugar
½ cup butter or margarine
2 eggs
1 teaspoon almond extract
½ teaspoon vanilla extract
2 cups all-purpose flour
2 teaspoons baking powder
½ teaspoon salt
½ cup light cream, half-and-half or milk

Cut cherries into halves while frozen. Set aside to thaw and drain. In large bowl, beat sugar and butter until light and fluffy. Add eggs, almond extract and vanilla, beating well. Crush ½ cup cherries with fork; stir into batter.

Combine flour, baking powder and salt. Fold half the flour mixture into batter with spatula, then half the cream. Fold in remaining flour and cream. Fold in remaining cherry halves. Portion batter evenly into 12 paper-lined or lightly greased muffin cups (2¾ inches in diameter). Sprinkle with additional sugar.

Bake in preheated 375°F oven 20 to 30 minutes or until golden brown.

Makes 12 muffins

Favorite recipe from **Cherry Marketing Institute**

Streusel Raspberry Muffins

Pecan Streusel Topping (recipe follows)
1½ cups all-purpose flour
½ cup sugar
2 teaspoons baking powder
½ cup milk
½ cup (1 stick) butter, melted and cooled
1 egg, beaten
1 cup fresh or individually frozen unsweetened raspberries

1. Preheat oven to 375°F. Grease 12 standard (2½-inch) muffin cups or line with paper baking cups. Prepare Pecan Streusel Topping; set aside.

2. Combine flour, sugar and baking powder in large bowl. Combine milk, butter and egg in small bowl until blended; stir into flour mixture just until moistened. Spoon half of batter into muffin cups. Divide raspberries among cups, then top with remaining batter. Sprinkle Pecan Streusel Topping over tops. Bake 25 to 30 minutes or until golden and toothpick inserted into centers comes out clean. Cool in pan on wire rack 5 minutes.

Makes 12 muffins

Pecan Streusel Topping: Combine ¼ cup *each* chopped pecans, packed brown sugar and all-purpose flour in small bowl. Stir in 2 tablespoons melted butter until mixture resembles moist crumbs.

Oatmeal Apple Cranberry Scones

2 cups all-purpose flour
1 cup uncooked rolled oats
⅓ cup sugar
2 teaspoons baking powder
½ teaspoon salt
½ teaspoon baking soda
½ teaspoon ground cinnamon
¾ cup MOTT'S® Natural Apple Sauce, divided
2 tablespoons margarine
½ cup coarsely chopped cranberries
½ cup peeled, chopped apple
¼ cup skim milk
¼ cup plus 2 tablespoons honey, divided

1. Preheat oven to 425°F. Spray baking sheet with nonstick cooking spray.

2. In large bowl, combine flour, oats, sugar, baking powder, salt, baking soda and cinnamon. Add ½ cup apple sauce and margarine; cut in with pastry blender or fork until mixture resembles coarse crumbs. Stir in cranberries and apple.

3. In small bowl, combine milk and ¼ cup honey. Add milk mixture to flour mixture; stir together until dough forms a ball.

4. Turn out dough onto well-floured surface; knead 10 to 12 times. Pat dough into 8-inch circle. Place on prepared baking sheet. Use tip of knife to score dough into 12 wedges.

5. In another small bowl, combine remaining ¼ cup apple sauce and 2 tablespoons honey. Brush mixture over top of dough.

6. Bake 12 to 15 minutes or until lightly browned. Immediately remove from baking sheet; cool on wire rack 10 minutes. Serve warm or cool completely. Cut into 12 wedges.

Makes 12 scones

helpful hint:

Cranberries are delicious when mixed with apples, pears or chocolate for pies, cookies and crisps. They are also a great addition to muffins, breads, chutneys and desserts.

Basic Cream Scones

2¼ cups all-purpose flour
¼ cup granulated sugar
1 tablespoon baking powder
½ teaspoon salt
6 tablespoons cold unsalted butter, cut into 6 pieces
⅔ cup whipping cream
2 eggs, beaten
Coarse white decorating sugar

1. Preheat oven to 425°F. Fit food processor with steel blade. Place flour, granulated sugar, baking powder and salt in work bowl. Pulse on/off to mix. Add butter; process 10 seconds or until mixture resembles coarse crumbs. Transfer to large bowl.

2. Combine cream and eggs; reserve 1 tablespoon mixture. Pour remaining cream mixture over flour mixture. Stir just until dry ingredients are moistened and dough is soft.

3. Turn dough out onto lightly floured surface. Shape into ball; pat into 8-inch circle. Cut into 8 wedges; place 2 inches apart on ungreased baking sheet. Brush reserved cream mixture over tops; sprinkle with coarse sugar.

4. Bake 12 to 14 minutes or until golden. Remove to wire rack to cool completely.

Makes 8 scones

Chocolate Lavender Scones: Add 1 teaspoon dried lavender to dry ingredients. Stir ½ cup coarsely chopped semisweet chocolate into dough before shaping.

Ginger Peach Scones: Stir 1 tablespoon finely chopped crystallized ginger and ⅓ cup chopped dried peaches into dough before shaping.

Lemon Poppy Seed Scones: Stir grated peel of 1 lemon (about 3½ teaspoons) and 1 tablespoon poppy seeds into dough before shaping. Omit coarse sugar topping. When scones have cooled slightly, drizzle with lemon icing made from 1 cup powdered sugar and 2 tablespoons lemon juice (add up to 1½ teaspoons more lemon juice, if necessary, for desired consistency).

Maple Pecan Scones: Stir ½ cup coarsely chopped pecans into dough before shaping. Omit coarse sugar topping. When scones have cooled slightly, drizzle with maple icing made from ¾ cup powdered sugar and 2 tablespoons maple syrup.

Mini Scones: Divide dough into 2 balls before shaping into rounds and cutting into wedges. Makes 16 mini scones.

Round Scones: Cut dough into rounds using lightly floured cookie or biscuit cutter.

Basic Cream Scone Variations

Rich Cranberry Scones

  3 cups all-purpose flour
  ⅓ cup plus 1 tablespoon sugar, divided
  1 tablespoon baking powder
  ½ teaspoon salt
  ½ cup I CAN'T BELIEVE IT'S NOT BUTTER!® Spread
  ¾ cup dried cranberries
  1 cup plus 1 tablespoon whipping or heavy cream, divided
  2 eggs

Preheat oven to 450°F.

In large bowl, combine flour, ⅓ cup sugar, baking powder and salt. With pastry blender or 2 knives, cut in I Can't Believe It's Not Butter!® Spread until mixture is size of fine crumbs. Stir in cranberries.

In small bowl, with wire whisk, blend 1 cup cream and eggs. Stir into flour mixture until dough forms. On floured surface, with floured hands, divide dough in half. Press each half into 6-inch circle. Cut each circle into 6 wedges; place on baking sheet. Brush with remaining 1 tablespoon cream, then sprinkle with remaining 1 tablespoon sugar.

Bake 12 minutes or until golden. Serve warm or cool completely on wire rack.

Makes 12 scones

Prep Time: 15 minutes | **Cook Time:** 12 minutes

Pineapple Citrus Muffins

  ⅓ cup honey
  ¼ cup butter or margarine, softened
  1 egg
  1 can (8 ounces) DOLE® Crushed Pineapple
  1 tablespoon grated orange peel
  1 cup all-purpose flour
  1 cup whole wheat flour
1½ teaspoons baking powder
  ¼ teaspoon salt
  ¼ teaspoon ground nutmeg
  1 cup DOLE® Chopped Dates
  ½ cup chopped walnuts, optional

• Preheat oven to 375°F. In large mixer bowl, beat together honey and butter 1 minute. Beat in egg, then undrained crushed pineapple and orange peel. In medium bowl, combine remaining ingredients; stir into pineapple mixture until just blended.

• Spoon batter into 12 greased muffin cups. Bake in preheated oven 25 minutes or until wooden pick inserted in center comes out clean. Cool slightly in pan before turning out onto wire rack. Serve warm.

Makes 12 muffins

Rich Cranberry Scones

Apple Butter Spice Muffins

½ cup sugar
1 teaspoon ground cinnamon
¼ teaspoon ground nutmeg
⅛ teaspoon ground allspice
½ cup pecans or walnuts, chopped
2 cups all-purpose flour
2 teaspoons baking powder
¼ teaspoon salt
1 cup milk
¼ cup vegetable oil
1 egg
¼ cup apple butter

1. Preheat oven to 400°F. Grease 12 standard (2½-inch) muffin cups or line with paper baking cups.

2. Combine sugar, cinnamon, nutmeg and allspice in large bowl. Toss 2 tablespoons sugar mixture with pecans in small bowl; set aside. Add flour, baking powder and salt to remaining sugar mixture.

3. Combine milk, oil and egg in medium bowl. Stir into flour mixture just until moistened.

4. Spoon 1 tablespoon batter into each prepared muffin cup. Spoon 1 teaspoon apple butter into each cup. Spoon remaining batter evenly over apple butter. Sprinkle reserved pecan mixture over each muffin. Bake 20 to 25 minutes or until golden brown and toothpick inserted into centers comes out clean. Immediately remove from pan; cool on wire rack 10 minutes. Serve warm or cool completely. *Makes 12 muffins*

Hearty Banana Carrot Muffins

2 ripe, medium DOLE® Bananas
1 package (14 ounces) oat bran muffin mix
¾ teaspoon ground ginger
1 medium DOLE® Carrot, shredded (½ cup)
⅓ cup light molasses
⅓ cup DOLE® Seedless or Golden Raisins
¼ cup chopped almonds

• Mash bananas with fork (1 cup).

• Combine muffin mix and ginger in large bowl. Add carrot, molasses, raisins and bananas. Stir just until moistened.

• Spoon batter into paper-lined muffin cups. Sprinkle tops with almonds.

• Bake at 425°F 12 to 14 minutes until browned. *Makes 12 muffins*

Prep Time: 20 minutes | **Bake Time:** 14 minutes

Apple Butter Spice Muffins

Pumpernickel Muffins

1 cup all-purpose flour
½ cup rye flour
½ cup whole wheat flour
2 teaspoons caraway seeds
1 teaspoon baking soda
½ teaspoon salt
1 cup buttermilk
¼ cup vegetable oil
¼ cup light molasses
1 egg
1 square (1 ounce) unsweetened chocolate, melted and cooled

1. Preheat oven to 400°F. Grease 12 standard (2½-inch) muffin cups or line with paper baking cups.

2. Combine flours, caraway seeds, baking soda and salt in large bowl.

3. Combine buttermilk, oil, molasses and egg in small bowl until blended. Stir in melted chocolate. Stir into flour mixture just until dry ingredients are moistened. Spoon evenly into prepared muffin cups.

4. Bake 20 to 25 minutes or until toothpick inserted into centers comes out clean. Immediately remove from pan. Cool on wire rack about 10 minutes. Serve warm or cold. Store at room temperature in tightly covered container up to 2 days.   *Makes 12 muffins*

Cheesy Ham and Pepper Muffins

2½ cups all-purpose flour
3 tablespoons sugar
1 tablespoon baking powder
¼ teaspoon black pepper
1 cup milk
6 tablespoons vegetable oil
2 eggs, beaten
2 tablespoons Dijon mustard
¾ cup (3 ounces) shredded Swiss cheese
¾ cup diced cooked ham
3 tablespoons chopped red or green bell pepper

1. Preheat oven to 400°F. Grease 12 standard (2½-inch) muffin cups or line with paper baking cups.

2. Combine flour, sugar, baking powder and black pepper in large bowl. Whisk together milk, oil, eggs and mustard in small bowl until blended. Stir into flour mixture just until moistened. Fold in cheese, ham and bell pepper. Spoon evenly into prepared muffin cups.

3. Bake 19 to 21 minutes or until toothpick inserted into centers comes out clean. Cool in pan on wire rack 5 minutes. Remove from pan and cool on wire rack 10 minutes.

Makes 12 muffins

Pumpernickel Muffins

Strawberry Muffins

1¼ cups all-purpose flour
2½ teaspoons baking powder
½ teaspoon salt
1 cup uncooked old-fashioned oats
½ cup sugar
1 cup milk
½ cup (1 stick) butter, melted
1 egg, beaten
1 teaspoon vanilla
1 cup chopped fresh strawberries

1. Preheat oven to 425°F. Grease bottoms only of 12 standard (2½-inch) muffin cups or line with paper baking cups; set aside.

2. Combine flour, baking powder and salt in large bowl. Stir in oats and sugar. Combine milk, butter, egg and vanilla in small bowl until well blended; stir into flour mixture just until moistened. Fold in strawberries. Spoon into prepared muffin cups, filling about two-thirds full.

3. Bake 15 to 18 minutes or until lightly browned and toothpick inserted into centers comes out clean. Remove from pan. Cool on wire rack 10 minutes. Serve warm or cool completely.

Makes 12 muffins

Buttermilk Oatmeal Scones

2 cups all-purpose flour, sifted
1 cup uncooked rolled oats
⅓ cup granulated sugar
1 tablespoon baking powder
½ teaspoon baking soda
⅛ teaspoon salt
6 tablespoons cold unsalted margarine, cut into small pieces
1 cup buttermilk

Preheat oven to 375°F. Grease baking sheets; set aside.

Combine flour, oats, sugar, baking powder, baking soda and salt in large bowl. Cut in margarine with pastry blender or process in food processor until mixture resembles coarse crumbs. Add buttermilk; stir with fork until soft dough forms. Turn out dough onto lightly floured surface; knead 10 to 12 times. Roll out dough to ½-inch-thick rectangle with lightly floured rolling pin. Cut dough into circles with lightly floured 1½-inch biscuit cutter. Place on prepared baking sheets. Brush tops with buttermilk and sprinkle with sugar. Bake 18 to 20 minutes or until golden brown and wooden pick inserted in center comes out clean. Remove from baking sheets. Cool on wire racks 10 minutes. Serve warm or cool completely.

Makes about 30 scones

Favorite recipe from **The Sugar Association, Inc.**

Strawberry Muffins

Cranberry Pecan Muffins

1½ cups fresh or frozen cranberries
¼ cup light corn syrup
1 package DUNCAN HINES® Bakery-Style Cinnamon Swirl Muffin Mix
1 egg
¾ cup water or milk
½ cup chopped pecans

1. Preheat oven to 400°F. Place 14 (2½-inch) paper liners in muffin cups. Place cranberries and corn syrup in heavy saucepan. Cook on medium heat, stirring occasionally, until cranberries pop and mixture is slightly thickened. Drain cranberries in strainer; set aside.

2. Empty muffin mix into medium bowl. Break up any lumps. Add egg and water. Stir until moistened, about 50 strokes. Stir in cranberries and pecans. Knead swirl packet from Mix for 10 seconds before opening. Cut off 1 end of swirl packet. Squeeze contents over top of batter. Swirl into batter with knife or spatula. *Do not completely mix in.* Spoon batter into muffin cups (see Tip). Sprinkle with contents of topping packet from Mix. Bake at 400°F for 18 to 22 minutes or until toothpick inserted into centers comes out clean. Cool in pans 5 to 10 minutes. Serve warm or cool completely. *Makes 14 muffins*

Tip: Fill an equal number of muffin cups in each muffin pan with batter. For more even baking, fill empty muffin cups with ½ inch of water.

Dill Sour Cream Scones

2 cups all-purpose flour
2 teaspoons baking powder
½ teaspoon baking soda
½ teaspoon salt
¼ cup (½ stick) cold butter, cut into pieces
2 eggs
½ cup sour cream
1 tablespoon chopped fresh dill *or* 1 teaspoon dried dill weed

1. Preheat oven to 425°F.

2. Combine flour, baking powder, baking soda and salt in medium bowl. Cut in butter with pastry blender or 2 knives until mixture resembles coarse crumbs. Beat eggs with fork in small bowl. Add sour cream and dill; beat until well blended. Stir into flour mixture until mixture forms soft dough that pulls away from side of bowl.

3. Turn out dough onto well-floured surface. Knead 10 times, careful not to overwork dough. Roll dough into 9×6-inch rectangle with lightly floured rolling pin. Cut dough into 6 (3-inch) squares. Cut each square diagonally in half, making 12 triangles. Place triangles 2 inches apart on ungreased baking sheets.

4. Bake 10 to 12 minutes or until golden brown and toothpick inserted into centers comes out clean. Cool on wire rack 10 minutes. Serve warm or cool completely. *Makes 12 scones*

Special Dark®
Chocolate Chip Scones

3¼ cups all-purpose flour
½ cup sugar
1 tablespoon plus 1 teaspoon baking powder
¼ teaspoon salt
2 cups (12-ounce package) HERSHEY'S SPECIAL DARK® Chocolate Chips
½ cup chopped nuts (optional)
2 cups whipping cream, chilled
2 tablespoons butter, melted
 Additional sugar
 Powdered sugar (optional)

1. Heat oven to 375°F. Lightly grease 2 baking sheets.

2. Stir together flour, ½ cup sugar, baking powder and salt in large bowl. Stir in chocolate chips and nuts, if desired.

3. Stir whipping cream into flour mixture just until ingredients are moistened.

4. Turn mixture out onto lightly floured surface. Knead gently until soft dough forms, about 2 minutes. Divide dough into three equal balls. One ball at a time, flatten into 7-inch circle; cut into 8 triangles. Transfer triangles to prepared baking sheets, spacing 2 inches apart. Brush with melted butter and sprinkle with additional sugar.

5. Bake 15 to 20 minutes or until lightly browned. Serve warm, sprinkled with powdered sugar, if desired.
Makes 24 scones

Tunnel of
Wisconsin Cheese Muffins

2 cups biscuit mix
5 slices bacon, crisply cooked and crumbled
¾ cup milk
1 egg, beaten
12 (½-inch) cubes Wisconsin Swiss cheese

Stir together biscuit mix and bacon in medium bowl. Add milk and egg, stirring just to mix. Spoon half of batter into 12 buttered muffin pan cups. Press one cheese cube in each cup. Top with remaining batter, covering cheese completely. Bake in preheated 400°F oven 25 minutes or until golden. Serve hot.
Makes 12 muffins

Favorite recipe from **Wisconsin Milk Marketing Board**

Calico Bell Pepper Muffins

¼ cup *each* finely chopped red, yellow and green bell pepper
2 tablespoons margarine
2 cups all-purpose flour
4 tablespoons sugar
1 tablespoon baking powder
¾ teaspoon salt
½ teaspoon dried basil leaves
1 cup low-fat milk
1 whole egg
2 egg whites

Preheat oven to 400°F. Paper-line 12 muffin cups or spray with cooking spray. In small skillet, cook peppers in margarine over medium-high heat until color is bright and peppers are tender-crisp, about 3 minutes. Set aside.

In large bowl, combine flour, sugar, baking powder, salt and basil. In small bowl, combine milk, whole egg and egg whites until blended. Add milk mixture and peppers with drippings to flour mixture and stir until just moistened. Spoon into prepared muffin cups. Bake 15 minutes or until golden and wooden pick inserted into centers comes out clean. Cool briefly and remove from pan.   *Makes 12 muffins*

Favorite recipe from **The Sugar Association, Inc.**

Peach-Almond Scones

2 cups all-purpose flour
¼ cup plus 1 tablespoon sugar, divided
2 teaspoons baking powder
½ teaspoon salt
5 tablespoons cold butter or margarine
½ cup sliced almonds, lightly toasted and divided
1 egg
2 tablespoons milk
1 can (16 ounces) peach halves or slices in juice, drained and finely chopped
½ teaspoon almond extract

1. Preheat oven to 425°F. Combine flour, ¼ cup sugar, baking powder and salt in large bowl. Cut in butter with pastry blender or 2 knives until mixture resembles coarse crumbs. Stir in ¼ cup almonds. Lightly beat egg and milk in small bowl. Reserve 2 tablespoons egg mixture; set aside. Stir peaches and almond extract into remaining egg mixture. Stir into flour mixture until soft dough forms.

2. Place dough onto well-floured surface. Gently knead 10 to 12 times. Roll dough into 9×6-inch rectangle. Cut into 6 (3-inch) squares using floured knife. Cut diagonally into halves, making 12 triangles; place 2 inches apart on ungreased baking sheets. Brush triangles with reserved egg mixture. Sprinkle with remaining ¼ cup almonds and 1 tablespoon sugar.

3. Bake 10 to 12 minutes or until golden brown. Remove from baking sheets and cool on wire racks 10 minutes. Serve warm.   *Makes 12 scones*

Calico Bell Pepper Muffins

Cinnamon Spiced Muffins

1½ cups all-purpose flour
¾ cup sugar, divided
2 teaspoons baking powder
½ teaspoon salt
½ teaspoon ground nutmeg
½ teaspoon ground coriander
½ teaspoon ground allspice
½ cup milk
⅓ cup butter, melted
1 egg
1 teaspoon ground cinnamon
¼ cup (½ stick) butter, melted

1. Preheat oven to 400°F. Grease 36 mini (1¾-inch) muffin cups.

2. Combine flour, ½ cup sugar, baking powder, salt, nutmeg, coriander and allspice in large bowl. Combine milk, ⅓ cup butter and egg in small bowl; stir into flour mixture just until moistened. Spoon evenly into prepared muffin cups.

3. Bake 10 to 13 minutes or until edges are lightly browned and toothpick inserted into centers comes out clean. Cool in pan on wire rack 2 minutes. Remove from pan.

4. Meanwhile, combine remaining ¼ cup sugar and cinnamon in shallow dish. Dip warm muffin tops in ¼ cup melted butter, then in sugar-cinnamon mixture. Serve warm.

Makes 36 mini muffins

Cheddar Olive Scones

2 cups all-purpose flour
1½ cups (6 ounces) shredded sharp Cheddar cheese
1 tablespoon sugar
2 teaspoons baking powder
1½ teaspoons cumin seed
¾ cup sour cream
¼ cup salad oil
1 large egg
½ cup pitted California ripe olives, cut into wedges

Mix flour, cheese, sugar, baking powder and cumin in large bowl. Beat sour cream, oil and egg in small bowl. Add egg mixture to flour mixture; stir just enough to moisten evenly. Gently stir in olives. Scrape dough onto lightly greased 15×10-inch baking sheet. Lightly flour hands; pat dough into 1-inch-thick round with lightly floured fingers. Cut round into 8 wedges with knife. Bake in preheated 375°F oven 30 to 35 minutes or until well browned. Serve warm or at room temperature. Cut or break scones into wedges.

Makes 8 servings

Favorite recipe from **California Olive Industry**

Prep Time: about 15 minutes | Bake Time: 30 to 35 minutes

Cinnamon Spiced Muffins

Peach Gingerbread Muffins

2 cups all-purpose flour
2 teaspoons baking powder
1 teaspoon ground ginger
½ teaspoon salt
½ teaspoon ground cinnamon
¼ teaspoon ground cloves
½ cup sugar
½ cup MOTT'S® Chunky Apple Sauce
¼ cup MOTT'S® Apple Juice
¼ cup GRANDMA'S® Molasses
1 egg
2 tablespoons vegetable oil
1 (16-ounce) can peaches in juice, drained and chopped

1. Preheat oven to 400°F. Line 12 (2½-inch) muffin cups with paper liners or spray with nonstick cooking spray.

2. In large bowl, combine flour, baking powder, ginger, salt and spices.

3. In small bowl, combine sugar, apple sauce, apple juice, molasses, egg and oil.

4. Stir apple sauce mixture into flour mixture just until moistened. Fold in peaches.

5. Spoon batter evenly into prepared muffin cups.

6. Bake 20 minutes or until toothpick inserted into centers comes out clean. Immediately remove from pan; cool on wire rack 10 minutes. Serve warm or cool completely.

Makes 12 servings

Sun-Dried Tomato Scones

2 cups buttermilk baking mix
¼ cup grated Parmesan cheese
1½ teaspoons dried basil
⅔ cup milk
½ cup chopped drained oil-packed sun-dried tomatoes
¼ cup chopped green onions

1. Preheat oven to 450°F. Lightly grease baking sheet; set aside. Combine baking mix, cheese and basil in medium bowl.

2. Stir in milk, tomatoes and onions. Mix just until dry ingredients are moistened. Drop by heaping teaspoonfuls onto prepared baking sheet.

3. Bake 8 to 10 minutes or until light golden brown. Remove baking sheet to wire rack; let stand 5 minutes. Remove scones and serve warm or at room temperature.

Makes 18 scones

Prep and Cook Time: 20 minutes

Peach Gingerbread Muffins

Brunch-Time Delights

Breakfast Empanadas

8 ounces bacon (about 10 slices)
1 package (15 ounces) refrigerated pie crusts
9 eggs
1 teaspoon water
1 teaspoon salt
   Dash black pepper
1 tablespoon butter
2 cups (8 ounces) shredded Mexican cheese blend, divided
4 tablespoons salsa
   All-purpose flour (optional)

1. Preheat oven to 425°F. Cook bacon in skillet over medium heat until crisp; drain on paper towels. Chop into small pieces; set aside. Spray large baking sheet with nonstick cooking spray. Cut pie crusts in half to make 4 semicircles; place on baking sheet.

2. Beat 1 egg with water in small bowl until well blended; set aside. Beat remaining 8 eggs, salt and pepper in medium bowl until well blended. Melt butter in large skillet over medium heat until hot; tilt skillet to coat bottom lightly. Sprinkle bacon evenly into skillet. Pour egg mixture into skillet; cook without stirring for 2 minutes. Gently stir until eggs are cooked but still slightly moist. Transfer to plate to cool.

3. Spoon one-fourth scrambled egg mixture onto half of each semicircle of pie crust. Sprinkle 1¾ cups cheese evenly over eggs. Spoon 1 tablespoon salsa into center of each mound of eggs and cheese.

4. Using pastry brush, brush edges of each semicircle with reserved egg-water mixture. Fold dough over egg mixture and seal edges with fork, making 4 empanadas. (Flour fork tines to prevent sticking, if necessary.)

5. Brush empanadas with remaining egg-water mixture; sprinkle with remaining ¼ cup cheese. Bake 15 to 20 minutes or until golden brown. *Makes 4 servings*

Tip: These empanadas make a great main dish for dinner, too. Plus, they can be prepared early in the day and reheated in a preheated 350°F oven for 20 to 25 minutes.

Chocolate Chip Coffeecake

    3 cups all-purpose flour, divided
 ⅓ cup sugar
    2 envelopes FLEISCHMANN'S® RapidRise™ Yeast
    1 teaspoon salt
 ½ cup milk
 ½ cup water
 ½ cup (1 stick) butter or margarine
    2 eggs
 ¾ cup semi-sweet chocolate morsels
    Chocolate Nut Topping (recipe follows)

In large bowl, combine 1 cup flour, sugar, undissolved yeast and salt. Heat milk, water and butter until very warm (120° to 130°F). Gradually add to dry ingredients. Beat 2 minutes at medium speed of electric mixer, scraping bowl occasionally. Add eggs and 1 cup flour; beat 2 minutes at high speed, scraping bowl occasionally. Stir in chocolate morsels and remaining flour to make a soft batter. Turn into greased 13×9×2-inch baking pan. Cover; let rise in warm, draft-free place until doubled in size, about 1 hour.

Bake at 400°F for 15 minutes; remove from oven and sprinkle with Chocolate Nut Topping. Return to oven and bake additional 10 minutes or until done. Cool in pan for 10 minutes. Remove from pan; cool on wire rack.   *Makes 1 cake*

Chocolate Nut Topping: In medium bowl, cut ½ cup butter into ⅔ cup all-purpose flour until crumbly. Stir in ⅔ cup sugar, 2 teaspoons ground cinnamon, 1 cup semi-sweet chocolate morsels and 1 cup chopped pecans.

helpful hint:

Try your hand at a cappuccino or a café latte to really impress brunch guests. Cappuccino is 2 parts espresso with 1 part steamed milk served in a standard-size cup and topped with the foam of steamed milk. Café latte is 1 part espresso with 2 parts steamed milk served in a tall mug and topped with the foam of steamed milk. Either may be dusted with sweetened cocoa powder or cinnamon.

Chocolate Chip Coffeecake

Oatmeal Brulée
with Raspberry Sauce

BRULÉE
   4 cups water
   ½ teaspoon salt
   3 cups uncooked old-fashioned oats
   1 cup whipping cream
   ½ teaspoon vanilla
   ¼ cup granulated sugar
   3 egg yolks
   3 tablespoons brown sugar

RASPBERRY SAUCE
   6 ounces frozen sweetened raspberries
   ½ cup granulated sugar
   ¼ cup water
   1 teaspoon orange extract

1. For brulée: Preheat oven to 300°F. Line baking sheet with foil; set aside. Heat 4 cups water and salt in medium saucepan over high heat until water comes to a boil. Add oats; reduce heat to low. Cook 4 to 5 minutes, stirring occasionally, until water is absorbed and oats are tender. Divide oatmeal among 4 ramekins or ovenproof bowls. Place on prepared baking sheet; set aside.

2. In separate medium saucepan, heat cream over high heat; do not boil. Remove from heat; stir in vanilla. Beat ¼ cup granulated sugar and egg yolks in large bowl with whisk. Slowly pour about ½ cup hot cream in thin stream into egg mixture, whisking constantly. Whisk remaining cream into egg mixture until well blended and smooth. Ladle cream mixture equally over oatmeal in ramekins. Bake 35 minutes or until nearly set. Remove from oven; preheat broiler to 500°F.

3. Meanwhile, for sauce, purée raspberries, ½ cup granulated sugar, water and orange extract in food processor. Pour sauce through strainer to remove seeds; discard seeds.

4. Sprinkle 1½ teaspoons brown sugar evenly over each brulée. Place baking sheet under broiler; broil 3 to 5 minutes or until tops are caramelized but not blackened. Cool 5 to 10 minutes before serving. Serve with raspberry sauce.   *Makes 4 servings*

Tip: This brulée has the texture of rice pudding and the taste of sweet custard with a creme brulée-like topping. *Brulée* (broo-LAY) comes from the French word for "burned."

Oatmeal Brulée with Raspberry Sauce

Spinach Sensation

  8 ounces bacon slices
  1 cup (8 ounces) sour cream
  3 eggs, separated
  2 tablespoons all-purpose flour
  ⅛ teaspoon black pepper
  1 package (10 ounces) frozen chopped spinach, thawed and squeezed dry
  ½ cup (2 ounces) shredded sharp Cheddar cheese
  ½ cup dry bread crumbs
  1 tablespoon butter or margarine, melted

1. Preheat oven to 350°F. Spray 2-quart round baking dish with nonstick cooking spray.

2. Place bacon in single layer in large skillet; cook over medium heat until crisp. Remove from skillet; drain on paper towels. Crumble and set aside.

3. Combine sour cream, egg yolks, flour and pepper in large bowl; set aside. Beat egg whites in medium bowl with electric mixer at high speed until stiff peaks form. Stir one fourth of egg whites into sour cream mixture; fold in remaining egg whites.

4. Arrange half of spinach in prepared dish. Top with half of sour cream mixture. Sprinkle ¼ cup cheese over sour cream mixture. Sprinkle bacon over cheese. Repeat layers, ending with remaining ¼ cup cheese.

5. Combine bread crumbs and butter in small bowl; sprinkle evenly over cheese. Bake, uncovered, 30 to 35 minutes or until egg mixture is set. Let stand 5 minutes before serving. *Makes 6 servings*

Apple & Raisin Oven Pancake

  1 large baking apple, cored and thinly sliced
  ⅓ cup golden raisins
  2 tablespoons packed brown sugar
  ½ teaspoon ground cinnamon
  4 eggs
  ⅔ cup milk
  ⅔ cup all-purpose flour
  2 tablespoons butter or margarine, melted
    Powdered sugar (optional)

1. Preheat oven to 350°F. Spray 9-inch pie plate with nonstick cooking spray.

2. Combine apple, raisins, brown sugar and cinnamon in medium bowl. Transfer to prepared pie plate. Bake, uncovered, 10 to 15 minutes or until apple begins to soften. Remove from oven. *Increase oven temperature to 450°F.*

3. Meanwhile, whisk eggs, milk, flour and butter in medium bowl until blended. Pour batter over apple mixture. Bake 15 minutes or until pancake is golden brown. Invert onto serving dish. Sprinkle with powdered sugar, if desired. *Makes 6 servings*

Spinach Sensation

Caramel-Nut Sticky Biscuits

TOPPING
⅔ cup firmly packed brown sugar
¼ cup light corn syrup
¼ cup (½ stick) margarine, melted
½ teaspoon ground cinnamon
1 cup pecan halves

BISCUITS
2 cups all-purpose flour
1 cup QUAKER® Oats (quick or old fashioned, uncooked)
¼ cup granulated sugar
1 tablespoon baking powder
¾ teaspoon baking soda
½ teaspoon salt (optional)
½ teaspoon ground cinnamon
⅓ cup (5⅓ tablespoons) margarine
1 cup buttermilk*

Sour milk can be substituted for buttermilk. To make 1 cup sour milk, combine 1 tablespoon vinegar or lemon juice and enough milk to make 1 cup; let stand 5 minutes.

Heat oven to 425°F. For topping, combine first four ingredients; mix well. Spread onto bottom of 9-inch square baking pan. Sprinkle with pecans; set aside. For biscuits, combine dry ingredients; mix well. Cut in margarine with pastry blender or two knives until crumbly. Stir in buttermilk, mixing just until moistened. Knead gently on lightly floured surface 5 to 7 times; pat into 8-inch square. Cut with knife into sixteen 2-inch square biscuits; place over topping in pan. Bake 25 to 28 minutes or until golden brown. Let stand 3 minutes; invert onto large platter. Serve warm.

Makes 16 servings

helpful hint:

The secret to making flaky, tender biscuits is to cut cold margarine, butter or shortening into the dry ingredients just until the mixture forms coarse crumbs. Don't worry about leaving some chunks of margarine. They'll melt and help make layers. Don't overwork the dough either. Knead no more than 10 times or the biscuits will be tough.

Caramel-Nut Sticky Biscuits

Country Buttermilk Biscuits

2 cups all-purpose flour
1 tablespoon baking powder
2 teaspoons sugar
½ teaspoon baking soda
½ teaspoon salt
⅓ cup shortening
⅔ cup buttermilk*

Sour milk can be substituted for buttermilk. To sour milk, combine 2½ teaspoons lemon juice plus enough milk to equal ⅔ cup in a 1-cup measure. Stir; let stand 5 minutes before using.

1. Preheat oven to 450°F.

2. Combine flour, baking powder, sugar, baking soda and salt in medium bowl. Cut in shortening with pastry blender or 2 knives until mixture resembles coarse crumbs. Make well in center of dry ingredients. Add buttermilk; stir until mixture forms soft dough that clings together and forms ball.

3. Turn dough out onto well-floured surface. Knead dough gently 10 to 12 times. Roll or pat dough to ½-inch thickness. Cut out dough with floured 2½-inch biscuit cutter.

4. Place biscuits 2 inches apart onto *ungreased* large baking sheet. Bake 8 to 10 minutes or until tops and bottoms are golden brown. Serve warm.   *Makes about 9 biscuits*

Drop Biscuits: Prepare Country Buttermilk Biscuits as directed in steps 1 and 2, except increase buttermilk to 1 cup. After adding buttermilk, stir batter with wooden spoon about 15 strokes. *Do not knead.* Drop dough by heaping tablespoonfuls, 1 inch apart, onto greased baking sheets. Bake as directed in step 4. Makes about 18 biscuits.

Sour Cream Dill Biscuits: Prepare Country Buttermilk Biscuits as directed in steps 1 through 2, except omit buttermilk. Combine ½ cup sour cream, ⅓ cup milk and 1 tablespoon chopped fresh dill *or* 1 teaspoon dried dill weed in small bowl until well blended. Stir into dry ingredients and continue as directed in steps 3 and 4. Makes about 9 biscuits.

Bacon 'n' Onion Biscuits: Prepare Country Buttermilk Biscuits as directed in steps 1 through 2, except add 4 slices crumbled crisp-cooked bacon (about ⅓ cup) and ⅓ cup chopped green onions to flour mixture before adding buttermilk. Continue as directed in steps 3 and 4. Makes about 9 biscuits.

Country Buttermilk Biscuits

Cheese-Filled Almond Braids

Sweet Yeast Dough (page 53)
2 packages (8 ounces each) cream cheese, softened
⅔ cup granulated sugar
2 eggs, separated
2 tablespoons all-purpose flour
1½ teaspoons almond extract
1 tablespoon water
¼ cup sliced almonds
Additional granulated sugar (optional)
Powdered sugar (optional)

1. Prepare Sweet Yeast Dough; let rise as directed. Grease 2 large baking sheets.

2. Beat cream cheese, ⅔ cup granulated sugar, egg yolks, flour and almond extract in large bowl with electric mixer at medium speed until smooth.

3. Cut dough into halves. Roll out one half of dough into 12×9-inch rectangle on lightly floured surface with lightly floured rolling pin. Carefully transfer dough to prepared baking sheet.

4. Score dough lengthwise into 3 (3-inch-wide) sections with tip of sharp knife, taking care not to cut completely through dough.

5. Spread half of cream cheese mixture on center section between score marks. Cut dough on outer sections into 1-inch-wide diagonal strips with scissors or sharp knife, cutting to within ½ inch of filling.

6. Starting at 1 end, fold strips over filling, alternating from left and right, overlapping strips in center to create a braided pattern. Repeat with remaining dough and cream cheese mixture.

7. Cover braids with towels; let rise in warm place about 45 minutes or until doubled in bulk.

8. Preheat oven to 350°F. Combine egg whites and 1 tablespoon water in small bowl. Brush braids with egg white mixture. Sprinkle almonds over braids. Sprinkle additional granulated sugar over almonds, if desired.

9. Bake 25 to 30 minutes or until braids are golden brown and sound hollow when tapped, rotating baking sheets from top to bottom racks halfway through baking. Immediately remove from baking sheets; cool completely on wire racks. Dust with powdered sugar, if desired.

Makes 24 servings (2 coffeecakes)

Fruit-Filled Almond Braids: Prepare dough for Cheese-Filled Almond Braids as directed above except substitute 2 cans or jars (about 10 to 12 ounces each) prepared prune, apple, peach or pineapple pie & pastry filling for cream cheese filling mixture. (Use 1 can to fill each braid.)

Sweet Yeast Dough

  4 to 4¼ cups all-purpose flour, divided
½ cup sugar
  2 packages active dry yeast
  1 teaspoon salt
¾ cup milk
¼ cup (½ stick) butter or margarine
  2 eggs
  1 teaspoon vanilla

1. Combine 1 cup flour, sugar, yeast and salt in large bowl. Combine milk and butter in 1-quart saucepan. Heat over low heat until mixture is 120° to 130°F. (Butter does not need to completely melt.)

2. Gradually beat milk mixture into dry ingredients with electric mixer at medium speed 2 minutes. Beat in eggs, vanilla and 1 cup flour at low speed. Increase speed to medium; beat 2 minutes. Stir in enough additional flour, about 2 cups, to make soft dough.

3. Turn out dough onto lightly floured surface; flatten slightly. Knead dough about 5 minutes or until smooth and elastic, adding remaining ¼ cup flour to prevent sticking if necessary. Shape dough into a ball.

4. Place in large greased bowl. Turn dough over so that top is greased. Cover with towel; let rise in warm place 1½ to 2 hours or until doubled in bulk.

5. Punch down dough. Knead dough on lightly floured surface 1 minute. Cover with towel; let rest 10 minutes.

Refrigerator Sweet Yeast Dough: Prepare Sweet Yeast Dough as directed in steps 1 through 3. Cover with greased plastic wrap; refrigerate 3 to 24 hours. Punch down dough. Knead dough on lightly floured surface 1 to 2 minutes. Cover with towel; let dough rest 20 minutes before shaping and second rising. (Second rising may take up to 1½ hours.)

Chili Cheese Puff

¾ cup all-purpose flour
1½ teaspoons baking powder
9 eggs
4 cups (16 ounces) shredded Monterey Jack cheese
2 cups (16 ounces) cottage cheese
2 cans (4 ounces each) diced green chilies, drained
1½ teaspoons sugar
¼ teaspoon salt
⅛ teaspoon hot pepper sauce
1 cup prepared salsa

1. Preheat oven to 350°F. Spray 13×9-inch baking dish with nonstick cooking spray.

2. Combine flour and baking powder in small bowl.

3. Whisk eggs in large bowl until blended; stir in Monterey Jack cheese, cottage cheese, chilies, sugar, salt and pepper sauce. Add flour mixture; stir just until blended. Pour into prepared dish.

4. Bake, uncovered, 45 minutes or until set. Let stand 5 minutes before serving. Serve with salsa.   *Makes 8 servings*

Turkey and Rice Quiche

3 cups cooked rice, cooled to room temperature
1½ cups chopped cooked turkey
1 medium tomato, seeded and finely diced
¼ cup sliced green onions
¼ cup finely diced green bell pepper
1 tablespoon chopped fresh basil *or* 1 teaspoon dried basil
½ teaspoon seasoned salt
⅛ to ¼ teaspoon ground red pepper
½ cup skim milk
3 eggs, beaten
Vegetable cooking spray
½ cup (2 ounces) shredded Cheddar cheese
½ cup (2 ounces) shredded mozzarella cheese

Combine rice, turkey, tomato, green onions, bell pepper, basil, salt, red pepper, milk and eggs in 13×9×2-inch pan coated with cooking spray. Top with cheeses. Bake at 375°F for 20 minutes or until knife inserted near center comes out clean. To serve, cut quiche into 8 squares; cut each square diagonally into 2 triangles.   *Makes 8 servings (2 triangles each)*

Favorite recipe from **USA Rice**

Chili Cheese Puff

Puff Pancake
with Summer Berries

Summer Berries (recipe follows)
4 tablespoons butter or margarine, divided
2 eggs
½ cup all-purpose flour
½ cup milk
1 tablespoon sugar
¼ teaspoon salt
Whipped cream (optional)

1. Prepare Summer Berries; set aside. Preheat oven to 425°F. Place 2 tablespoons butter in ovenproof skillet. Place skillet in oven 3 minutes or until butter is bubbly. Swirl pan to coat bottom and sides.

2. Beat eggs in medium bowl with electric mixer at high speed. Add flour, milk, remaining 2 tablespoons butter, sugar and salt; beat until smooth.

3. Pour batter into prepared skillet. Bake 15 minutes. *Reduce oven temperature to 350°F.* Continue baking 10 to 15 minutes or until pancake is puffed and golden brown.

4. Serve pancake in skillet with Summer Berries. Top with whipped cream, if desired.

Makes 6 servings

Summer Berries

2 cups blueberries
1 cup sliced strawberries
1 cup raspberries
Sugar to taste

Combine blueberries, strawberries and raspberries in medium bowl. Gently toss with sugar. Let stand 5 minutes.

Makes 4 cups

helpful hint:

Berries are perishable and expensive. They should be used as soon as possible after purchase. Look for berries that are plump and fresh-looking. Wash them gently just before using.

Puff Pancake with Summer Berries

Strawberry Cinnamon French Toast

  1 egg
¼ cup fat-free (skim) milk
½ teaspoon vanilla
  4 (1-inch-thick) diagonally cut slices French bread (about 1 ounce each)
  2 teaspoons reduced-fat margarine
  2 packets sugar substitute
¼ teaspoon ground cinnamon
  1 cup sliced strawberries

1. Preheat oven to 450°F.

2. Spray nonstick baking sheet with nonstick cooking spray; set aside.

3. Combine egg, milk and vanilla in shallow dish or pie plate. Lightly dip bread slices in egg mixture until completely coated. Place on baking sheet; bake 15 minutes or until golden, turning over halfway through baking time.

4. Meanwhile, combine margarine, sugar substitute and cinnamon in small bowl; stir until well blended. Spread mixture evenly over French toast. Top with strawberries.

Makes 4 servings

Note: This recipe was tested with aspartame sugar substitute.

Mini Sausage Quiches

½ cup butter or margarine, softened
  3 ounces cream cheese, softened
  1 cup all-purpose flour
½ pound BOB EVANS® Italian Roll Sausage
  1 cup (4 ounces) shredded Swiss cheese
  1 tablespoon snipped fresh chives
  2 eggs
  1 cup half-and-half
¼ teaspoon salt
    Dash cayenne pepper

Beat butter and cream cheese in medium bowl until creamy. Blend in flour; refrigerate 1 hour. Roll into 24 (1-inch) balls; press each into ungreased mini-muffin cup to form pastry shell. Preheat oven to 375°F. To prepare filling, crumble sausage into small skillet. Cook over medium heat until browned, stirring occasionally. Drain off any drippings. Sprinkle evenly into pastry shells in muffin cups; sprinkle with Swiss cheese and chives. Whisk eggs, half-and-half, salt and cayenne until blended; pour into pastry shells. Bake 20 to 30 minutes or until set. Remove from pans. Serve hot. Refrigerate leftovers.

Makes 24 appetizers

Tip: Pour mixture into 12 standard 2½-inch muffin cups to make larger individual quiches. Serve for breakfast.

Strawberry Cinnamon French Toast

Baked Banana Doughnuts

2 ripe bananas, mashed
2 egg whites
1 tablespoon vegetable oil
1 cup packed brown sugar
1½ cups all-purpose flour
¾ cup whole wheat flour
2 teaspoons baking powder
½ teaspoon baking soda
¼ teaspoon pumpkin pie spice
1 tablespoon granulated sugar
2 tablespoons chopped walnuts (optional)

Preheat oven to 425°F. Spray baking sheet with nonstick cooking spray. Beat bananas, egg whites, oil and brown sugar in large bowl or food processor. Add flours, baking powder, baking soda and pumpkin pie spice. Mix until well blended. Let stand for five minutes for dough to rise. Scoop out heaping tablespoonfuls of dough onto prepared baking sheet. Using thin rubber spatula or butter knife round out doughnut hole in center of dough (if dough sticks to knife or spatula, spray with cooking spray). With spatula, smooth outside edges of dough into round doughnut shape. Repeat until all dough is used. Sprinkle with granulated sugar and walnuts, if desired. Bake 6 to 10 minutes or until tops are golden.

Makes about 22 doughnuts

Variation: Use 8 ounces solid pack pumpkin instead of bananas to make pumpkin doughnuts.

Favorite recipe from **The Sugar Association, Inc.**

Spring Vegetable Quiche

4 eggs
1½ cups milk
1 package (10 ounces) frozen chopped spinach, thawed and squeezed dry
1 cup shredded Swiss cheese (about 4 ounces)
1 package KNORR® Recipe Classics™ Spring Vegetable recipe mix
1 (9-inch) frozen deep-dish pie crust

• Preheat oven and cookie sheet to 350°F.

• In large bowl, with wire whisk, beat eggs lightly. Blend in milk, spinach, cheese and recipe mix. Pour into frozen pie crust.

• Bake on cookie sheet 50 minutes or until knife inserted halfway between center and edge comes out clean.

Makes about 6 servings

Prep Time: 10 minutes | **Cook Time:** 50 minutes

Baked Banana Doughnuts

Spicy Sausage Popover Pizza

½ pound turkey breakfast sausage patties
½ pound 93% lean ground turkey
⅓ cup chopped onion
1 clove garlic, minced
¾ cup chopped red bell pepper
1½ cups all-purpose flour
¼ teaspoon salt
¼ teaspoon crushed red pepper
1 cup fat-free (skim) milk
¾ cup egg substitute *or* 3 eggs
1 cup (4 ounces) shredded reduced-fat Cheddar cheese
½ cup (2 ounces) shredded part-skim mozzarella cheese
½ cup prepared pizza sauce

1. Preheat oven to 425°F. Generously spray 13×9-inch baking dish with nonstick cooking spray; set aside.

2. Crumble turkey sausage patties into large skillet. Add ground turkey, onion and garlic to skillet. Cook over medium heat until turkey is no longer pink. Drain fat. Stir in bell pepper. Set aside.

3. Combine flour, salt and crushed red pepper in medium bowl. Combine milk and egg substitute in another medium bowl; whisk into flour mixture until smooth. Pour into prepared baking dish. Sprinkle sausage mixture over top. Sprinkle with Cheddar and mozzarella cheeses. Bake, uncovered, 21 to 23 minutes or until puffed and golden brown. Cut into 8 rectangles before serving.

4. Meanwhile, microwave pizza sauce at HIGH 1 minute. Top each rectangle with 1 tablespoon pizza sauce.

Makes 8 servings

Prep Time: 15 minutes | **Bake Time:** 21 to 23 minutes

Spicy Sausage Popover Pizza

French Toast Strata

4 ounces day-old French or Italian bread, cut into ¾-inch cubes (4 cups)
⅓ cup golden raisins
1 package (3 ounces) cream cheese, cut into ¼-inch cubes
3 eggs
1½ cups milk
½ cup maple-flavored pancake syrup
1 teaspoon vanilla
2 tablespoons sugar
1 teaspoon ground cinnamon
Additional maple-flavored pancake syrup (optional)

1. Spray 11×7-inch baking dish with nonstick cooking spray. Place bread cubes in even layer in prepared dish; sprinkle raisins and cream cheese evenly over bread.

2. Beat eggs in medium bowl with electric mixer at medium speed until blended. Add milk, ½ cup pancake syrup and vanilla; mix well. Pour egg mixture evenly over bread mixture. Cover; refrigerate at least 4 hours or overnight.

3. Preheat oven to 350°F. Combine sugar and cinnamon in small bowl; sprinkle evenly over strata.

4. Bake, uncovered, 40 to 45 minutes or until puffed, golden brown and knife inserted into center comes out clean. Cut into squares and serve with additional pancake syrup.

Makes 6 servings

Festive Cornmeal Biscuits

1¾ cups all-purpose flour
½ cup yellow cornmeal
1 tablespoon baking powder
1 tablespoon sugar
1 teaspoon salt
¼ teaspoon baking soda
3 tablespoons butter
¾ cup buttermilk
1 egg white, beaten
Peach or strawberry fruit spread (optional)

1. Preheat oven to 425°F. Spray baking sheet with nonstick cooking spray. Combine flour, cornmeal, baking powder, sugar, salt and baking soda in large bowl; mix well. Cut in butter with pastry blender or two knives until mixture forms coarse crumbs. Add buttermilk; mix just until dough holds together.

2. Turn dough out onto lightly floured surface; knead 8 to 10 times. Pat dough to ½-inch thickness; cut with decorative 2-inch cookie or biscuit cutter. Place biscuits onto prepared baking sheet. Brush tops lightly with egg white.

3. Bake 12 to 13 minutes or until light golden brown. Serve with preserves, if desired.

Makes 12 servings

French Toast Strata

Cinnamon Buns

1 recipe Sweet Yeast Dough (page 53)
½ cup granulated sugar
2 teaspoons ground cinnamon
2 tablespoons butter, melted
½ cup raisins (optional)
2 cups sifted powdered sugar
3 tablespoons milk
½ teaspoon vanilla

1. Prepare Sweet Yeast Dough; let rise as directed.

2. Combine granulated sugar and cinnamon in small bowl; set aside. Grease two 9-inch round cake pans.

3. Cut dough in half. Roll one half of dough into 12×8-inch rectangle on lightly floured surface with lightly floured rolling pin. Brush rectangle with half of melted butter; sprinkle with half of sugar mixture and half of raisins, if desired. Starting with long side, roll up jelly-roll style. (Do not roll dough too tightly because centers of rolls will pop up as they rise.) Repeat with remaining dough.

4. Cut each roll into 12 (1-inch slices) with unflavored dental floss or floured sharp knife. To use dental floss, position it under roll; bring up ends of floss, cross over center and gently pull floss to cut each slice.

5. Place slices ½ inch apart in prepared pans. Rolls will spread as they rise. Cover pans with towels; let rise in warm place about 1 hour or until doubled in bulk.

6. Preheat oven to 350°F. Bake 20 to 25 minutes or until rolls are golden brown. Cool in pans on wire racks 5 minutes.

7. Combine powdered sugar, milk and vanilla in small bowl until smooth. Spread mixture over rolls. Serve warm.

Makes 24 buns

Basil Biscuits

2 cups all-purpose flour
4 tablespoons grated Parmesan cheese, divided
1 tablespoon baking powder
½ teaspoon baking soda
¼ teaspoon salt
4 tablespoons Neufchâtel cheese
2 tablespoons butter, divided
6 ounces plain nonfat yogurt
⅓ cup slivered fresh basil leaves

1. Combine flour, 2 tablespoons Parmesan, baking powder, baking soda and salt in large bowl. Cut in Neufchâtel and 1 tablespoon butter with pastry blender or two knives until mixture forms coarse crumbs. Stir in yogurt and basil, mixing just until dough clings together. Turn dough out onto lightly floured surface and gently pat into ball. Knead just until dough holds together. Pat and roll dough into 7-inch log. Cut into 7 (1-inch-thick) slices.

2. Spray 10-inch cast iron skillet or Dutch oven with nonstick cooking spray; arrange biscuits in skillet. Melt remaining 1 tablespoon butter and brush over biscuit tops. Sprinkle with remaining 2 tablespoons Parmesan. Place skillet on grid set 4 to 6 inches above medium-hot coals (about 375°F); cover grill. Bake 20 to 40 minutes or until golden and firm on top. *Makes 7 biscuits*

Note: To prepare a charcoal grill for baking, arrange a single, solid, even layer of medium coals in bottom of charcoal grill. If necessary, reduce temperature by either allowing coals to burn down or removing 3 or 4 coals at a time to a fireproof container until desired temperature is reached. For a gas grill, begin on medium heat and adjust heat as necessary. Besides raising or lowering the temperature setting, you can turn off one side of the grill or set each side to a different temperature.

Breakfast in a Loaf

    Scrambled Eggs (recipe follows)
 1 round loaf bread (8- to 9-inch diameter)
 4 ounces sliced ham
½ red bell pepper, thinly sliced crosswise
½ cup (2 ounces) shredded Monterey Jack cheese
½ cup (2 ounces) shredded Cheddar cheese
½ cup sliced pitted ripe olives
 1 medium tomato, thinly sliced
 8 ounces mushrooms, sliced and cooked

1. Preheat oven to 350°F. Prepare Scrambled Eggs. Remove from heat; cover to keep warm.

2. Cut 2-inch slice from top of loaf; set aside for lid. Remove soft interior of loaf, leaving 1-inch-thick wall and bottom.

3. Place ham on bottom of loaf. Top with bell pepper rings; sprinkle with half of cheeses. Layer Scrambled Eggs, olives and tomato over cheeses. Top with remaining cheeses and mushrooms.

4. Place lid on loaf. Wrap in foil. Place on baking sheet. Bake about 30 minutes or until heated through. Cut into wedges. *Makes 4 servings*

Scrambled Eggs

  1 tablespoon butter or margarine
  6 eggs, lightly beaten
½ teaspoon salt
¼ teaspoon black pepper

1. Melt butter in 10-inch skillet over medium heat.

2. Season eggs with salt and pepper. Add eggs to skillet; cook, stirring gently and lifting to allow uncooked eggs to flow under cooked portion. Do not overcook; eggs should be soft with no liquid remaining. *Makes 4 servings*

Breakfast in a Loaf

Ham-Egg-Brie Strudel

4 eggs
1 tablespoon minced green onion
1 tablespoon minced parsley
¼ teaspoon salt
⅛ teaspoon black pepper
1 tablespoon vegetable oil
4 sheets phyllo pastry
2 tablespoons butter or margarine, melted
3 ounces sliced ham
3 ounces Brie cheese

1. Preheat oven to 375°F. Lightly beat eggs; add green onion, parsley, salt and pepper. Heat oil in medium skillet over medium-low heat. Add egg mixture; cook and stir until softly scrambled. Set aside.

2. Place 1 phyllo sheet on large piece of waxed paper. Brush lightly with butter. Top with second phyllo sheet; brush with butter. Repeat with remaining phyllo sheets. Arrange half of ham slices near short end of pastry, leaving 2-inch border around short end and sides. Place scrambled eggs over ham. Cut cheese into small pieces. Place over eggs; top with remaining ham.

3. Fold in long sides of phyllo; fold short end over ham. Use waxed paper to roll pastry to enclose filling. Place on lightly greased baking sheet, seam side down. Brush with remaining butter. Bake about 15 minutes or until lightly browned. Slice and serve immediately.

Makes 4 servings

Date-Nut Granola

2 cups uncooked old-fashioned oats
2 cups barley flakes
1 cup sliced almonds
⅓ cup vegetable oil
⅓ cup honey
1 teaspoon vanilla
1 cup chopped dates

1. Preheat oven to 350°F. Grease 13×9-inch baking pan.

2. Combine oats, barley flakes and almonds in large bowl; set aside.

3. Combine oil, honey and vanilla in small bowl. Pour honey mixture over oat mixture; stir well. Pour into prepared pan.

4. Bake about 25 minutes or until toasted, stirring frequently after the first 10 minutes. Stir in dates while mixture is still hot. Cool. Store tightly covered

Makes 6 cups

Honey Sweet Potato Biscuits

2 cups all-purpose flour
1 tablespoon baking powder
½ teaspoon salt
¼ cup vegetable shortening
1 tablespoon grated orange peel
1 tablespoon grated lemon peel
¾ cup mashed cooked sweet potato (1 large sweet potato baked until tender, peeled and mashed)
⅓ cup honey
½ cup milk (about)

Combine flour, baking powder and salt in large bowl. Cut in shortening until mixture is size of small peas. Add orange and lemon peels, sweet potato and honey; mix well. Add enough milk to make soft, but not sticky, dough. Knead 3 or 4 times on lightly floured surface. Pat dough to 1-inch thickness and cut into 2¼-inch rounds. Place on ungreased baking sheet.

Bake in preheated 400°F oven 15 to 18 minutes or until lightly browned. Serve warm.

Makes 10 biscuits

Favorite recipe from **National Honey Board**

Easy Morning Strata

1 pound BOB EVANS® Original Recipe Roll Sausage
8 eggs
10 slices bread, cut into cubes (about 10 cups)
3 cups milk
2 cups (8 ounces) shredded Cheddar cheese
2 cups (8 ounces) sliced fresh mushrooms
1 (10-ounce) package frozen cut asparagus, thawed and drained
2 tablespoons butter or margarine, melted
2 tablespoons all-purpose flour
1 tablespoon dry mustard
2 teaspoons dried basil leaves
1 teaspoon salt

Crumble sausage into large skillet. Cook over medium heat until browned, stirring occasionally. Drain off any drippings. Whisk eggs in large bowl. Add sausage and remaining ingredients; mix well. Spoon into greased 13×9-inch baking dish. Cover; refrigerate 8 hours or overnight. Preheat oven to 350°F. Bake 60 to 70 minutes or until knife inserted near center comes out clean. Let stand 5 minutes before cutting into squares; serve hot. Refrigerate leftovers.

Makes 10 to 12 servings

Onion-Parmesan Mini Bagels

4 to 4½ cups all-purpose flour, divided
2 tablespoons dried minced onion
2 tablespoons plus 1 teaspoon sugar, divided
1 package (¼ ounce) active dry yeast
1 teaspoon salt
1½ cups warm water (120° to 130°F)
6 cups plus 1 tablespoon cold water, divided
1 egg white
½ cup finely shredded Parmesan cheese

1. Combine 2 cups flour, onion, 2 tablespoons sugar, yeast and salt in large bowl. Add 1½ cups warm water. Beat with electric mixer at low speed 1 minute or until blended. Increase speed to high; beat 3 minutes.

2. On lightly floured surface, knead in enough remaining flour to make moderately stiff dough. Cover with plastic wrap; let rest 10 minutes.

3. Spray 2 baking sheets with nonstick cooking spray; set aside. Divide dough into 24 equal portions. Shape each portion into ball. Press thumbs through center of each ball. Stretch to form 1½-inch hole. Place on prepared baking sheets. Cover with plastic wrap and clean kitchen towel. Let rise in warm place 30 minutes or until doubled in bulk.

4. Preheat broiler. Broil bagels about 5 inches from heat source 2 to 3 minutes, turning once. (Bagels should not brown.) Bring 6 cups cold water and remaining 1 teaspoon sugar to a boil in Dutch oven. Drop 7 or 8 bagels into boiling water mixture. Gently simmer 3 minutes, turning once. Drain on paper towels. Repeat with remaining bagels.

5. Preheat oven to 375°F. Place bagels on baking sheets sprayed with cooking spray. Beat egg white and remaining 1 tablespoon water in small bowl. Brush tops of bagels with egg white mixture. Sprinkle with Parmesan cheese. Bake about 20 minutes or until golden brown. *Makes 24 bagels*

Prep Time: 40 minutes | **Rise Time:** 30 minutes | **Bake Time:** 20 minutes

Onion-Parmesan Mini Bagels

Breakfast Pizza

1 can (10 ounces) refrigerated biscuit dough
8 ounces bacon slices
2 tablespoons butter or margarine
2 tablespoons all-purpose flour
¼ teaspoon salt
⅛ teaspoon black pepper
1½ cups milk
½ cup (2 ounces) shredded sharp Cheddar cheese
¼ cup sliced green onions
¼ cup chopped red bell pepper

1. Preheat oven to 350°F. Spray 13×9-inch baking dish with nonstick cooking spray.

2. Separate biscuit dough; arrange in rectangle on lightly floured surface. Roll into 14×10-inch rectangle. Place in prepared dish; pat edges up sides of dish. Bake 15 minutes. Remove from oven; set aside.

3. Meanwhile, place bacon in single layer in large skillet; cook over medium heat until crisp. Remove from skillet; drain on paper towels. Crumble; set aside.

4. Melt butter in medium saucepan over medium heat. Stir in flour, salt and black pepper until smooth. Gradually stir in milk; cook and stir until thickened. Stir in cheese until melted. Spread sauce evenly over baked crust. Arrange bacon, green onions and bell pepper over sauce.

5. Bake, uncovered, 20 minutes or until crust is golden brown. Cut into 6 wedges before serving.

Makes 6 servings

helpful hint:

This breakfast pizza is a way to get more vegetables into your diet. Whatever you have in the refrigerator will work great in this recipe. Try sliced mushrooms, chopped broccoli, diced onion or halved cherry tomatoes. Leftovers are perfect for lunch too!

Breakfast Pizza

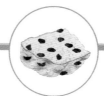

Sweet & Savory Quick Breads

Cheddar-Apple Bread

2 cups all-purpose flour
2 teaspoons baking powder
1 teaspoon baking soda
¼ teaspoon salt
1 cup sour cream
¼ cup milk
1 cup packed light brown sugar
½ cup (1 stick) butter, softened
2 eggs
1 teaspoon vanilla
1½ cups diced dried apples
1 cup (4 ounces) shredded Cheddar cheese

1. Preheat oven to 350°F. Spray 9×5-inch loaf pan with nonstick cooking spray; set aside.

2. Combine flour, baking powder, baking soda and salt in small bowl. Combine sour cream and milk in another small bowl. Beat brown sugar and butter in large bowl with electric mixer at medium speed until light and fluffy. Beat in eggs and vanilla until blended. Add flour mixture to butter mixture alternately with sour cream mixture, beginning and ending with flour mixture. Beat well after each addition. Stir in apples and cheese until blended. Spoon into prepared pan.

3. Bake 50 to 55 minutes or until toothpick inserted into center comes out clean. Cool in pan on wire rack 15 minutes. Remove from pan and cool completely on wire rack.

Makes 1 loaf (about 12 servings)

Tip: Brown sugar can become hard during storage, making it difficult to measure. To soften it, place the brown sugar in a microwavable bowl and microwave on HIGH 30 to 60 seconds or until softened.

Dazzling Orange Quick Bread

BREAD

- 1 cup all-purpose flour
- 1 cup whole wheat flour
- ¾ cup packed light brown sugar
- ¼ cup WATKINS® Vanilla Dessert Mix
- 1 teaspoon baking soda
- 1 teaspoon WATKINS® Baking Powder
- 1 teaspoon WATKINS® Ground Cinnamon
- 1 teaspoon WATKINS® Nutmeg
- ½ teaspoon salt
- ⅔ cup diet orange soda
- ½ cup honey
- 3 tablespoons egg substitute
- 1 teaspoon WATKINS® Butter Extract
- ½ cup ground pecans
- 1 can (11 ounces) mandarin oranges, drained and chopped

GLAZE

- 1 cup powdered sugar, sifted
- 1 to 2 tablespoons hot milk
- 1 teaspoon WATKINS® Vanilla
- ½ teaspoon WATKINS® Orange Extract
- ½ cup honey-roasted pecan halves or coarsely chopped pecans

Preheat oven to 350°F. Grease and flour 9×5-inch loaf pan. For bread, combine flours, brown sugar, dessert mix, baking soda, baking powder, cinnamon, nutmeg and salt in large bowl. Add orange soda, honey, egg substitute and butter extract; mix well. Stir in ground pecans and mandarin oranges. Pour into prepared pan. Bake for 50 to 60 minutes or until toothpick inserted into center comes out clean. Cool in pan on wire rack for 10 minutes; remove from pan and cool completely on wire rack.

For glaze, combine powdered sugar, milk, vanilla and orange extract in small bowl; beat until smooth. Drizzle over cake in lattice fashion. Arrange pecan halves between lattices or sprinkle with chopped pecans. *Makes 12 servings*

Favorite recipe from **Janice Green, Trenton, TN**

Mott's® Cinnamania Bread

½ cup GRANDMA'S® Molasses
½ cup water
 1 cup chopped dates
 1 (4-ounce) container red cinnamon imperial candies
½ cup MOTT'S® Natural Apple Sauce
 2 egg whites
1½ cups whole wheat flour
½ cup unprocessed bran
 3 teaspoons cinnamon
 1 teaspoon baking soda
 1 teaspoon baking powder

TOPPING
¼ cup MOTT'S® Natural Apple Sauce
½ teaspoon cinnamon
¼ cup crushed walnuts

1. Preheat oven to 350°F. Spray 8½×4½×2½-inch loaf pan with nonstick cooking spray.

2. Combine Grandma's Molasses, water, dates and candies in microwavable bowl. Microwave for 4 minutes on high power or until boiling. Stir in ½ cup Mott's Natural Apple Sauce and let mixture cool approximately 15 minutes. Stir in egg whites.

3. In separate large bowl, mix together wheat flour, bran, 3 teaspoons cinnamon, baking soda and baking powder. Pour in molasses mixture and stir just until moistened.

4. Pour batter into prepared loaf pan. Prepare Topping. Mix together ¼ cup Mott's Natural Apple Sauce and ½ teaspoon cinnamon. Spread evenly over top of batter with the back of spoon. Sprinkle crushed walnuts on top. Bake for 1 hour or until knife inserted in center comes out clean.   *Makes 9 servings*

Aloha Bread

   1 (10-ounce) jar maraschino cherries
1¾ cups all-purpose flour
   2 teaspoons baking powder
   ½ teaspoon salt
   ⅔ cup firmly packed brown sugar
   ⅓ cup butter or margarine, softened
   2 eggs
   1 cup mashed ripe bananas
   ½ cup chopped macadamia nuts or walnuts

Drain maraschino cherries, reserving 2 tablespoons juice. Cut cherries into quarters; set aside.

Combine flour, baking powder and salt in small bowl; set aside.

In medium bowl, combine brown sugar, butter, eggs and reserved cherry juice; mix at medium speed of electric mixer until ingredients are thoroughly combined. Add flour mixture alternately with mashed bananas, beginning and ending with flour mixture. Stir in cherries and nuts. Lightly spray 9×5×3-inch loaf pan with nonstick cooking spray. Spread batter evenly in pan.

Bake in preheated 350°F oven 1 hour or until loaf is golden brown and wooden pick inserted near center comes out clean. Remove from pan and cool on wire rack. Store in tightly covered container or wrapped in foil.   *Makes 1 loaf (about 16 slices)*

Favorite recipe from **Cherry Marketing Institute**

Spicy Onion Bread

   2 tablespoons instant minced onion
   ⅓ cup water
1½ cups biscuit mix
   ½ cup milk
   1 egg, lightly beaten
   ½ teaspoon TABASCO® brand Pepper Sauce
   2 tablespoons butter, melted
   ½ teaspoon caraway seeds (optional)

Preheat oven to 400°F. Soak instant minced onion in water 5 minutes. Combine biscuit mix, milk, egg and TABASCO® Sauce in large bowl and stir until blended. Stir in onion. Turn into greased 8-inch pie plate. Brush with melted butter. Sprinkle with caraway seeds. Bake 20 to 25 minutes or until golden brown.   *Makes 8 servings*

Aloha Bread

Zucchini-Orange Bread

1 package (about 17 ounces) cranberry-orange muffin mix
1½ cups shredded zucchini (about 6 ounces)
1 cup water
1 teaspoon ground cinnamon
1 teaspoon grated orange peel (optional)
Cream cheese (optional)

1. Preheat oven 350°F. Grease 8×4-inch loaf pan; set aside.

2. Combine muffin mix, zucchini, water, cinnamon and orange peel, if desired, in medium bowl; stir until just moistened. Spoon batter into prepared loaf pan; bake 40 minutes or until toothpick inserted into center comes out almost clean.

3. Cool in pan on wire rack 5 minutes. Remove bread from pan to wire rack; cool completely. Serve with cream cheese, if desired.   *Makes 1 loaf (about 16 slices)*

Poppy Seed Bread

BREAD
3 cups all-purpose flour
1½ teaspoons salt
1½ teaspoons WATKINS® Baking Powder
2¼ cups granulated sugar
3 eggs
1½ cups milk
1 cup plus 2 tablespoons WATKINS® Original Grapeseed Oil
1½ to 4 tablespoons WATKINS® Poppy Seed
1½ teaspoons WATKINS® Vanilla
1½ teaspoon WATKINS® Almond Extract
1½ teaspoons WATKINS® Butter Extract

GLAZE
¾ cup powdered sugar
¼ cup orange juice
½ teaspoon WATKINS® Vanilla
½ teaspoon WATKINS® Almond Extract
½ teaspoon WATKINS® Butter Extract

Preheat oven to 350°F. Grease and flour two 8½×4½-inch loaf pans. Combine all bread ingredients in large bowl in order listed above; beat 2 minutes. Pour into prepared pans. Bake for 55 minutes or until toothpick inserted into centers comes out clean.

Meanwhile, blend all glaze ingredients in small bowl until smooth. Drizzle over bread while loaves are warm.   *Makes 2 loaves*

Favorite recipe from **Susan Residence, Minnesota**

Zucchini-Orange Bread

Cranberry Raisin Nut Bread

1½ cups all-purpose flour
¾ cup packed light brown sugar
1½ teaspoons baking powder
½ teaspoon baking soda
½ teaspoon ground cinnamon
½ teaspoon ground nutmeg
1 cup coarsely chopped fresh or frozen cranberries
½ cup golden raisins
½ cup coarsely chopped pecans
1 tablespoon grated orange peel
2 eggs
¾ cup milk
3 tablespoons butter, melted
1 teaspoon vanilla
Cranberry-Orange Spread (recipe follows)

1. Preheat oven to 350°F. Grease 8½×4½-inch loaf pan.

2. Combine flour, brown sugar, baking powder, baking soda, cinnamon and nutmeg in large bowl. Stir in cranberries, raisins, pecans and orange peel. Mix eggs, milk, butter and vanilla in small bowl until blended; stir into flour mixture just until moistened. Spoon into prepared pan.

3. Bake 55 to 60 minutes or until toothpick inserted into center comes out clean. Cool in pan 15 minutes. Remove from pan and cool completely on wire rack. Store tightly wrapped in plastic wrap at room temperature. Serve with Cranberry-Orange Spread.

Makes 1 loaf

Cranberry-Orange Spread

1 package (8 ounces) cream cheese, softened
1 package (3 ounces) cream cheese, softened
1 container (12 ounces) cranberry-orange sauce
¾ cup chopped pecans

Combine cream cheese and cranberry-orange sauce in small bowl; stir until blended. Stir in pecans. Store in refrigerator.

Makes about 3 cups spread

Cranberry Raisin Nut Bread

Lemon Raisin Quick Bread

1¼ cups all-purpose flour
¾ cup whole wheat flour
4 tablespoons sugar, divided
2 teaspoons baking powder
½ teaspoon baking soda
¼ teaspoon salt
1½ cups (12 ounces) lemon-flavored low-fat yogurt
¼ cup (½ stick) unsalted butter, melted and cooled slightly
1 egg
½ teaspoon grated lemon peel
1 cup raisins
¾ cup chopped walnuts (optional)

1. Preheat oven to 350°F. Grease 8½×4½-inch loaf pan. Combine flours, 3 tablespoons sugar, baking powder, baking soda and salt in large bowl. Combine yogurt, butter, egg and lemon peel in medium bowl; stir until well blended.

2. Pour yogurt mixture into flour mixture. Add raisins and walnuts, if desired; stir just until dry ingredients are moistened. Pour into prepared pan and smooth top. Sprinkle with remaining 1 tablespoon sugar.

3. Bake 40 to 45 minutes or until lightly browned and toothpick inserted into center comes out clean. Cool in pan on wire rack 30 minutes. Remove from pan; cool completely.

Makes 1 loaf

Apricot Honey Bread

3 cups whole wheat flour
3 teaspoons baking powder
1 teaspoon ground cinnamon
½ teaspoon salt
¼ teaspoon ground nutmeg
1¼ cups 2% low-fat milk
1 cup honey
1 egg, slightly beaten
2 tablespoons vegetable oil
1 cup chopped dried apricots
½ cup sunflower seeds, chopped walnuts or almonds
½ cup raisins

Combine dry ingredients in large bowl. Combine milk, honey, egg and oil in separate large bowl. Pour milk mixture over dry ingredients and stir until just moistened. Gently fold in apricots, sunflower seeds and raisins. Pour into greased 9×5×3-inch loaf pan. Bake at 350°F 55 to 60 minutes or until wooden pick inserted near center comes out clean.

Makes 12 servings

Favorite recipe from **National Honey Board**

Mini Chip Harvest Ring

¾ cup whole-wheat flour*
¾ cup all-purpose flour
¾ cup granulated sugar
½ cup packed light brown sugar
2 teaspoons ground cinnamon
1¼ teaspoons baking soda
½ teaspoon salt
3 eggs
¾ cup vegetable oil
1½ teaspoons vanilla extract
2 cups grated carrots, apples *or* zucchini, drained
¾ cup HERSHEY'S MINI CHIPS™ Semi-Sweet Chocolate Chips
½ cup chopped walnuts
Cream Cheese Glaze (recipe follows)

All-purpose flour can be substituted for whole-wheat flour.

1. Heat oven to 350°F. Grease and flour 6- or 8-cup fluted tube pan.

2. Stir together whole-wheat flour, all-purpose flour, granulated sugar, brown sugar, cinnamon, baking soda and salt in large bowl. Beat eggs, oil and vanilla in small bowl. Add to dry ingredients; blend well. Stir in carrots, small chocolate chips and walnuts. Pour batter into prepared pan.

3. Bake 45 to 50 minutes or until wooden pick inserted in center comes out clean. Cool 30 minutes; remove from pan to wire rack.

4. Prepare Cream Cheese Glaze; spread over top of cake, allowing glaze to run down sides. Garnish as desired.   *Makes 8 to 10 servings*

Cream Cheese Glaze

1½ ounces (½ of 3-ounce package) cream cheese, softened
¾ cup powdered sugar
2 teaspoons milk
½ teaspoon vanilla extract

Beat cream cheese, powdered sugar, milk and vanilla in small bowl until smooth and of desired consistency. Add additional milk, ½ teaspoon at a time, if needed.

Onion-Zucchini Bread

1 large zucchini (¾ pound), shredded
2½ cups all-purpose flour*
1⅓ cups *French's®* French Fried Onions
⅓ cup grated Parmesan cheese
1 tablespoon baking powder
1 tablespoon chopped fresh basil *or* 1 teaspoon dried basil
½ teaspoon salt
¾ cup milk
½ cup (1 stick) butter or margarine, melted
¼ cup packed light brown sugar
2 eggs

You can substitute 1¼ cups whole wheat flour for 1¼ cups all-purpose flour.

1. Preheat oven to 350°F. Grease 9×5×3-inch loaf pan.

2. Drain zucchini in colander. Combine flour, French Fried Onions, cheese, baking powder, basil and salt in large bowl.

3. Combine milk, butter, brown sugar and eggs in medium bowl; whisk until well blended. Place zucchini in kitchen towel; squeeze out excess liquid. Stir zucchini into milk mixture.

4. Stir milk mixture into flour mixture, stirring just until moistened. Do not overmix. (Batter will be very stiff and dry.) Spread batter in prepared pan. Run knife down center of batter.

5. Bake 50 to 65 minutes or until toothpick inserted in center comes out clean. Cool in pan on wire rack 10 minutes. Remove bread from pan to wire rack; cool completely. Cut into slices to serve.**   *Makes 10 to 12 servings*

**For optimum flavor, wrap bread overnight and serve the next day. It's great when toasted!*

Prep Time: 20 minutes | **Bake Time:** about 1 hour

helpful hint:

Choose zucchini that are heavy for their size, firm and well shaped. They should have a bright color and be free of cuts and soft spots. Small zucchini are more tender because they were harvested when they were young. Although they are available all year, the peak season for zucchini is July to September.

Onion-Zucchini Bread

Mini Pumpkin Cranberry Breads

    3 cups all-purpose flour
    1 tablespoon plus 2 teaspoons pumpkin pie spice
    2 teaspoons baking soda
 1½ teaspoons salt
    3 cups granulated sugar
    1 can (15 ounces) LIBBY'S® 100% Pure Pumpkin
    4 large eggs
    1 cup vegetable oil
    ½ cup orange juice or water
    1 cup sweetened dried, fresh or frozen cranberries

PREHEAT oven to 350°F. Grease and flour five or six 5×3-inch mini disposable pans.

COMBINE flour, pumpkin pie spice, baking soda and salt in large bowl. Combine sugar, pumpkin, eggs, vegetable oil and orange juice in large mixer bowl; beat just until blended. Add pumpkin mixture to flour mixture; stir just until moistened. Fold in cranberries. Spoon batter into prepared loaf pans.

BAKE for 50 to 55 minutes or until wooden pick inserted into center comes out clean. Cool in pans on wire racks for 10 minutes; remove to wire racks to cool completely.

Makes 5 or 6 mini loaves

Walnut Cheddar Apple Bread

    2 cups all-purpose flour
    2 teaspoons baking powder
    1 teaspoon baking soda
 ¼ teaspoon salt
 ½ cup (2 sticks) butter, softened
    1 cup packed light brown sugar
    2 eggs
    1 teaspoon vanilla
    1 cup sour cream
 ¼ cup milk
    1 cup (4 ounces) shredded Cheddar cheese
    1 cup diced dried apples
 ½ cup coarsely chopped walnuts

1. Preheat oven to 350°F. Grease 9×5-inch loaf pan. Combine flour, baking powder, baking soda and salt in small bowl.

2. Beat butter and sugar in large bowl with electric mixer on medium speed until light and fluffy. Beat in eggs and vanilla. Add flour mixture to butter mixture on low speed alternately with sour cream and milk, beginning and ending with flour mixture. Mix well after each addition. Stir in cheese, apples and walnuts. Spoon batter into prepared pan.

3. Bake 50 to 55 minutes or until toothpick inserted in center comes out clean. Cool in pan 15 minutes. Remove from pan; cool completely on wire rack. *Makes 1 loaf (16 slices)*

Mini Pumpkin Cranberry Bread

Brunch-Time Zucchini-Date Bread

BREAD
1 cup chopped pitted dates
1 cup water
1 cup whole wheat flour
1 cup all-purpose flour
2 tablespoons granulated sugar
1 teaspoon baking powder
½ teaspoon baking soda
½ teaspoon salt
½ teaspoon ground cinnamon
¼ teaspoon ground cloves
2 eggs
1 cup shredded zucchini, pressed dry with paper towels

CREAM CHEESE SPREAD
1 package (8 ounces) cream cheese
¼ cup powdered sugar
1 tablespoon vanilla
⅛ teaspoon ground cinnamon
Dash ground cloves

1. Preheat oven to 350°F. Spray 8×4-inch loaf pan with nonstick cooking spray; set aside.

2. For bread, combine dates and water in small saucepan. Bring to a boil over medium-high heat. Remove from heat; let stand 15 minutes.

3. Combine flours, granulated sugar, baking powder, baking soda, salt, cinnamon and cloves in large bowl. Beat eggs in medium bowl; stir in date mixture and zucchini. Stir egg mixture into flour mixture just until dry ingredients are moistened. Pour batter evenly into prepared pan.

4. Bake 30 to 35 minutes or until toothpick inserted into center comes out clean. Cool 5 minutes. Remove from pan. Cool completely on wire rack.

5. Meanwhile, for cream cheese spread, combine cream cheese, powdered sugar, vanilla, cinnamon and cloves in small bowl. Beat until smooth. Cover and refrigerate until ready to use.

6. Cut bread into 16 slices. Serve with cream cheese spread. *Makes 16 servings*

Brunch-Time Zucchini-Date Bread

Boston Brown Bread

½ cup rye flour
½ cup yellow cornmeal
½ cup whole wheat flour
3 tablespoons sugar
1 teaspoon baking soda
¾ teaspoon salt
½ cup chopped walnuts
½ cup raisins
1 cup buttermilk*
⅓ cup molasses
Boiling water

Or, substitute soured fresh milk. To sour milk, place 1 tablespoon lemon juice plus enough milk to equal 1 cup in 2-cup measure. Stir; let stand 5 minutes before using.

1. Generously grease 3 (16-ounce) cans and 1 side of 3 (6-inch) square foil pieces with shortening; set aside.

2. Combine rye flour, cornmeal, whole wheat flour, sugar, baking soda and salt in large bowl. Stir in walnuts and raisins. Whisk buttermilk and molasses in medium bowl until smooth. Add buttermilk mixture to dry ingredients; stir until well mixed.

3. Spoon mixture evenly into prepared cans. Place 1 piece of foil, greased side down, on top of each can. Secure foil with rubber bands or cotton string. Place filled cans in deep 4-quart saucepan or Dutch oven.** Pour boiling water around cans so water comes halfway up sides of cans. (Make sure foil tops do not touch boiling water.)

4. Bring to a boil over high heat. Reduce heat to low. Cover; simmer (water should be bubbling very slowly) 1¼ to 1½ hours or until wooden skewer inserted in center of bread comes out clean. Remove cans from saucepan. Immediately run knife around inside edges of cans to loosen breads. Invert and gently shake breads out of cans. Cool completely on wire rack.

Makes 3 loaves

**To bake loaves, preheat oven to 325°F. Prepare batter as directed in steps 1 through 3 and spoon into prepared cans. Do not cover with foil. Bake 45 to 50 minutes or until tops are brown and wooden skewer inserted in center comes out clean. Immediately run knife around inside edges of cans. Invert and gently shake breads out of cans. Cool completely on wire rack.*

Boston Brown Bread

Banana Nut Bread

½ cup granulated sugar
2 tablespoons brown sugar
5 tablespoons margarine
1⅓ cups mashed ripe bananas (2 medium)
1 egg
2 egg whites
2½ cups all-purpose flour
1 teaspoon baking soda
½ teaspoon salt
⅓ cup walnuts

Preheat oven to 375°F. Spray large loaf pan with nonstick cooking spray; set aside.

Beat sugars and margarine in large bowl with electric mixer until light and fluffy. Add bananas, egg and egg whites. Sift together flour, baking soda and salt in medium bowl; add to banana mixture. Stir in walnuts. Pour into prepared loaf pan.

Bake 1 hour or until wooden pick inserted into center comes out clean. Remove from pan. Cool on wire rack 10 minutes. Serve warm or cool completely.

Makes 1 loaf (16 servings)

Favorite recipe from **The Sugar Association, Inc.**

Lemon Cranberry Loaves

1¼ cups finely chopped fresh cranberries
½ cup finely chopped walnuts
¼ cup granulated sugar
1 package DUNCAN HINES® Moist Deluxe® Lemon Supreme Cake Mix
¾ cup milk
1 package (3 ounces) cream cheese, softened
4 eggs
Confectioners' sugar

1. Preheat oven to 350°F. Grease and flour two 8½×4½-inch loaf pans.

2. Stir together cranberries, walnuts and granulated sugar in large bowl; set aside.

3. Combine cake mix, milk and cream cheese in large bowl. Beat at medium speed with electric mixer for 2 minutes. Add eggs, 1 at a time, beating for 2 minutes. Fold in cranberry mixture. Pour into prepared pans. Bake at 350°F for 45 to 50 minutes or until toothpick inserted in centers comes out clean. Cool in pans 15 minutes. Loosen loaves from pans. Invert onto cooling rack. Turn right side up. Cool completely. Dust with confectioners' sugar.

Makes 24 slices

Tip: To quickly chop cranberries or walnuts, use a food processor fitted with a steel blade and pulse until evenly chopped.

Banana Nut Bread

Honey Soda Bread

    2 cups all-purpose flour
    1 cup whole wheat flour
    2 teaspoons baking soda
    ½ teaspoon salt
    ¼ cup butter or margarine, cut up
    1 cup golden raisins
    2 teaspoons caraway seeds
    1 cup plain low-fat yogurt
    ⅓ cup honey
    2 tablespoons milk

In large bowl, combine flours, baking soda and salt; mix well. Cut in butter until mixture resembles coarse crumbs; mix in raisins and caraway seeds.

In small bowl, whisk together yogurt and honey. Add to flour mixture; stir until just combined. Turn dough onto lightly floured surface; knead 10 times or until dough is smooth. Form dough into ball; place on lightly greased baking sheet. With sharp knife, cut an "X" ¼ inch deep into top of loaf; brush with milk. Bake at 325°F for 45 to 50 minutes or until golden. Cool on wire rack.   *Makes 1 loaf*

Favorite recipe from **National Honey Board**

Jalapeño-Bacon Corn Bread

    4 slices bacon, crisp-cooked and drippings reserved
    ¼ cup minced green onions
    2 jalapeño peppers,* stemmed, seeded and minced
    1 cup yellow cornmeal
    1 cup all-purpose flour
 2½ teaspoons baking powder
    ½ teaspoon *each* baking soda and salt
    ¾ cup plain yogurt
    1 egg, beaten
    ¾ cup milk
    ¼ cup (½ stick) butter, melted
    ½ cup (2 ounces) shredded Cheddar cheese

Jalapeño peppers can sting and irritate the skin, so wear rubber gloves when handling them and do not touch your eyes.

1. Preheat oven to 400°F. Pour 2 tablespoons bacon drippings into 9-inch square baking pan. Crumble bacon into small bowl; add green onions and peppers.

2. Combine cornmeal, flour, baking powder, baking soda and salt in large bowl. Whisk yogurt and egg in medium bowl until smooth. Whisk in milk and butter. Pour liquid mixture into dry ingredients; stir just until moistened. Stir in bacon mixture. Pour into prepared pan; sprinkle with cheese. Bake 20 to 25 minutes or until toothpick inserted into center comes out clean. Cut into squares; serve hot.   *Makes 9 to 12 servings*

Molasses Brown Bread

1 cup all-purpose flour
1 cup graham or rye flour
1 cup whole wheat flour
1 teaspoon baking soda
½ teaspoon salt
1 cup buttermilk
1 cup light molasses
½ cup golden or dark raisins
½ cup chopped walnuts or pecans
   Cream cheese (optional)

1. Preheat oven to 350°F. Spray 9×5-inch loaf pan with nonstick cooking spray. Combine all-purpose flour, graham flour, whole wheat flour, baking soda and salt in large bowl. Add buttermilk and molasses; mix well. Stir in raisins and nuts.

2. Spoon batter evenly into prepared pan. Bake 50 to 55 minutes or until toothpick inserted into center comes out clean.

3. Transfer pan to wire rack; let stand 10 minutes. Remove bread from pan to wire rack; cool completely. Serve at room temperature with cream cheese, if desired.

Makes 1 loaf (about 16 slices)

Chippy Banana Bread

⅓ cup butter or margarine, softened
⅔ cup sugar
2 eggs
2 tablespoons milk
1¾ cups all-purpose flour
1¼ teaspoons baking powder
¾ teaspoon salt
½ teaspoon baking soda
1 cup mashed ripe bananas
1 cup HERSHEY'S Semi-Sweet Chocolate Chips or HERSHEY'S Cinnamon
   Chips

1. Heat oven to 350°F. Lightly grease 8×4×2-inch loaf pan.

2. Beat butter and sugar in large bowl on medium speed of mixer until creamy. Add eggs, one at a time, beating well after each addition. Add milk; beat until blended.

3. Stir together flour, baking powder, salt and baking soda; add alternately with bananas to butter mixture, beating until smooth after each addition. Gently fold in chocolate chips. Pour batter into prepared pan.

4. Bake 60 to 65 minutes or until wooden pick inserted near center comes out clean. Cool 10 minutes. Remove from pan to wire rack; cool completely. For easier slicing, wrap in foil and store overnight.

Makes 12 servings

Malty Maple Corn Bread

1 cup coarse ground cornmeal
1 cup porter* or dark ale
¼ cup maple syrup
1 cup all-purpose flour
1 tablespoon baking powder
½ teaspoon salt
2 eggs, beaten
¼ cup (½ stick) melted butter

Porter is a dark beer with a strong flavor of roasted malt.

1. Preheat oven to 400°F. Grease 9-inch square baking pan. Combine cornmeal, porter and maple syrup in small bowl; set aside.

2. Sift flour, baking powder and salt into large bowl. Add cornmeal mixture, eggs and melted butter. Stir until well blended.

3. Pour batter into prepared baking pan. Bake 20 to 25 minutes or until toothpick inserted into center comes out clean. Cool in pan 10 minutes. Slice and serve.

Makes 8 servings

Note: For an extra-flavorful crust, place the greased pan in the oven for several minutes to preheat. When batter is ready, pour it into the hot pan and bake as directed. The corn bread will develop a thick, brown crust with a deep, rich flavor.

Soda Bread

1½ cups whole wheat flour
1 cup all-purpose flour
½ cup rolled oats
¼ cup sugar
1½ teaspoons baking powder
½ teaspoon baking soda
¼ teaspoon ground cinnamon
⅓ cup raisins (optional)
¼ cup walnuts (optional)
1¼ cups low-fat buttermilk
1 tablespoon vegetable oil

Preheat oven to 375°F. Combine whole wheat flour, all-purpose flour, oats, sugar, baking powder, baking soda and cinnamon in large bowl. Stir in raisins and walnuts, if desired. Gradually stir in buttermilk and oil until dough forms. Knead in bowl for 30 seconds. Spray 8×4-inch loaf pan with nonstick cooking spray; place dough in pan. Bake 40 to 50 minutes or until wooden toothpick inserted into center comes out clean. *Makes 16 slices*

Favorite recipe from **The Sugar Association, Inc.**

Malty Maple Corn Bread

Herb-Cheese Biscuit Loaf

1½ cups all-purpose flour
¼ cup grated Parmesan cheese
2 tablespoons yellow cornmeal
2 teaspoons baking powder
½ teaspoon salt
¼ cup (½ stick) cold butter, cut into pieces
2 eggs
½ cup whipping cream
¾ teaspoon dried basil
¾ teaspoon dried oregano
⅛ teaspoon garlic powder
Additional grated Parmesan cheese (optional)

1. Preheat oven to 425°F. Grease large baking sheet; set aside.

2. Combine flour, ¼ cup cheese, cornmeal, baking powder and salt in large bowl. Cut in butter with pastry blender or two knives until mixture resembles coarse crumbs.

3. Beat eggs in medium bowl. Add cream, basil, oregano and garlic powder; beat until well blended. Add cream mixture to flour mixture; stir until mixture forms soft dough that clings together and forms ball.

4. Turn dough out onto well-floured surface. Knead dough gently 10 to 12 times. Place dough on prepared baking sheet. Roll or pat dough into 7-inch round, about 1 inch thick.

5. Starting from center, score top of dough into 8 wedges with tip of sharp knife. (Do not cut completely through dough.) Sprinkle with additional cheese, if desired.

6. Bake 20 to 25 minutes or until toothpick inserted into center comes out clean. Cool on baking sheet on wire rack 10 minutes. Serve warm.   *Makes 8 servings*

helpful hint:

Cornmeal is a meal ground from dried corn kernels. Fine grade cornmeal comes from white, yellow or blue corn. It can be stone-ground, in which the germ and hull of the corn is ground too, so the meal has more vitamins. More typical is steel-ground cornmeal, produced by a modern process that removes the husk and germ so the meal is more highly refined.

Herb-Cheese Biscuit Loaf

Hawaiian Fruit and Nut Quick Bread

2 cups all-purpose flour
1 tablespoon orange-flavored instant drink powder
2 teaspoons baking soda
1 teaspoon ground cinnamon
¾ cup granulated sugar
¾ cup light brown sugar
¾ cup chopped macadamia nuts
½ cup shredded coconut
¾ cup canola oil
2 eggs
2 teaspoons rum extract
2 cups chopped fresh mango

1. Preheat oven to 350°F. Lightly grease 9×5-inch loaf pan. Set aside.

2. Sift flour, drink powder, baking soda and cinnamon into medium bowl. Stir in sugars, macadamia nuts and coconut. Combine oil, eggs and rum extract in separate medium bowl. Add to dry mixture; stir to mix well. Stir in mango.

3. Spoon batter into prepared pan. Bake 60 to 70 minutes or until bread is light golden brown and pulls away from sides of pan. Cool in pan 10 minutes. Remove to wire rack; cool completely.

Makes 1 loaf

Oatmeal Pumpkin Bread

1 cup quick-cooking oats
1 cup low-fat milk, heated
¾ cup cooked or canned pumpkin
2 eggs, beaten
¼ cup margarine, melted
2 cups all-purpose flour
1 cup sugar
1 tablespoon baking powder
1 teaspoon ground cinnamon
¼ teaspoon ground nutmeg
¼ teaspoon salt
1 cup raisins
½ cup chopped pecans

Preheat oven to 350°F. In large bowl, combine oats and milk; let stand about 5 minutes. Stir in pumpkin, eggs and margarine. In separate bowl, mix together flour, sugar, baking powder, cinnamon, nutmeg and salt. Gradually add dry ingredients to oatmeal mixture. Stir in raisins and nuts; mix well. Place in greased 9×5-inch loaf pan. Bake 55 to 60 minutes or until done. Cool on wire rack.

Makes one loaf (16 slices)

Favorite recipe from **The Sugar Association, Inc.**

Hawaiian Fruit and Nut Quick Bread

Rising Yeast Breads

Petit Pain au Chocolate

3 to 3½ cups all-purpose flour
3 tablespoons granulated sugar
1 package (¼ ounce) active dry yeast
1 teaspoon salt
1 cup plus 1 tablespoon milk, divided
3 tablespoons butter or margarine, at room temperature
1 egg, lightly beaten
1 milk chocolate candy bar (6 ounces), cut into 16 pieces
2 teaspoons colored sugar

1. Combine 3 cups flour, granulated sugar, yeast and salt in large bowl; set aside.

2. Combine 1 cup milk and butter in small saucepan. Heat over low heat until mixture is 120° to 130°F. (Butter does not need to completely melt.)

3. Gradually stir milk mixture and egg into flour mixture until dough forms ball.

4. Turn out dough onto lightly floured surface; flatten slightly. Knead dough 8 to 10 minutes or until smooth and elastic, adding remaining ½ cup flour to prevent sticking if necessary.

5. Shape dough into ball; place in large greased bowl. Turn dough over so that top is greased. Cover with towel; let rise in warm place about 1 hour or until doubled in bulk.

6. Punch down dough. Knead dough on lightly floured surface 1 minute. Roll dough back and forth, forming loaf.

7. Cut loaf into 8 pieces. Roll 1 dough piece into 6-inch round. Place 2 chocolate pieces in center. Fold edges into center around chocolate. Place seam side down on lightly greased baking sheet. Repeat with remaining dough pieces, placing rolls 3 inches apart on baking sheet.

8. Cover rolls lightly with towel and let rise in warm place 20 to 30 minutes or until slightly puffed. Meanwhile, preheat oven to 400°F. Brush tops with remaining 1 tablespoon milk. Sprinkle with colored sugar.

9. Bake 12 to 15 minutes or until rolls are golden brown. Serve immediately.

Makes 8 rolls

Berry-Cheese Braid

DOUGH
1 cup milk
1 egg, lightly beaten
3 tablespoons butter, softened
1 teaspoon salt
3 cups bread flour
5 tablespoons sugar
1½ teaspoons active dry yeast

FILLING
1 package (8 ounces) cream cheese, softened
1 egg
¼ cup sugar
½ teaspoon vanilla
1 cup fresh raspberries
1 cup fresh blueberries

TOPPING
1 tablespoon sugar

BREAD MACHINE DIRECTIONS

1. Measuring carefully, place all dough ingredients in bread machine pan in order specified by owner's manual. Program dough cycle setting; press start. (Do not use delay cycle.) Lightly grease 2 baking sheets; set aside.

2. For filling, beat cream cheese, egg, sugar and vanilla in large bowl until well blended; cover and refrigerate.

3. When cycle is complete, remove dough to lightly floured surface. If necessary, knead in additional bread flour to make dough easy to handle. Divide dough in half. Roll each half into 12×9-inch* rectangle; carefully place rectangles on prepared baking sheets.

4. Spread cream cheese filling lengthwise down center third of each dough rectangle, leaving 1-inch border at short ends. Sprinkle evenly with raspberries and blueberries. Fold 1-inch short-end dough borders over filling. Make 5 cuts on each long side of dough rectangles, just up to filling, to form 6 strips on each side. Gently fold strips in toward centers, alternating left and right, and allowing some filling to show through. Sprinkle braids with 1 tablespoon sugar. Cover with clean towels; let rise in warm, draft-free place 45 minutes or until doubled in size.

5. Preheat oven to 325°F. Bake braids 25 to 30 minutes or until golden brown. Remove from baking sheets; cool on wire racks. Serve at room temperature.

Makes 2 braids (24 servings)

For a slightly flatter appearance, roll dough into 14×9-inch rectangle.

Berry-Cheese Braid

Bread Bowls

1¼ cups water
1 teaspoon salt
1½ teaspoons sugar
3 tablespoons white cornmeal
3¾ cups bread flour
2¼ teaspoons (1 packet) RED STAR® Active Dry Yeast or QUICK•RISE™ Yeast
　　or Bread Machine Yeast

BREAD MACHINE METHOD

Place room temperature ingredients in pan in order listed. Select dough cycle. Check dough consistency after 5 minutes of kneading, making adjustments, if necessary.

TRADITIONAL METHOD

Combine yeast, 1 cup flour and other dry ingredients. Heat water to 120° to 130°F; add to flour mixture. Beat 3 minutes on medium speed. By hand, stir in enough remaining flour to make firm dough. Knead on floured surface 5 to 7 minutes until smooth and elastic. Use additional flour, if necessary. Place dough in lightly greased bowl. Cover; let rise until dough tests ripe.*

Place two fingers into the risen dough up to second knuckle and take out. If the indentations remain the dough is ripe and ready to punch down.

SHAPING, RISING AND BAKING

Turn dough onto lightly floured surface; punch down to remove air bubbles. Divide and shape into three round balls. Place on greased baking sheet covered with cornmeal. Cover; let rise until indentation remains after lightly touching sides of balls. Bake in preheated 425°F oven 20 to 30 minutes. Spray or brush balls with cold water several times during first 10 minutes of baking for a crispy crust. Remove from baking sheet; cool.

TO MAKE BOWLS

Cut thin slice off the top. Hollow out inside, leaving half-inch sides. Placing bowls in a 300°F oven for 10 minutes will dry sides and prevent premature soaking from salads and soups.　　　　　　　　　　　　　　　　　　　　　　*Makes 3 bread bowls*

Note: Fill bread bowls with your favorite thick soup, such as chili, hearty seafood, corn or potato chowder, or a crisp vegetable, seafood or fruit salad. Because of the thin walls, the bowls are not suitable for thin soups like chicken noodle or French onion. Fill bowls with your favorite dip and use inside pieces as dunkers.

Bread Bowl

Parker House Rolls

4¾ to 5¼ cups all-purpose flour, divided
⅓ cup sugar
2 envelopes FLEISCHMANN'S® RapidRise™ Yeast
1½ teaspoons salt
¾ cup milk
¾ cup water
¼ cup butter or margarine
1 egg
¼ cup butter or margarine, melted

In large bowl, combine 2 cups flour, sugar, undissolved yeast and salt. Heat milk, water and ¼ cup unmelted butter until very warm (120° to 130°F). Stir into dry ingredients. Beat 2 minutes at medium speed of electric mixer, scraping bowl occasionally. Add egg and ½ cup flour; beat 2 minutes at high speed. Stir in enough remaining flour to make a soft dough. Knead on lightly floured surface until smooth and elastic, about 8 to 10 minutes. Cover;* let rest 10 minutes.

Divide dough in half; roll each half into 12-inch square, about ¼-inch thick. Cut each into 6 (12×2-inch) strips. Cut each strip into 3 (4×2-inch) rectangles. Brush each rectangle with melted butter. Crease rectangles slightly off center with dull edge of knife and fold at crease. Arrange rolls side by side in rows, slightly overlapping, on greased baking sheets, with shorter side of each roll facing down. Allow ¼ inch of space between each row. Cover; let rise in warm, draft-free place until doubled in size, about 30 minutes.

Bake at 400°F for 13 to 15 minutes or until done. Remove from sheets; cool on wire rack. Brush with remaining melted butter. *Makes 36 rolls*

If desired, allow dough to rise in refrigerator 12 to 24 hours.

helpful hint:

The Parker House roll was given its name at a 19th century Boston hotel, the Parker House. It's a light yeast roll with a characteristic shape of a round piece of dough that is folded in half on an off-center crease.

Parker House Rolls

Maple-Pumpkin-Pecan Rings

1 can (15 ounces) solid-pack pumpkin
1 cup water
½ cup shortening
7 to 8 cups all-purpose flour, divided
2 cups pecans, coarsely chopped
½ cup sugar
2 packages (¼ ounce each) active dry yeast
2 teaspoons salt
2 eggs
2 teaspoons maple flavoring, divided
6 to 8 tablespoons milk
2 cups powdered sugar

1. Combine pumpkin, water and shortening in medium saucepan over medium heat until shortening is melted and temperature reaches 120° to 130°F. Remove from heat.

2. Combine 4 cups flour, pecans, sugar, yeast and salt in large bowl. Add pumpkin mixture, eggs and 1 teaspoon maple flavoring; beat vigorously 2 minutes. Add remaining flour, ¼ cup at a time, until dough begins to pull away from side of bowl. Turn dough out onto lightly floured work surface; flatten slightly. Knead 10 minutes or until smooth and elastic, using additional flour to prevent sticking, if necessary. Shape dough into ball. Place in large, lightly greased bowl; turn dough over once to grease top. Cover with clean kitchen towel; let rise in warm place about 1 hour or until doubled in bulk.

3. Turn dough out onto lightly greased work surface; divide into four pieces. Shape each piece into 24-inch-long rope. Twist two ropes together. Tuck ends under loaf to prevent untwisting. Place on lightly greased baking sheet. Repeat with remaining two ropes. Form each twisted rope into a ring; pinch edges to seal. Cover; let rise in warm place 45 minutes.

4. Preheat oven to 375°F. Bake bread 25 minutes or until deep golden brown. Immediately remove bread from baking sheets and cool on wire racks 20 minutes.

5. Combine remaining 1 teaspoon maple flavoring and 6 tablespoons milk in small bowl. Whisk milk mixture into powdered sugar in medium bowl. If icing is too thick, add remaining milk, 1 teaspoon at a time, until of desired consistency. Drizzle over loaves.

Makes 2 large rings

Maple-Pumpkin-Pecan Rings

Peanut Butter & Chocolate Pull-Apart Rolls

DOUGH
½ cup milk
⅓ cup water (70° to 80°F)
¼ cup creamy peanut butter, at room temperature
½ teaspoon salt
2¼ cups bread flour
¼ cup sugar
1½ teaspoons FLEISCHMANN'S® Bread Machine Yeast

FILLING
½ cup (3 ounces) semisweet chocolate pieces
2 tablespoons creamy peanut butter

ICING
½ cup sifted powdered sugar
1 tablespoon creamy peanut butter or cocoa powder
2 to 4 teaspoons milk

BREAD MACHINE RECIPE

To make dough, add dough ingredients to bread machine pan in the order suggested by manufacturer. Select dough/manual cycle.

To make filling, combine filling ingredients in small bowl; blend well. To shape and fill, when cycle is complete, remove dough to floured surface. If necessary, knead in additional flour to make dough easy to handle.

Roll dough into 14-inch circle. Cut into 6 wedges; place filling, dividing evenly, at wide end of each wedge. Beginning at wide end, roll up tightly; curve to form crescent. Arrange crescents, seam side down, in spoke fashion on greased large baking sheet. Pinch ends at center to seal. Cover and let rise in warm, draft-free place until doubled in size, about 30 to 45 minutes. Bake at 375°F for 15 to 20 minutes or until done. Remove from pan; cool on wire rack.

To make icing, combine icing ingredients in small bowl; stir until smooth. Drizzle on rolls.

Makes 6 rolls

Note: Dough can be prepared in all size bread machines.

Peanut Butter & Chocolate Pull-Apart Rolls

Apricot Ring

FILLING
1 cup dried apricots, chopped
1 cup apple juice
¾ cup sugar

DOUGH
1 package (¼ ounce) active dry yeast
4 tablespoons sugar, divided
1 cup warm water (110°F)
4 cups all-purpose flour, divided
1 teaspoon salt
2 eggs, beaten
¼ cup (½ stick) butter or margarine, softened
1 egg white, lightly beaten
2 tablespoons sliced almonds

1. To make filling, combine apricots and apple juice in small saucepan over medium heat. Cover and cook, stirring occasionally, about 12 minutes or until apricots are tender and juice is absorbed. Stir in sugar to taste. Cook, stirring constantly, about 3 minutes or until mixture becomes thick paste; remove from heat and let cool.

2. To make dough, dissolve yeast and 1 tablespoon sugar in water in large bowl of electric mixer. Let stand 10 minutes. Add remaining 3 tablespoons sugar, 1 cup flour and salt.

3. Beat with electric mixer at medium speed 3 minutes. Add 2 eggs and butter. Stir in enough of remaining 3 cups flour to make soft dough.

4. Knead dough on lightly floured surface about 10 minutes or until smooth, using additional flour if necessary to prevent sticking. Cover and let rest 20 minutes.

5. Grease large baking sheet. Roll dough into 18×11-inch rectangle on lightly floured surface. Spread filling over dough. Roll up jelly-roll style; seal edge. Form into ring on prepared baking sheet, sealing ends.

6. Cut ring at 1-inch intervals about two thirds of the way through dough, using kitchen scissors or sharp knife. Turn each slice outward to form a petal as you cut.

7. Cover with damp cloth; let rise in warm place about 45 minutes or until doubled in bulk.

8. Preheat oven to 350°F. Brush ring with egg white and sprinkle with almonds. Bake about 30 minutes or until browned.   *Makes 1 large coffeecake (15 to 18 servings)*

Swedish Limpa Bread

1¾ to 2 cups all-purpose flour, divided
½ cup rye flour
1 package (¼ ounce) active dry yeast
1 tablespoon sugar
1½ teaspoons grated orange peel
1 teaspoon salt
½ teaspoon fennel seeds, crushed
½ teaspoon caraway seeds, crushed
¾ cup plus 4 teaspoons water, divided
4 tablespoons molasses, divided
2 tablespoons butter or margarine
1 teaspoon instant coffee granules
¼ teaspoon whole fennel seeds
¼ teaspoon whole caraway seeds

1. Combine 1½ cups all-purpose flour, rye flour, yeast, sugar, orange peel, salt and crushed seeds in large bowl. Heat ¾ cup water, 3 tablespoons molasses and butter in small saucepan over low heat until temperature reaches 120° to 130°F. Stir in coffee granules. Stir water mixture into flour mixture with rubber spatula to form soft but sticky dough. Gradually add additional all-purpose flour to form rough dough.

2. Turn out dough onto lightly floured surface. Knead 2 minutes or until soft dough forms, gradually adding remaining all-purpose flour to prevent sticking, if necessary. Cover with inverted bowl; let rest 5 minutes. Continue kneading 5 to 8 minutes or until smooth and elastic. Shape dough into ball; place in large greased bowl. Turn dough over to grease top. Loosely cover with lightly greased sheet of plastic wrap. Let rise in warm place 75 minutes or until almost doubled in bulk.

3. Punch down dough. Grease 8½×4½-inch loaf pan. Roll dough into 12×7-inch rectangle. Starting with one short end, roll up tightly, jelly-roll style. Pinch seams and ends to seal. Place seam-side down in prepared pan. Cover loosely with plastic wrap. Let rise in warm place 1 hour or until doubled in bulk.

4. Preheat oven to 350°F. Stir together remaining 1 tablespoon molasses and 4 teaspoons water in small bowl; set aside. Uncover loaf; make 3 diagonal slashes on top of dough using sharp knife. Bake 40 to 45 minutes or until loaf sounds hollow when tapped; brush top with molasses mixture and sprinkle with whole fennel and caraway seeds halfway through baking time. Brush again with molasses mixture about 10 minutes before removing loaf from oven. Cool in pan on wire rack 5 minutes. Remove from pan. Cool completely on wire rack.

Makes 1 loaf (12 servings)

Rye Bread

2 packages active dry yeast
1 tablespoon sugar
1¾ cups warm water (105° to 115°F)
3 cups rye flour, divided
2 to 3 cups bread flour, divided
½ cup molasses
2 tablespoons caraway seeds
2 tablespoons white vinegar
2 tablespoons vegetable oil
2 teaspoons salt
1 egg
1 egg white
1 tablespoon water
Additional caraway seeds (optional)

1. Sprinkle yeast and sugar over 1¾ cups warm water in large bowl of electric mixer; stir until yeast is dissolved. Let stand 5 minutes or until mixture is bubbly.

2. Gradually beat 2 cups rye flour and 1 cup bread flour into yeast mixture with electric mixer at low speed. Add molasses, caraway seeds, vinegar, oil and salt; beat 1 minute. Increase speed to medium; beat 2 minutes.

3. Reduce speed to low. Beat in 1 egg and remaining 1 cup rye flour. Increase speed to medium; beat 2 minutes. Stir in enough additional bread flour, about 1 cup, with wooden spoon to make soft dough.

4. Turn out dough onto lightly floured surface; flatten slightly. Knead dough 10 to 15 minutes or until smooth and elastic, adding remaining 1 cup bread flour to prevent sticking if necessary. Shape dough into a ball; place in large greased bowl. Turn dough over to grease top. Cover with clean kitchen towel; let rise in warm place about 1¼ hours or until doubled in bulk.

5. Punch down dough. Knead dough on lightly floured surface 1 minute. Cut dough in half. Cover with towel; let rest 10 minutes. Grease large baking sheet. Shape each half into oval loaf about 9 inches long. Place loaves 6 inches apart on prepared baking sheet. Cover with towel; let rise in warm place about 1 hour or until doubled in bulk.

6. Preheat oven to 350°F. Combine egg white and 1 tablespoon water in small cup. Make 3 (½-inch-deep) diagonal slashes with tip of sharp knife across top of each loaf. Brush loaves with egg white mixture. Sprinkle with additional caraway seeds, if desired.

7. Bake 30 to 35 minutes or until loaves are browned and sound hollow when tapped. Immediately remove from baking sheet; cool completely on wire racks.   *Makes 2 loaves*

Rye Bread

Braided Sandwich Ring

DOUGH

¾ cup buttermilk, at 80°F
2 eggs, at room temperature
2 tablespoons vegetable oil
3 tablespoons sugar
1½ teaspoons salt
4 cups bread flour
2¼ teaspoons (1 packet) RED STAR® Active Dry Yeast or QUICK•RISE™ Yeast
    or Bread Machine Yeast

GLAZE

1 egg
1 tablespoon milk
1 tablespoon sesame or poppy seeds

FILLING

Mayonnaise, leaf lettuce, sliced tomatoes, onion rings, sliced black olives,
    thinly sliced deli meats (ham, roast beef, prosciutto, salami), sliced
    cheeses (brick, mozzarella, Swiss), Dijon mustard

BREAD MACHINE METHOD

Place room temperature dough ingredients in pan in order listed. Select dough cycle.
Check dough consistency after 5 minutes of kneading, making adjustments if necessary.

HAND-HELD MIXER METHOD

Combine 2 cups flour, sugar, yeast and salt. Heat buttermilk to 120° to 130°F. Combine
flour mixture, buttermilk, 2 eggs and oil in mixing bowl on low speed. Beat 2 to 3 minutes
on medium speed. By hand, stir in enough remaining flour to make firm dough. Knead on
floured surface 5 to 7 minutes or until smooth and elastic. Use additional flour, if
necessary. Place dough in lightly oiled bowl and turn to grease top. Cover; let rise until
dough tests ripe.*

*Place two fingers into the risen dough up to the second knuckle and take out. If the indentations
remain the dough is ripe and ready to punch down.*

STAND MIXER METHOD

Combine 2 cups flour, sugar, yeast and salt. Heat buttermilk to 120° to 130°F. Combine
flour mixture, buttermilk, 2 eggs and oil in mixing bowl with paddle or beaters 4 minutes
on medium speed. Gradually add remaining flour and knead with dough hook 5 to
7 minutes or until smooth and elastic. Use additional flour, if necessary. Place dough in
lightly oiled bowl and turn to grease top. Cover; let rise until dough tests ripe.*

continued on page 124

Braided Sandwich Ring

Braided Sandwich Ring, continued

SHAPING AND BAKING

Punch down dough. Divide into three parts. On lightly floured surface, roll each third into 24-inch rope. On greased baking sheet lightly sprinkled with cornmeal, loosely braid ropes from center to ends. Shape into circle; fasten ends by pinching dough together. Cover; let rise until indentation remains after touching.

For glaze, combine remaining 1 egg and milk; gently brush risen dough. Sprinkle with sesame seeds. Bake in preheated 375°F oven 25 to 35 minutes or until golden brown; cool.

Using serrated knife, slice ring crosswise to create large sandwich. Spread bottom half with mayonnaise; arrange filling ingredients. Spread top section with mustard; place on top of filling. To serve slice into serving portions. *Makes 1 large sandwich ring (12 to 18 servings)*

Cranberry-Cheese Batter Bread

1¼ **cups milk**
  3 **cups all-purpose flour**
  ½ **cup sugar**
  1 **package active dry yeast**
  1 **teaspoon salt**
  ½ **cup (1 stick) cold butter**
  ½ **cup (4 ounces) cold cream cheese**
  1 **cup (3 ounces) dried cranberries**

1. Heat milk in small saucepan over low heat until temperature reaches 120° to 130°F. Grease 8-inch square pan; set aside.

2. Combine flour, sugar, yeast and salt in large bowl. Cut butter and cream cheese into 1-inch chunks; add to flour mixture. Cut in butter and cream cheese with pastry blender until mixture resembles coarse crumbs. Stir in cranberries. Add warm milk; beat 1 minute or until dough looks stringy.

3. Place batter in prepared pan. Cover with towel; let rise in warm place about 1 hour.

4. Preheat oven to 375°F. Bake 35 minutes or until golden brown.

Makes 1 loaf (16 servings)

Cranberry-Cheese Batter Bread

Focaccia

1 cup water
1 tablespoon olive oil, plus additional for brushing
1 teaspoon salt
1 tablespoon sugar
3 cups bread flour
2¼ teaspoons (1 packet) RED STAR® Active Dry Yeast or QUICK•RISE™ Yeast
    or Bread Machine Yeast
    Suggested toppings: sun-dried tomatoes, roasted bell pepper slices,
    sautéed onion rings, fresh and dried herbs in any combination, grated
    hard cheese

BREAD MACHINE METHOD

Place room temperature ingredients, except toppings, in pan in order listed. Select dough cycle. Check dough consistency after 5 minutes of kneading, making adjustments if necessary.

HAND-HELD MIXER METHOD

Combine yeast, 1 cup flour, sugar and salt. Combine water and 1 tablespoon oil; heat mixture to 120° to 130°F. Combine dry and liquid mixtures in mixing bowl on low speed. Beat 2 to 3 minutes on medium speed. By hand, stir in enough remaining flour to make a firm dough. Knead on floured surface 5 to 7 minutes or until smooth and elastic. Add additional flour, if necessary.

STAND MIXER METHOD

Combine yeast, 1 cup flour, sugar and salt. Combine water and 1 tablespoon oil; heat mixture to 120° to 130°F. Combine dry and liquid mixtures in mixing bowl with paddle or beaters for 4 minutes on medium speed. Gradually add remaining flour and knead with dough hook 5 to 7 minutes or until smooth and elastic. Add additional flour, if necessary.

FOOD PROCESSOR METHOD

In 2-cup measure, heat ¼ cup water to 110° to 115°F; keep remaining ¾ cup water cold. Add yeast; set aside. Insert dough blade in work bowl; add bread flour, sugar and salt. Pulse to combine. Add cold water and olive oil to yeast mixture; stir to combine. With machine running, add liquid mixture through feed tube in a steady stream only as fast as flour will absorb it. Open lid to check dough consistency. If dough is stiff and somewhat dry, add 1 teaspoon water; if soft and sticky, add 1 tablespoon flour. Close lid and process for 10 seconds. Check dough consistency again, making additional adjustments if necessary.

RISING, SHAPING AND BAKING

Place dough in lightly oiled bowl and turn to grease top. Cover; let rise until dough tests ripe.* Turn dough onto lightly floured surface; punch down to remove air bubbles. On lightly floured surface, shape dough into a ball. Place on greased baking sheet. Flatten to

continued on page 128

Focaccia

Focaccia, continued

14-inch circle. With knife, cut circle in dough about 1 inch from edge, cutting almost through to baking sheet. Pierce center with fork. Cover; let rise about 15 minutes. Brush with oil and sprinkle with desired toppings. Bake in preheated 375°F oven 25 to 30 minutes or until golden brown. Remove from baking sheet to cool. Serve warm or at room temperature.

Makes 1 (14-inch) loaf

*Place two fingers into the risen dough up to the second knuckle and take out. If the indentations remain the dough is ripe and ready to punch down.

Baker's Note: When flattening dough into circle, if the dough does not stretch easily, let it rest a couple of minutes and then press it out. Repeat if necessary.

No-Knead Sandwich Bread

    2 packages (2¼ teaspoons) active dry yeast
    ¾ cup warm water (110° to 115°F)
    3 tablespoons canola oil
    1 cup all-purpose flour
    ⅔ cup uncooked old-fashioned oats
    ¼ cup soy flour*
    ¼ cup wheat gluten*
    ¼ cup sesame seeds
    2 teaspoons sugar substitute
    1 teaspoon salt

* Soy flour, wheat gluten and sesame seeds are available in the natural foods sections of many supermarkets and at health food stores.

1. Stir yeast into water in small bowl; let stand 5 minutes. Add oil.

2. Combine all-purpose flour, oats, soy flour, gluten, sesame seeds, sugar substitute and salt in food processor fitted with plastic dough blade. Using on/off pulses, process until well blended.

3. With processor running, slowly pour yeast mixture through feed tube; then using on/off pulses, process until dough comes together and forms a mass. Unlock processor lid, but do not remove; let dough rise 1 hour or until doubled in bulk.

4. Spray 8×4-inch loaf pan with nonstick cooking spray. Using on/off pulses, process briefly until dough comes together and forms a ball. Turn dough out onto floured work surface. Shape into disc. (Dough will be slightly sticky.) Roll dough on floured surface into 12×8-inch rectangle. Roll up from short side; fold under ends and place in prepared pan. Cover with towel; let rise in warm place 45 minutes or until doubled in bulk.

5. Preheat oven to 375°F. Bake 35 minutes or until bread is golden brown and sounds hollow when tapped. Remove from pan and cool completely on wire rack. Cut into 30 (¼-inch-thick) slices before serving.

Makes 30 servings

No-Knead Sandwich Bread

Pecan Sticky Buns

DOUGH*
4½ to 5½ cups all-purpose flour, divided
½ cup granulated sugar
1½ teaspoons salt
2 packages active dry yeast
¾ cup warm milk (105° to 115°F)
½ cup warm water (105° to 115°F)
¼ cup (½ stick) margarine or butter, softened
2 eggs

GLAZE
½ cup KARO® Light or Dark Corn Syrup
½ cup packed light brown sugar
¼ cup (½ stick) margarine or butter
1 cup pecans, coarsely chopped

FILLING
½ cup firmly packed light brown sugar
1 teaspoon ground cinnamon
2 tablespoons margarine or butter, melted

To use frozen bread dough, omit ingredients for dough. Thaw two 1-pound loaves frozen bread dough in refrigerator overnight. In step 3, press loaves together and roll to a 20×12-inch rectangle; complete as recipe directs.

1. For Dough: In large bowl combine 2 cups flour, granulated sugar, salt and yeast. Stir in milk, water and softened margarine until blended. Stir in eggs and enough additional flour (about 2 cups) to make a soft dough. Knead on floured surface until smooth and elastic, about 8 minutes. Cover dough and let rest on floured surface 10 minutes.

2. For Glaze: Meanwhile, in small saucepan over low heat stir corn syrup, brown sugar and margarine until smooth. Pour into 13×9×2-inch baking pan. Sprinkle with pecans; set aside.

3. For Filling: Combine brown sugar and cinnamon; set aside. Roll dough to a 20×12-inch rectangle. Brush dough with 2 tablespoons melted margarine; sprinkle with brown sugar mixture. Starting from a long side, roll up jelly-roll fashion. Pinch seam to seal. Cut into 15 slices. Place slices, cut sides up, into prepared pan. Cover tightly. Refrigerate 2 to 24 hours.

4. To bake, preheat oven to 375°F. Uncover pan and let stand at room temperature 10 minutes. Bake 28 to 30 minutes or until tops are browned. Invert onto serving tray. Serve warm or cool completely.

Makes 15 rolls

Prep Time: 30 minutes plus chilling | **Bake Time:** 28 to 30 minutes

Pecan Sticky Buns

Cheddar-Onion Loaf

1 cup water
1 package (¼ ounce) active dry yeast
2 teaspoons sugar
2 cups all-purpose flour
4 tablespoons butter, softened, divided
2 eggs
¼ teaspoon salt
1 cup whole wheat flour
1 large onion, finely chopped
1 cup (4 ounces) shredded sharp Cheddar cheese
½ teaspoon poppy seeds

1. Heat water in small saucepan over low heat until temperature reaches 105° to 110°F. To proof yeast, sprinkle yeast and sugar over heated water in large bowl; stir until dissolved. Let stand 5 minutes or until mixture is bubbly. Add all-purpose flour, 2 tablespoons butter, eggs and salt. Beat with electric mixer at low speed until blended. Increase speed to high; beat 10 minutes. Stir in whole wheat flour until soft dough forms. Cover with plastic wrap; let rise in warm place 1 hour or until doubled in bulk.

2. Meanwhile, cook onion in remaining 2 tablespoons butter in small skillet over medium heat about 4 minutes or until tender. Remove from heat; cool.

3. Spray 9-inch pie plate with nonstick cooking spray. Sprinkle dough with cheese and half of onion; stir until evenly distributed. Turn dough out into pie plate. Spoon remaining onion over dough; sprinkle with poppy seeds. Let rise in warm place, covered, about 1 hour or until doubled in bulk.

4. Preheat oven to 375°F. Uncover loaf. Bake 30 minutes or until loaf sounds hollow when tapped. Remove from pie plate. Cool on wire rack 30 minutes. Cut into 12 wedges before serving.

Makes 1 loaf (12 servings)

helpful hint:

Whole wheat flour is milled from the entire wheat kernel and retains all of the grain's natural flavor, color and nutrients. It is generally used in combination with all-purpose or bread flour to avoid overly dense or poorly risen loaves. Whole wheat flour is more perishable than all-purpose flour, so make sure to check the expiration date before using it.

Pumpkin Yeast Rolls

16 slivered almonds
¼ teaspoon liquid green food coloring
1 package (16 ounces) hot roll mix
1 to 1¼ teaspoons pumpkin pie spice*
⅔ cup apple cider
⅓ cup water
2 tablespoons butter, softened
1 whole egg, lightly beaten
1 egg white
2 tablespoons cold water

Substitute ½ teaspoon ground cinnamon, ¼ teaspoon ground ginger and ⅛ teaspoon each ground allspice and ground nutmeg for 1 teaspoon pumpkin pie spice.

1. Place almonds in small resealable food storage bag. Add food coloring; seal bag. Shake bag until almonds are evenly colored. Place almonds on paper-towel-lined plate; let dry.

2. Combine hot roll mix, yeast package from mix and pumpkin pie spice in large bowl; mix well.

3. Combine cider and water in small saucepan. Heat over medium heat until cider mixture is hot (120° to 130°F); pour over dry ingredients. Add butter and whole egg; stir until dough pulls away from side of bowl.

4. Place dough on lightly floured surface; knead about 5 minutes or until smooth and elastic. Let rest 5 minutes. Cut dough into 16 equal pieces; roll each piece into ball. Combine egg white and cold water in small bowl; beat lightly with fork until well blended.

5. Brush egg white mixture evenly onto rolls, covering completely.

6. With sharp knife, lightly score surface of each roll, beginning at top center and coming down around sides of roll, to resemble pumpkin. Insert 1 almond sliver into top of each roll for stem.

7. Lightly grease baking sheet. Place rolls 2 inches apart on prepared baking sheet. Cover loosely with towel; let rise in warm place 20 to 30 minutes or until doubled in size.

8. Preheat oven to 375°F. Bake 15 to 20 minutes or until golden brown.   *Makes 16 rolls*

Greek Flat Breads

Basic Yeast Bread (recipe follows)
8 ounces crumbled feta cheese
1 cup chopped kalamata olives
6 cloves garlic, minced
2 tablespoons olive oil
2 eggs
2 tablespoons water
Coarse salt (optional)

1. Prepare Basic Yeast Bread through Step 4. Grease 2 baking sheets; set aside. Turn out dough onto lightly oiled work surface; divide in half. Keep one half of dough covered. Divide other half of dough into 16 equal pieces. Form each piece into ball. Cover with towel; let rest 5 minutes.

2. Combine cheese, olives, garlic and oil in medium bowl; set aside. Beat eggs and water in small bowl.

3. Flatten each ball of dough to ½-inch thickness. Place 2 inches apart on prepared baking sheet. Brush dough with beaten egg. Sprinkle each round of dough with olive mixture; press topping into dough slightly. Cover with towel; let rise 45 minutes. Repeat with remaining half of dough.

4. Place heavy baking or roasting pan on lower rack of oven. Preheat oven to 400°F.

5. Sprinkle tops of dough with coarse salt, if desired. Place bread in oven. Carefully place 4 to 5 ice cubes in heavy pan; close door. Bake 15 minutes or until lightly browned. Immediately remove bread from baking sheets and place on wire rack to cool.

Makes 32 flat breads

Basic Yeast Bread

2 cups milk
¼ cup (½ stick) unsalted butter, softened
6½ to 7½ cups bread or all-purpose flour, divided
2 packages active dry yeast
2 teaspoons salt
¼ cup sugar
2 eggs

1. Heat milk and butter in small saucepan over medium heat just until butter is melted. Remove from heat; cool to about 120° to 130°F.

2. Combine 4 cups flour, yeast, salt and sugar in large bowl. Add milk mixture and eggs. Beat vigorously 2 minutes. Add remaining flour, ¼ cup at a time, until dough begins to pull away from sides of bowl.

3. Turn out dough onto lightly floured work surface; flatten slightly. Knead 10 minutes or until smooth and elastic, adding flour if necessary to prevent sticking.

continued on page 136

Greek Flat Breads

Greek Flat Breads, continued

4. Shape dough into ball. Place in large lightly oiled bowl; turn dough over once to oil surface. Cover with clean kitchen towel; let rise in warm place about 1 hour or until doubled in bulk.

5. Grease two 9×5-inch loaf pans; set aside. Turn out dough onto lightly oiled work surface; divide in half. Shape each half of dough into loaf; place in prepared pans. Cover with towel; let rise in warm place 45 minutes.

6. Preheat oven to 375°F. Bake 25 minutes or until loaves are golden and sound hollow when tapped. Immediately remove bread from pans and cool on wire rack.

Makes 2 loaves

Freezer Rolls

1¼ cups warm water (100° to 110°F)
2 envelopes FLEISCHMANN'S® Active Dry Yeast
½ cup sugar
½ cup warm milk (100° to 110°F)
⅓ cup butter or margarine, softened
1½ teaspoons salt
5½ to 6 cups all-purpose flour
2 large eggs

Place ½ cup warm water in large bowl. Sprinkle yeast over water; stir until dissolved. Add remaining ¾ cup warm water, sugar, warm milk, butter, salt and 2 cups flour. Beat 2 minutes at medium speed of electric mixer. Add eggs and ½ cup flour. Beat at high speed for 2 minutes. Stir in enough remaining flour to make soft dough. Turn out onto lightly floured surface. Knead until smooth and elastic, about 8 to 10 minutes. Cover with plastic wrap; let rest for 20 minutes.

Punch dough down. Shape into desired shapes for dinner rolls. Place on greased baking sheets. Cover with plastic wrap and foil, sealing well. Freeze up to 1 week.*

Once frozen, rolls may be placed in plastic freezer bags.

Remove rolls from freezer; unwrap and place on greased baking sheets. Cover; let rise in warm, draft-free place until doubled in size, about 1½ hours.

Bake at 350°F for 15 minutes or until done. Remove from baking sheets; cool on wire racks.

Makes about 2 dozen rolls

To bake without freezing: After shaping, let rise in warm, draft-free place until doubled in size, about 1 hour. Bake according to above directions.

Shaping the Dough: Crescents: Divide dough in half; roll each half to 14-inch circle. Cut each into 12 pie-shaped wedges. Roll up tightly from wide end. Curve ends slightly to form crescents. **Knots:** Divide dough into 24 equal pieces; roll each to 9-inch rope. Tie once loosely. **Coils:** Divide dough into 24 equal pieces; roll each to 9-inch rope. Coil each rope and tuck end under the coil. **Twists:** Divide dough into 24 equal pieces; roll each into 12-inch rope. Fold each rope in half and twist three to four times. Pinch ends to seal.

Freezer Rolls

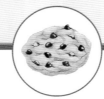

Cookie Extravaganza

Peanut Butter, Oatmeal, Cherry and Chip Mini Cookies

½ cup granulated sugar
⅓ cup butter, softened
¼ cup packed brown sugar
¼ cup creamy peanut butter
1 egg *or* ¼ cup egg substitute
½ teaspoon vanilla
1 cup uncooked quick oats
⅓ cup all-purpose flour
¼ cup whole wheat flour
½ teaspoon baking powder
¼ teaspoon baking soda
⅓ cup mini semisweet chocolate chips
¼ cup dried cherries, coarsely chopped

1. Preheat oven to 375°F.

2. Beat granulated sugar, butter, brown sugar and peanut butter in large bowl with electric mixer at medium speed until creamy. Add egg and vanilla; beat until well blended. Add oats, flours, baking powder and baking soda. Beat at low speed until blended. Stir in chocolate chips and cherries.

3. Drop mixture by slightly rounded measuring teaspoonfuls onto ungreased baking sheets. Bake 8 to 9 minutes or until light brown. Let stand on cookie sheets 1 minute. Transfer to wire racks; cool completely. *Makes 96 mini cookies*

Prep Time: 10 minutes | **Bake Time:** 8 minutes

Chocolate Gingersnaps

¾ cup sugar
1 package (18¼ ounces) chocolate cake mix *without* pudding in the mix
1 tablespoon ground ginger
2 eggs
⅓ cup vegetable oil

1. Preheat oven to 350°F. Spray cookie sheets with nonstick cooking spray. Place sugar in shallow bowl.

2. Combine cake mix and ginger in large bowl. Add eggs and oil; stir until well blended.

3. Shape tablespoonfuls of dough into 1-inch balls; roll in sugar to coat. Place 2 inches apart on prepared cookie sheets.

4. Bake about 10 minutes. Remove to wire racks to cool completely.

Makes about 3 dozen cookies

Island Cookies

1⅔ cups all-purpose flour
¾ teaspoon baking powder
½ teaspoon baking soda
½ teaspoon salt
¾ cup (1½ sticks) butter, softened
¾ cup packed brown sugar
⅓ cup granulated sugar
1 teaspoon vanilla extract
1 egg
1¾ cups (11.5-ounce package) NESTLÉ® TOLL HOUSE® Milk Chocolate Morsels
1 cup flaked coconut, toasted, if desired
1 cup chopped walnuts

PREHEAT oven to 375°F.

COMBINE flour, baking powder, baking soda and salt in small bowl. Beat butter, brown sugar, granulated sugar and vanilla extract in large mixer bowl until creamy. Beat in egg. Gradually beat in flour mixture. Stir in morsels, coconut and nuts. Drop by slightly rounded tablespoon onto ungreased baking sheets.

BAKE for 8 to 11 minutes or until edges are lightly browned. Cool on baking sheets for 2 minutes; remove to wire racks to cool completely. *Makes about 3 dozen cookies*

Note: NESTLÉ® TOLL HOUSE® Semi-Sweet Chocolate Morsels, Semi-Sweet Chocolate Mini Morsels, Premier White Morsels or Butterscotch Flavored Morsels can be substituted for the Milk Chocolate Morsels.

Chocolate Gingersnaps

Toasted Almond and Cranberry Biscotti

4 tablespoons butter, softened, divided
1 cup whole blanched almonds
2½ cups all-purpose flour
1 cup granulated sugar
1 teaspoon baking powder
½ teaspoon baking soda
2 eggs
1 teaspoon almond extract
¼ teaspoon vanilla
½ cup milk
1 cup dried cranberries
2 tablespoons packed brown sugar

1. Preheat oven to 350°F. Lightly grease cookie sheets.

2. Melt 1 tablespoon butter in small skillet. Remove from heat; add almonds. Stir gently to coat almonds. Place in single layer on ungreased cookie sheet. Bake 8 to 10 minutes or until golden brown and fragrant, stirring frequently. Almonds can easily burn so watch carefully. Immediately remove almonds from pan; cool completely.

3. Combine flour, sugar, baking powder and baking soda in large bowl. Add eggs, almond extract, vanilla and 2 tablespoons butter; beat with electric mixer at medium-low speed until soft dough forms. Continue beating adding only enough milk, 1 tablespoon at a time, to make smooth dough. Add almonds and cranberries. Knead dough gently in bowl until well blended. Transfer dough to floured surface; divide in half. Shape each half into 12×2-inch loaf on prepared cookie sheet.

4. Bake about 15 minutes or until lightly browned on top. Remove from oven and turn logs over, exposing unbrowned bottoms. Return to oven; bake 15 minutes more or until evenly brown all over (loaf will sound hollow when tapped). Cool on wire rack 12 to 15 minutes or until cool enough to handle with bare hands.

5. While still warm, slice diagonally into ½-inch-thick pieces. Place slices on ungreased cookie sheets. Bake 10 minutes more on each side or until brown. Remove to wire racks; cool completely.

6. Melt remaining 1 tablespoon butter with brown sugar in small skillet over medium-high heat. Cook and stir until dark golden brown, careful not to burn. Drizzle in thin ribbons over warm cookies.

Makes about 4 dozen cookies

Toasted Almond and Cranberry Biscotti

Choco-Peanut Butter-Brickle Cookies

1 (14-ounce) can EAGLE BRAND® Sweetened Condensed Milk (NOT evaporated milk)
1 cup crunchy peanut butter
2 eggs
1 teaspoon vanilla extract
1½ cups all-purpose flour
1 teaspoon baking soda
½ teaspoon baking powder
½ teaspoon salt
1 cup (6 ounces) semisweet chocolate chips
1 cup chocolate-covered toffee bits or almond brickle chips

1. Preheat oven to 350°F. In large bowl, beat EAGLE BRAND®, peanut butter, eggs and vanilla until well blended.

2. In medium bowl, combine flour, baking soda, baking powder and salt. Add to peanut butter mixture; beat until blended. Stir in chocolate chips and toffee bits. Drop by heaping tablespoonfuls onto lightly greased baking sheets.

3. Bake 12 minutes or until lightly browned. Cool slightly on baking sheets; remove to wire racks to cool.

Makes 3 dozen cookies

Prep Time: 15 minutes | **Bake Time:** 12 minutes

Thumbprint Cookies

1½ cups all-purpose flour
1 teaspoon baking soda
¼ teaspoon salt
⅔ cup sugar
¼ cup (½ stick) butter, softened
1 egg white
1 teaspoon vanilla
½ cup raspberry or apricot fruit spread

1. Combine flour, baking soda and salt in medium bowl; set aside. Beat sugar, butter, egg white and vanilla in large bowl with electric mixer at high speed until blended. Add flour mixture; mix well. Press mixture together to form ball. Cover with plastic wrap. Refrigerate 30 minutes or overnight.

2. Preheat oven to 375°F. Lightly coat cookie sheet with nonstick cooking spray; set aside.

3. With lightly floured hands, shape dough into 20 (1-inch) balls; place on cookie sheet. Press down with thumb in center of each ball to form indentation. Fill each indentation with about 1 teaspoon fruit spread.

4. Bake 10 to 12 minutes or until golden brown. Remove to wire rack to cool.

Makes 20 cookies

Choco-Peanut Butter-Brickle Cookies

Browned Butter Spritz Cookies

1½ cups (3 sticks) unsalted butter
2½ cups all-purpose flour
¼ cup cake flour
¼ teaspoon salt
½ cup granulated sugar
¼ cup powdered sugar
1 egg yolk
1 teaspoon vanilla
⅛ teaspoon almond extract

1. Heat butter in heavy medium saucepan over medium heat until melted and light amber in color, stirring frequently. Transfer butter to large bowl. Cover and refrigerate about 2 hours or until solid. Let butter stand at room temperature about 15 minutes to soften before completing recipe.

2. Preheat oven to 350°F. Combine all-purpose flour, cake flour and salt in small bowl.

3. Beat browned butter, granulated sugar and powdered sugar in large bowl with electric mixer at medium speed until light and fluffy. Add egg yolk, vanilla and almond extract; beat until well blended. Add flour mixture to butter mixture; beat until well blended.

4. Fit cookie press with desired plate (or change plates for different shapes after first batch). Fill press with dough; press dough 1 inch apart on ungreased cookie sheets. Bake 10 to 12 minutes or until just lightly browned. Cool 5 minutes on cookie sheets; transfer to wire racks to cool completely. *Makes about 8 dozen cookies*

Decorating Tip: To add holiday sparkle to these delicious cookies, before baking, sprinkle them with red or green decorating sugar, or press red or green glacé cherry halves into the centers. For pretty trees or wreaths, tint the dough with green food color before using the tree or wreath plate in your cookie press. Sprinkle with colored nonpareils as ornaments before baking, or pipe red icing bows on the baked and cooled cookies.

helpful hint:

Spritz are a Scandinavian cookie. By using different plates in a cookie press, spritz cookies can be formed into many shapes. If your first efforts are not successful, just transfer the dough back to the cookie press and try again. They are a great cookie to make if you want to make a lot of cookies quickly!

Browned Butter Spritz Cookies

Lollipop Cookies

3 cups all-purpose flour
1 teaspoon baking powder
1⅓ cups granulated sugar
1 cup (2 sticks) butter, softened
2 eggs
2 teaspoons vanilla
2 ounces unsweetened chocolate, melted
   Royal Icing (page 148)
   Liquid or paste food coloring
   Assorted decors (optional)
   Decorator Frosting (page 148)
   Craft sticks*

Available where cake decorating supplies are sold.

1. Preheat oven to 350°F. Combine flour and baking powder in small bowl. Beat sugar and butter in large bowl with electric mixer at medium speed until light and fluffy. Beat in eggs and vanilla until well blended. Gradually add flour mixture. Beat at low speed until blended.

2. Remove half of dough from bowl; shape into disk. Wrap disk in plastic wrap; refrigerate while working with remaining half of dough. Add melted chocolate to remaining dough in bowl. Beat at low speed until well blended. Place chocolate dough on lightly floured surface; press into 6-inch square. Cut lengthwise into 4 equal strips. Cut crosswise into 4 equal strips to form 16 squares.

3. Roll each square into a ball. Place balls 3 inches apart on ungreased baking sheets. Place craft stick under each ball. Press balls into 2½-inch circles using lightly floured bottom of drinking glass. Bake, one sheet at a time, 10 to 12 minutes or until edges are set. Immediately remove cookies with spatula to wire racks; cool completely. Repeat with remaining chocolate and plain dough.

4. To marbleize cookies, prepare Royal Icing. Divide icing among bowls. Tint with desired food coloring. (Liquid food coloring will thin frosting to the right consistency. If using paste colors, stir in water, 1 drop at a time, with spoon until slightly thickened.)

5. Place large sheet of heavy-duty foil on counter. Place cookies on foil. Spread thin layer of icing on cookies to within ⅛ inch of edge. Dip spoon into contrasting color of icing. Drizzle or drop icing onto base color. Repeat with 1 or 2 more colors. Swirl colors with tip of toothpick. Do not over mix or colors will turn muddy. Decorate with candies or sprinkles while icing is still soft, if desired. Let stand 30 minutes or until icing is set.

6. To add additional piped decorations, use colored Decorator Frosting or stir sifted powdered sugar into Royal Icing until thick enough to hold shape when dropped from spoon. Spoon frosting or icing into resealable plastic freezer bag with one small corner cut off. Decorate as desired. Let cookies stand 1 hour or until piping is set.

Makes 32 lollipops

Royal Icing

4 egg whites*
4 cups powdered sugar, sifted
1 teaspoon almond extract or clear vanilla extract**

Use only grade A clean, uncracked eggs.

**Icing remains very white when clear flavorings are used.*

Beat egg whites in large bowl with electric mixer at high speed until foamy. Gradually add sugar and almond extract. Beat at high speed until thickened.

Makes 2 cups

Note: When dry, Royal Icing is very hard and resistant to damage that can occur during shipping.

Decorator Frosting

¾ cup (1½ sticks) butter, softened
4½ cups powdered sugar, sifted
3 tablespoons water
1 teaspoon vanilla
¼ teaspoon almond extract

Beat butter in medium bowl with electric mixer at medium speed until smooth. Add 2 cups sugar. Beat at medium speed until light and fluffy. Add water and extracts. Beat at low speed until well blended, scraping down side of bowl once. Beat in remaining 2½ cups sugar until mixture is creamy.

Makes 2 cups

Note: This frosting is perfect for piping, but is less durable than Royal Icing. Bumping, stacking and handling may damage decorations.

helpful hint:

For sandwich cookie lollipops, bake only the chocolate cookies with a craft stick. Spread 1½ tablespoons Decorator Frosting on flat side of chocolate cookie to within ¼ inch of edge with small spatula. Place vanilla cookie, flat-side down, over frosting. Gently press cookies together. Repeat. Let stand 20 minutes or until frosting is set. Store tightly covered at room temperature for up to 2 weeks. Makes 16 sandwich cookies.

Black and White Sandwich Cookies

1 package (18¼ ounces) chocolate cake mix with pudding in the mix
1½ cups (3 sticks) unsalted butter, softened, divided
2 egg yolks, divided
½ to ¾ cup milk, divided
1 package (18¼ ounces) butter recipe yellow cake mix with pudding in the mix
4 cups powdered sugar
¼ teaspoon salt
2 tablespoons unsweetened cocoa (optional)

1. Preheat oven to 325°F. For chocolate cookies, place half of chocolate cake mix in large bowl. Add ½ cup (1 stick) butter; beat with electric mixer at high speed until well blended. Add 1 egg yolk and remaining cake mix; beat just until dough forms. Beat in 1 to 2 tablespoons milk if dough is too crumbly.

2. Shape dough into 36 balls, using about 1 tablespoon dough for each cookie. Place 2 inches apart on ungreased cookie sheets; flatten slightly. Bake 20 minutes or until cookies are firm. Let cookies stand on cookie sheets 5 minutes; transfer to wire racks to cool completely.

3. For vanilla cookies, place half of yellow cake mix in large bowl. Add ½ cup (1 stick) butter; beat with electric mixer at high speed until well blended. Add remaining egg yolk and cake mix; beat just until dough forms. Beat in 1 to 2 tablespoons milk if dough is too crumbly.

4. Shape dough into 36 balls, using about 1 tablespoon dough for each cookie. Place 2 inches apart on ungreased cookie sheets; flatten slightly. Bake 20 minutes or until cookies are firm. Let cookies stand on cookie sheets 5 minutes; transfer to wire racks to cool completely.

5. Cut remaining ½ cup (1 stick) butter into small pieces. Beat butter, powdered sugar, salt and 6 tablespoons milk in large bowl with electric mixer at low speed 1 minute; beat at medium speed until light and fluffy. Add additional 2 tablespoons milk if necessary for more spreadable frosting. If desired, divide frosting in half. Add cocoa and 1 tablespoon milk to one half to create chocolate frosting.

6. Spread frosting on flat sides of chocolate cookies, using about 1 tablespoon per cookie. Top with vanilla cookies.

Makes 3 dozen sandwich cookies

Black and White Sandwich Cookies

Chocolate Malt Delights

1 package (18 ounces) refrigerated chocolate chip cookie dough
⅓ cup plus 3 tablespoons malted milk powder, original or chocolate flavor, divided
1¼ cups prepared chocolate frosting
1 cup coarsely chopped malted milk balls

1. Let dough stand at room temperature about 15 minutes. Preheat oven to 350°F. Grease cookie sheets.

2. Beat dough and ⅓ cup malted milk powder in large bowl with electric mixer at medium speed until well blended. Drop rounded tablespoonfuls of dough onto prepared cookie sheets.

3. Bake 10 to 12 minutes or until lightly browned at edges. Cool on cookie sheets 5 minutes; remove to wire racks to cool completely.

4. Combine frosting and remaining 3 tablespoons malted milk powder. Top each cookie with rounded tablespoonful of frosting; garnish with malted milk balls.

Makes about 1½ dozen cookies

Chocolate Chip & Macadamia Cookies

2 squares (1 ounce each) unsweetened chocolate
½ cup (1 stick) butter, softened
1 cup packed light brown sugar
1 egg
1 teaspoon vanilla
1¼ cups all-purpose flour
½ teaspoon baking soda
1 cup (6 ounces) semisweet chocolate chips
¾ cup macadamia nuts, roughly chopped

1. Preheat oven to 350°F. Lightly grease cookie sheets or line with parchment paper.

2. Melt unsweetened chocolate in top of double boiler over hot, not boiling, water. Remove from heat; cool.

3. Beat butter, melted chocolate and sugar in large bowl with electric mixer at medium speed until blended. Add egg and vanilla; beat until light. Blend in flour, baking soda, chocolate chips and macadamia nuts.

4. Drop dough by rounded teaspoonfuls 2 inches apart onto prepared cookie sheets. Bake 10 to 12 minutes or until firm. *Do not overbake.* Remove to wire racks to cool.

Makes about 4 dozen cookies

Chocolate Malt Delights

Peanut Butter & Jelly Pockets

1 package (18 ounces) refrigerated peanut butter cookie dough
1 jar (10 ounces) strawberry or raspberry pastry filling
Coarse decorating sugar

1. Freeze dough 1 hour or until firm but not frozen.

2. Preheat oven to 350°F. Lightly grease cookie sheets.

3. Cut dough into ¼-inch slices; place half of dough slices 2 inches apart on prepared cookie sheets. Spoon about 1 teaspoon pastry filling each onto centers of dough slices; top with remaining dough slices. Sprinkle tops with decorating sugar.

4. Bake 12 to 15 minutes or until edges are light brown. Cool on cookie sheets 3 minutes. Remove to wire racks; cool completely. *Makes about 1½ dozen cookies*

Mexican Sugar Cookies (Polvorones)

1 cup (2 sticks) butter, softened
½ cup powdered sugar
2 tablespoons milk
1 teaspoon vanilla
1 teaspoon ground cinnamon, divided
1½ to 1¾ cups all-purpose flour
1 teaspoon baking powder
1 cup granulated sugar
1 square (1 ounce) semisweet chocolate, finely grated

1. Preheat oven to 325°F. Grease cookie sheets; set aside.

2. Beat butter, powdered sugar, milk, vanilla and ½ teaspoon cinnamon in large bowl with electric mixer at medium speed until light and fluffy. Gradually add 1½ cups flour and baking powder. Beat at low speed until well blended. Stir in additional flour with spoon if dough is too soft to shape.

3. Shape tablespoonfuls of dough into 1¼-inch balls. Place balls 3 inches apart on prepared cookie sheets. Flatten each ball into 2-inch round with bottom of glass dipped in granulated sugar.

4. Bake 20 to 25 minutes or until edges are golden brown. Let stand on cookie sheets 3 to 4 minutes.

5. Meanwhile, combine granulated sugar, grated chocolate and remaining ½ teaspoon cinnamon in small bowl. Transfer cookies, one at a time, to sugar mixture; coat both sides. Remove to wire racks; cool completely.

6. Store tightly covered at room temperature or freeze up to 3 months.
Makes about 2 dozen cookies

Peanut Butter & Jelly Pockets

Two-Toned Biscotti with Pistachios and Chocolate Raisins

⅔ cup granulated sugar
⅓ cup butter, softened
 2 teaspoons baking powder
⅛ teaspoon salt
 2 eggs
 2 cups all-purpose flour
¼ cup chopped pistachio nuts
 2 tablespoons unsweetened cocoa powder
½ cup chocolate-covered raisins
¼ teaspoon ground nutmeg

1. Preheat oven to 375°F. Lightly grease 2 cookie sheets.

2. Beat sugar and butter in large bowl with electric mixer at medium speed until light and fluffy. Add baking powder and salt; beat until well blended. Add eggs, one at a time, beating well after each addition. Gradually add flour, beating until well blended.

3. Divide dough in half. Stir nuts and cocoa into 1 portion of dough. Stir raisins and nutmeg into remaining dough. Divide each dough mixture in half.

4. Pat 1 portion chocolate dough into 8×6-inch rectangle. Shape 1 portion raisin dough into log; place in center of chocolate rectangle. Wrap chocolate dough around raisin log, flattening slightly. Place log on prepared cookie sheet, seam side down. Repeat with remaining dough.

5. Bake 40 to 50 minutes or until log sounds slightly hollow when tapped. Cool on cookie sheets 15 to 20 minutes or until warm but not hot. *Reduce oven temperature to 325°F.*

6. Cut each warm log diagonally into ¾-inch slices with sharp serrated knife. Place on ungreased cookie sheets. Bake 7 to 8 minutes. Turn slices; bake 7 to 8 minutes or until crisp.

Makes about 2 dozen cookies

helpful hint:

When buying unshelled pistachios make sure the shells are partially open. This helps in getting the nut meat out and ensures that the nuts are mature. Pistachio nuts are rich in calcium, thiamin, phosphorus, iron and Vitamin A.

Two-Toned Biscotti with Pistachios and Chocolate Raisins

Chocolate Toffee Crescents

1 package (18 ounces) refrigerated triple chocolate cookie dough
½ cup all-purpose flour
1 package (8 ounces) toffee baking bits
¾ cup butterscotch chips or semisweet chocolate chips

1. Lightly grease cookie sheets. Let dough stand at room temperature about 15 minutes.

2. Combine dough and flour in large bowl; beat until well blended. Stir in 1 cup toffee bits. Shape rounded tablespoonfuls of dough into crescent shapes; place 2 inches apart on prepared cookie sheets. Freeze 20 minutes.

3. Preheat oven to 350°F. Bake crescents 9 to 11 minutes or until set. Cool on cookie sheets 2 minutes. Remove to wire racks; cool completely.

4. Place butterscotch chips in small resealable food storage bag. Microwave on MEDIUM (50%) 1 minute; knead bag lightly. Microwave and knead at additional 30-second intervals until completely melted. Cut off tiny corner of bag. Drizzle melted chips over crescents; sprinkle with remaining toffee bits. Let stand until set.   *Makes about 2 dozen cookies*

Whirligigs

1 package (18 ounces) refrigerated sugar cookie dough
¼ cup all-purpose flour
½ teaspoon *each* banana and strawberry extract (optional)
    Red and yellow food colorings
    Colored sugar (optional)
12 (8-inch) lollipop sticks or wooden popsicle sticks*

Lollipop and popsicle sticks are available at crafts stores and where cake decorating supplies are sold.

1. Remove dough from wrapper; place in large bowl. Let dough stand at room temperature about 15 minutes.

2. Preheat oven to 350°F. Grease cookie sheets.

3. Add flour to dough; beat with electric mixer at medium speed until well blended. Divide dough in half; place in separate bowls. Add banana extract, if desired, and yellow food coloring to dough in one bowl. Add strawberry extract, if desired, and red food coloring to dough in remaining bowl. Beat doughs separately with electric mixer at medium speed until well blended and evenly colored. Wrap doughs separately in plastic wrap; freeze dough 30 minutes.

4. Shape red dough into rope about 18 inches long on lightly floured surface. Repeat with yellow dough. Twist ropes together. Divide rope into 3 equal pieces. Working with one piece at a time, shape dough into rope about 20 inches long. Cut into 4 equal pieces. Coil each piece into circle; place 2 inches apart on prepared cookie sheets. (Make sure to leave room for lollipop sticks.) Sprinkle cookies with colored sugar, if desired. Refrigerate about 15 minutes. Repeat with remaining dough.

5. Carefully poke lollipop stick into edge of each cookie. Bake 12 to 15 minutes or until edges are lightly browned. Cool completely on cookie sheets.   *Makes 1 dozen (3-inch) cookies*

Chocolate Toffee Crescents

Waikiki Cookies

1¾ cups all-purpose flour
½ teaspoon salt
¼ teaspoon baking soda
1½ cups packed light brown sugar
⅔ cup shortening
1 tablespoon water
1 teaspoon vanilla
2 eggs
1 cup white chocolate chunks
1 cup macadamia nuts, coarsely chopped

1. Preheat oven to 375°F.

2. Combine flour, salt and baking soda in medium bowl; set aside.

3. Combine brown sugar, shortening, water and vanilla in large bowl. Beat with electric mixer at medium speed until well blended. Add eggs; beat well. Add flour mixture; beat at low speed just until blended. Stir in white chocolate chunks and nuts.

4. Drop dough by rounded tablespoonfuls 2 inches apart onto ungreased cookie sheet.

5. Bake 7 to 9 minutes or until cookies are set. Do not overbake. Cool 2 minutes on baking sheet. Remove cookies to wire rack; cool completely.

Makes about 3 dozen cookies

Glazed Donut Cookies

1 package (18 ounces) refrigerated oatmeal raisin cookie dough in squares
    or rounds (12 count)
Prepared white or chocolate frosting
Assorted colored sprinkles

1. Remove dough from wrapper. Separate dough into 12 pieces; let stand at room temperature about 15 minutes.

2. Preheat oven to 350°F. Grease 12 standard (2½-inch) muffin cups.

3. Shape each dough piece into 12-inch-long rope on lightly floured surface. Coil ropes into muffin cups, leaving centers open.

4. Bake 12 minutes; remove from oven and reshape center hole with round handle of wooden spoon. Return to oven; bake 3 to 4 minutes or until set.

5. Remove from oven; reshape holes, if necessary. Cool in pan 4 minutes; transfer cookies to wire racks to cool completely.

6. Spread frosting over cookies; decorate with sprinkles.

Makes 12 large cookies

Waikiki Cookies

Norwegian Pepper Cookies (Pepperkaker)

    4 to 4½ cups all-purpose flour, divided
    1 teaspoon baking soda
    1 teaspoon ground cardamom
    1 teaspoon ground cinnamon
    1 teaspoon ground cloves
    ½ teaspoon black pepper
    ½ teaspoon salt
    ½ cup (1 stick) butter, softened
 2½ cups powdered sugar
    4 eggs
    3 tablespoons lemon juice
    1 tablespoon grated lemon peel
    ½ teaspoon almond extract
    ½ cup diced candied citron, finely chopped
    Lemon Glaze (recipe follows)

1. Combine 4 cups flour, baking soda, cardamom, cinnamon, cloves, pepper and salt in medium bowl. Beat butter and half of powdered sugar in large bowl with electric mixer at medium speed until light and fluffy. Beat in eggs and remaining powdered sugar.

2. Gradually add flour mixture. Beat at low speed until well blended. Beat in lemon juice, lemon peel and almond extract. Stir in citron and enough remaining flour until stiff dough forms.

3. Shape tablespoonfuls of dough into 1-inch balls. Place balls on large cookie sheets or tray; cover with plastic wrap and refrigerate until firm, 2 hours or overnight.

4. Preheat oven to 350°F. Grease cookie sheets. Place balls 1 inch apart on prepared cookie sheets. Bake 13 to 15 minutes or until firm and light golden brown. Remove cookies to wire racks.

5. Meanwhile, prepare Lemon Glaze. While still warm, brush cookies with Lemon Glaze. Let stand at room temperature 1 hour or until set.

6. Store tightly covered at room temperature or freeze up to 3 months.

Makes about 7 dozen cookies

Lemon Glaze

    2 cups sifted powdered sugar
    3 to 4 tablespoons lemon juice

Combine powdered sugar and lemon juice in large bowl. Stir until smooth and spreadable. If mixture is too stiff, add more lemon juice.

Makes about ½ cup glaze

Double Lemon Delights

2¼ cups all-purpose flour
½ teaspoon baking powder
½ teaspoon salt
1 cup (2 sticks) butter, softened
¾ cup granulated sugar
1 egg
2 tablespoons grated lemon peel, divided
1 teaspoon vanilla
Additional granulated sugar
1 cup powdered sugar
4 to 5 teaspoons lemon juice

1. Preheat oven to 375°F.

2. Combine flour, baking powder and salt in small bowl; set aside. Beat butter and granulated sugar in large bowl with electric mixer at medium speed until light and fluffy. Beat in egg, 1 tablespoon lemon peel and vanilla until well blended. Gradually beat in flour mixture at low speed until blended.

3. Drop dough by level ¼ cupfuls onto ungreased cookie sheets, spacing 3 inches apart. Flatten dough until 3 inches in diameter with bottom of glass that has been dipped in additional granulated sugar.

4. Bake 12 to 14 minutes or until cookies are just set and edges are golden brown. Cool on cookie sheets 2 minutes; transfer to wire racks. Cool completely.

5. Combine powdered sugar, lemon juice and remaining 1 tablespoon lemon peel in small bowl; drizzle over cookies. Let stand until icing is set.

Makes about 1 dozen (4-inch) cookies

Variation: To make smaller cookies, drop 2 tablespoons dough 2 inches apart onto ungreased cookie sheets. Bake 8 to 10 minutes or until cookies are just set and edges are golden brown. Cool on cookie sheets 2 minutes; transfer to wire racks. Cool completely. Continue with Step 5. Makes about 2 dozen cookies

helpful hint:

For even baking and browning of cookies, bake them in the center of the oven. If the heat distribution in your oven is uneven, turn the cookie sheet halfway through the baking time. Most cookies bake quickly and should be watched carefully to avoid overbaking. It's generally better to slightly underbake, rather than to overbake cookies.

Apple Cinnamon Chunkies

1 package (18 ounces) refrigerated oatmeal raisin cookie dough
1 cup chopped dried apples
½ cup cinnamon baking chips
½ teaspoon apple pie spice*

*Substitute ¼ teaspoon ground cinnamon, ⅛ teaspoon ground nutmeg and pinch of ground allspice or ground cloves for ½ teaspoon apple pie spice.

1. Let dough stand at room temperature about 15 minutes. Preheat oven to 350°F. Lightly grease cookie sheets.

2. Combine dough, apples, cinnamon chips and apple pie spice in large bowl; beat until well blended. Drop dough by rounded tablespoonfuls 2 inches apart onto prepared cookie sheets.

3. Bake 10 to 12 minutes or until golden brown. Cool on cookie sheets 2 to 3 minutes. Remove to wire racks; cool completely.

Makes 2 dozen cookies

Danish Raspberry Cookies

2 squares (1 ounce each) unsweetened chocolate
½ cup (1 stick) butter, softened
½ cup sugar
1 egg
2 cups cake flour
1 teaspoon vanilla
¼ teaspoon salt
1 cup (6 ounces) milk chocolate or white chocolate chips or ½ cup of each
1 to 1¼ cups seedless raspberry jam

1. Melt unsweetened chocolate in top of double boiler over hot, not boiling, water. Remove from heat; cool. Beat butter and sugar in large bowl with electric mixer at medium speed until light. Add egg and melted chocolate; beat until fluffy. Stir in flour, vanilla and salt until well blended. Cover; refrigerate until firm, about 1 hour.

2. Preheat oven to 400°F. Lightly grease cookie sheets or line with parchment paper. Divide dough into 4 equal parts. Divide each part into 2 pieces. Shape each piece into rope 12 inches long on lightly floured board. (The ropes should be about the thickness of a finger.) Place 2 inches apart on prepared cookie sheets. With side of finger, make an indentation along length of each rope. Bake 8 minutes or until firm.

3. Meanwhile, melt chocolate chips in small bowl over hot water. Stir until smooth. (If using both kinds of chips, melt separately.) Stir preserves; spoon into pastry bag fitted with ¼-inch tip or into small heavy-duty plastic bag. (If using plastic bag, snip off small corner from one side of bag.) Pipe preserves down length of each cookie strip. Return to oven for 2 minutes, then remove to wire racks. While cookies are still warm, drizzle with melted chocolate, then cut strips into 1-inch diagonal pieces. Refrigerate until chocolate is set.

Makes 8 dozen cookies

Apple Cinnamon Chunkies

Chunky Chocolate Chip Peanut Butter Cookies

1¼ cups all-purpose flour
½ teaspoon baking soda
½ teaspoon salt
½ teaspoon ground cinnamon
¾ cup (1½ sticks) butter or margarine, softened
½ cup packed granulated sugar
½ cup brown sugar
½ cup creamy peanut butter
1 egg
1 teaspoon vanilla extract
2 cups (12-ounce package) NESTLÉ® TOLL HOUSE® Semi-Sweet Chocolate Morsels
½ cup coarsely chopped peanuts

PREHEAT oven to 375°F.

COMBINE flour, baking soda, salt and cinnamon in small bowl. Beat butter, granulated sugar, brown sugar and peanut butter in large mixer bowl until creamy. Beat in egg and vanilla extract. Gradually beat in flour mixture. Stir in morsels and peanuts.

DROP dough by rounded tablespoon onto ungreased baking sheets. Press down slightly to flatten into 2-inch circles.

BAKE for 7 to 10 minutes or until edges are set but centers are still soft. Cool on baking sheets for 4 minutes; remove to wire racks to cool completely.

Makes about 3 dozen cookies

helpful hint:

Peanut butter is a blend of ground roasted peanuts, vegetable oil and salt. Commercial brands contain a stabilizer that prevents the oil from separating. It can be stored after opening for three months at room temperature or longer if refrigerated. Natural peanut butters are 100 percent peanuts contain no additives to keep them from separating; they need to be stirred before using. Natural peanut butters must be refrigerated after opening and will keep up to 6 months.

Chunky Chocolate Chip Peanut Butter Cookies

Oatmeal Scotchies

1¼ cups all-purpose flour
1 teaspoon baking soda
½ teaspoon salt
½ teaspoon ground cinnamon
1 cup (2 sticks) butter or margarine, softened
¾ cup granulated sugar
¾ cup packed brown sugar
2 eggs
1 teaspoon vanilla extract *or* grated peel of 1 orange
3 cups quick or old-fashioned oats
1⅔ cups (11-ounce package) NESTLÉ® TOLL HOUSE® Butterscotch Flavored Morsels

PREHEAT oven to 375°F.

COMBINE flour, baking soda, salt and cinnamon in small bowl. Beat butter, granulated sugar, brown sugar, eggs and vanilla extract in large mixer bowl. Gradually beat in flour mixture. Stir in oats and morsels. Drop by rounded tablespoon onto ungreased baking sheets.

BAKE for 7 to 8 minutes for chewy cookies or 9 to 10 minutes for crispy cookies. Cool on baking sheets for 2 minutes; remove to wire racks to cool completely.

Makes about 4 dozen cookies

Pan Cookie Variation: GREASE 15×10-inch jelly-roll pan. Spread dough into prepared pan. Bake for 18 to 22 minutes or until light brown. Cool completely in pan on wire rack. Makes 4 dozen bars.

Quick-Fix Gingersnaps

1 package (about 17 ounces) sugar cookie mix
½ cup (1 stick) butter, melted
1 egg
1 tablespoon light molasses
1 teaspoon ground ginger
½ teaspoon ground cinnamon
¼ cup sugar
½ cup finely chopped pecans

1. Preheat oven to 375°F.

2. Combine cookie mix, butter, egg, molasses, ginger and cinnamon in large bowl; mix well. Form dough into 1-inch balls. (Dampen hands when handling dough to prevent sticking.)

3. Place sugar in shallow bowl. Roll balls of dough in sugar to coat completely. Arrange 2 inches apart on ungreased cookie sheets; flatten slightly with back of metal spatula. Sprinkle with pecans; press gently with fingers.

4. Bake 8 to 10 minutes or until lightly browned. Cool 1 minute on cookie sheets. Transfer to wire racks; cool completely. Store in airtight container. *Makes about 4 dozen cookies*

Oatmeal Scotchies

Butterscotch Almond Crescents

1 cup (2 sticks) unsalted butter, softened
½ cup plus 1 tablespoon powdered sugar
¼ teaspoon salt
1 teaspoon almond extract
1¾ cups all-purpose flour
¾ cup ground almonds
Butterscotch Glaze (recipe follows)
½ cup sliced almonds

1. Preheat oven to 300°F. Line cookie sheets with parchment paper.

2. Beat butter, sugar and salt in large bowl with electric mixer at medium speed until light and fluffy. Add almond extract; beat until well blended. Gradually add flour, beating until well blended. Stir in ground almonds until well blended.

3. Shape dough by tablespoonfuls into 3-inch ropes. Shape ropes into crescents; place on prepared cookie sheets. Bake 20 to 25 minutes or until lightly browned. Cool 5 minutes on cookie sheets; transfer to wire racks to cool completely.

4. Prepare Butterscotch Glaze. Drizzle glaze over crescents; sprinkle with almonds. Let stand 30 minutes or until glaze is set. *Makes 3 to 3½ dozen cookies*

Butterscotch Glaze

½ cup packed brown sugar
2 tablespoons half-and-half
1½ tablespoons unsalted butter
¼ teaspoon salt

Combine brown sugar, half-and-half, butter and salt in small saucepan. Cook over low heat, stirring constantly, until butter melts and sugar dissolves.

Butterscotch Almond Crescents

Banana Sandies

2⅓ cups all-purpose flour
1 cup (2 sticks) butter, softened
¾ cup granulated sugar
¼ cup packed light brown sugar
½ cup ¼-inch slices banana (about 1 medium)
1 teaspoon vanilla
¼ teaspoon salt
⅔ cup chopped pecans
Prepared cream cheese frosting
Yellow food coloring (optional)

1. Preheat oven to 350°F. Grease cookie sheets.

2. Beat flour, butter, sugars, banana slices, vanilla and salt in large bowl with electric mixer at medium speed 2 to 3 minutes or until well blended. Stir in pecans. Shape dough into 1-inch balls. Place 2 inches apart on prepared cookie sheets; flatten to ¼-inch thickness with bottom of glass dipped in sugar. Bake 12 to 15 minutes or until edges are lightly browned. Remove immediately to wire racks; cool completely.

3. Tint frosting with food coloring, if desired. Spread 1 tablespoon frosting over bottoms of half the cookies. Top with remaining cookies.   *Makes about 2 dozen sandwich cookies*

Chocolate-Edged Lace Cookies

⅔ cup ground almonds
½ cup (1 stick) butter
½ cup sugar
2 tablespoons milk
1 tablespoon flour
4 ounces dark sweet or bittersweet chocolate candy bar, broken into pieces

1. Preheat oven to 325°F. Grease cookie sheets very lightly. Combine almonds, butter, sugar, milk and flour in large skillet. Cook and stir over low heat until well blended. Keep mixture warm over very low heat while forming and baking cookies.

2. Drop tablespoonfuls of batter 2 inches apart onto prepared cookie sheets. Bake 6 minutes or until cookies are golden brown. Let cookies stand on cookie sheets 30 seconds to 1 minute before loosening with thin spatula. (If cookies become too brittle to remove, warm them briefly in oven.) Remove cookies to wire rack;* cool.

3. Melt chocolate in small, heavy saucepan over low heat, stirring constantly. Tilt saucepan to pool chocolate at one end; dip edge of each cookie in chocolate, turning cookie slowly so entire edge is lightly rimmed with chocolate. Let cookies stand on waxed paper until chocolate is set.   *Makes about 2 dozen cookies*

For tuile-shaped cookies, balance a wooden spoon over two cans of the same height. Working quickly while cookies are still hot, drape the cookies (bottom side down) over the handle of the spoon so that both sides hang down and form a taco shape. When firm, transfer to wire rack to cool completely. Dip both edges of cooled cookies into chocolate.

Banana Sandies

Brownie & Bar Cookie Bonanza

Crispy Cookie Treats

1 package (18 ounces) refrigerated bite-size miniature chocolate chip cookie dough (40 count)
½ cup (1 stick) butter
½ teaspoon ground cinnamon
1 package (16 ounces) miniature marshmallows
4 cups crisp rice cereal
2 cups unsweetened granola

1. Bake cookies according to package directions. Reserve 24 cooled cookies. Coarsely chop remaining 16 cookies. Place chopped cookies in resealable food storage bag; seal bag. Freeze at least 1 hour.

2. Melt butter in large saucepan over medium heat; stir in cinnamon. Add marshmallows; cook and stir until melted and smooth. Remove from heat; let stand 10 minutes, stirring every few minutes.

3. Meanwhile, lightly grease 13×9-inch baking pan and rubber spatula. Combine cereal, granola and frozen chopped cookies in large bowl. Pour marshmallow mixture over cereal mixture; stir with spatula until well blended.

4. Press mixture into prepared pan; flatten into bars with lightly greased waxed paper or hands. Press reserved 24 cookies on top of bars, spacing evenly. Let stand at room temperature about 2 hours or until set. Cut into 2×2¼-inch bars. *Makes 2 dozen bars*

Cappuccino Crunch Bars

1¾ cups all-purpose flour, sifted
1 teaspoon baking soda
1 teaspoon salt
½ teaspoon ground cinnamon
1 cup (2 sticks) butter, softened
1½ cups packed brown sugar
½ cup granulated sugar
2 eggs
2 teaspoons instant coffee granules or espresso powder, dissolved in
    1 tablespoon hot water and cooled to room temperature
2 teaspoons vanilla
1 teaspoon freshly grated orange peel (optional)
1 cup white chocolate chips
1 cup chocolate-covered toffee baking bits

1. Preheat oven to 350°F. Grease 13×9-inch baking pan.

2. Combine flour, baking soda, salt and cinnamon in large bowl; set aside.

3. Beat butter and sugars in large bowl with electric mixer at medium speed until fluffy. Add eggs, one at a time, beating well after each addition. Add coffee mixture, vanilla and orange peel, if desired; beat well. Add flour mixture; beat until well blended. Stir in white chocolate chips and toffee bits.

4. Spread batter evenly in prepared pan. Bake 25 to 35 minutes or until golden brown. Cool completely in pan on wire rack; cut into bars.   *Makes about 2½ dozen bars*

helpful hint:

Instant coffee granules and powders are the result of removing water from brewed coffee through drying. Store instant and freeze-dried coffees in a cool place. Instant coffee should always be dissolved in hot water before adding to a recipe.

Cappuccino Crunch Bars

Shortbread Turtle Cookie Bars

1¼ cups (2½ sticks) butter, softened, divided
1 cup all-purpose flour
1 cup uncooked old-fashioned oats
1¼ cups packed brown sugar, divided
1 teaspoon ground cinnamon
¼ teaspoon salt
1½ cups chopped pecans
4 squares (1 ounce each) white chocolate, finely chopped
6 squares (1 ounce each) bittersweet or semisweet chocolate, finely chopped

1. Preheat oven to 350°F.

2. Beat ½ cup (1 stick) butter in large bowl with electric mixer at medium speed 2 minutes or until light and fluffy. Add flour, oats, ¾ cup brown sugar, cinnamon and salt; beat at low speed until coarse crumbs form. Pat firmly onto bottom of ungreased 13×9-inch baking pan. Set aside.

3. To prepare caramel, heat remaining ¾ cup (1½ sticks) butter and ¾ cup brown sugar in heavy medium saucepan over medium-high heat, stirring constantly until butter melts. Bring mixture to a boil; cook 1 minute without stirring. Remove from heat; stir in pecans. Pour caramel over crust.

4. Bake 18 to 22 minutes on center rack of oven or until caramel begins to bubble. Immediately sprinkle with white and bittersweet chocolates; swirl (do not spread) with knife after 45 seconds to 1 minute or when slightly softened. Cool completely in pan on wire rack; cut into 2×1-inch bars. *Makes about 4½ dozen bars*

Strawberry Streusel Bars

2 cups all-purpose flour
1 cup sugar
1 cup (2 sticks) butter, softened
¾ cup pecans, coarsely chopped
1 egg
1 jar (10 ounces) strawberry preserves

1. Preheat oven to 350°F. Grease 9-inch square baking pan. Set aside.

2. Combine flour, sugar, pecans, butter and egg in large mixer bowl. Beat with electric mixer at low speed 2 to 3 minutes or until mixture is crumbly. Reserve 1 cup crumb mixture; press remaining crumb mixture onto bottom of prepared baking pan. Spread preserves to within ½ inch of edges. Crumble remaining crumb mixture over preserves. Bake 42 to 50 minutes or until lightly browned. Cool completely. Cut into bars. *Makes about 24 bars*

Shortbread Turtle Cookie Bars

Baklava

4 cups slivered almonds and/or walnuts (1 pound)
1¼ cups sugar, divided
2 teaspoons ground cinnamon
¼ teaspoon ground cloves
1 package (16 ounces) frozen phyllo dough (about 20 sheets), thawed
1 cup (2 sticks) butter, melted
1½ cups water
¾ cup honey
2 (2-inch-long) strips lemon peel
1 tablespoon fresh lemon juice
1 cinnamon stick
3 whole cloves

1. Place half the nuts in work bowl of food processor. Process using on/off pulsing action until nuts are finely chopped, but not pasty. Remove nuts to medium bowl. Repeat with remaining nuts.

2. Add ½ cup sugar, cinnamon and ground cloves to nuts; mix well.

3. Unroll phyllo dough and place on large sheet of waxed paper. Cut phyllo sheets in half crosswise to form 2 stacks, each about 13×9 inches. Cover phyllo with plastic wrap and damp, clean kitchen towel. (Phyllo dough dries out quickly if not covered.)

4. Preheat oven to 325°F. Brush 13×9-inch baking dish with some melted butter.

5. Place 1 phyllo sheet in bottom of dish, folding in edges if too long; brush surface with butter. Repeat with 7 more phyllo sheets, brushing surface of each sheet with butter as they are layered. Sprinkle about ½ cup nut mixture evenly over layered phyllo.

6. Top nuts with 3 more layers of phyllo, brushing each sheet with butter. Sprinkle another ½ cup nut mixture on top. Repeat layering and brushing of 3 phyllo sheets with butter and sprinkling with ½ cup nut mixture until there are a total of eight 3-sheet layers. Top final layer of nut mixture with remaining 8 phyllo sheets, brushing each sheet with butter.

7. Cut Baklava lengthwise into 4 equal sections, then cut diagonally at 1½-inch intervals to form diamond shapes. Sprinkle top lightly with some water to prevent top phyllo layers from curling up during baking. Bake 50 to 60 minutes or until golden brown.

8. To prepare syrup, combine water, remaining ¾ cup sugar, honey, lemon peel, lemon juice, cinnamon stick and whole cloves in medium saucepan. Bring to a boil over high heat. Reduce heat to low; simmer 15 minutes.

9. Strain hot syrup; drizzle evenly over hot Baklava. Cool completely before serving.

Makes about 32 pieces

Toffee Brownie Bars

CRUST
¾ cup butter or margarine, softened
¾ cup firmly packed brown sugar
1 egg yolk
¾ teaspoon vanilla extract
1½ cups all-purpose flour

FILLING
1 (21-ounce) package DUNCAN HINES® Family-Style Chewy Fudge Brownie Mix
1 egg
⅓ cup water
⅓ cup vegetable oil

TOPPING
1 package (12 ounces) milk chocolate chips, melted
¾ cup finely chopped pecans

1. Preheat oven to 350°F. Grease 15½×10½×1-inch pan.

2. For crust, combine butter, brown sugar, egg yolk and vanilla extract in large bowl. Stir in flour. Spread in prepared pan. Bake at 350°F for 15 minutes or until golden.

3. For filling, prepare brownie mix following package directions. Spread over hot crust. Bake at 350°F for 15 minutes or until surface appears set. Cool 30 minutes.

4. For topping, spread melted chocolate on top of brownie layer; sprinkle with pecans. Cool completely.

Makes 48 bars

Tip: Bars can be made ahead and frozen in an airtight container for several weeks.

Oatmeal Date Bars

       2 packages (18 ounces each) refrigerated oatmeal raisin cookie dough
    2½ cups uncooked old-fashioned oats, divided
       2 packages (8 ounces each) chopped dates
       1 cup water
    ½ cup sugar
       1 teaspoon vanilla

1. Let both doughs stand at room temperature about 15 minutes. Preheat oven to 350°F. Lightly grease 13×9-inch baking pan.

2. For topping, combine ¾ of one package of dough and 1 cup oats in medium bowl; beat until well blended. Set aside.

3. For crust, combine remaining 1¼ packages dough and remaining 1½ cups oats in large bowl; beat until well blended. Press dough evenly onto bottom of prepared pan. Bake 10 minutes.

4. Meanwhile for filling, combine dates, water and sugar in medium saucepan; bring to a boil over high heat. Boil 3 minutes; remove from heat and stir in vanilla. Spread date mixture evenly over partially baked crust; sprinkle evenly with topping mixture.

5. Bake 25 to 28 minutes or until bubbly. Cool completely in pan on wire rack.

Makes about 2 dozen bars

Mystical Layered Bars

    ⅓ cup butter
       1 cup graham cracker crumbs
    ½ cup uncooked old-fashioned or quick oats
       1 can (14 ounces) sweetened condensed milk
       1 cup flaked coconut
    ¾ cup semisweet chocolate chips
    ¾ cup raisins
       1 cup coarsely chopped pecans

1. Preheat oven to 350°F. Melt butter in 13×9-inch baking pan. Remove from oven.

2. Sprinkle graham cracker crumbs and oats evenly over butter; press with fork. Drizzle condensed milk over oats. Layer coconut, chocolate chips, raisins and pecans over milk.

3. Bake 25 to 30 minutes or until lightly browned. Cool in pan on wire rack 5 minutes; cut into 2×1½-inch bars. Cool completely in pan on wire rack. Store tightly covered at room temperature or freeze up to 3 months.

Makes 3 dozen bars

Oatmeal Date Bars

Jam Jam Bars

1 package (18¼ ounces) yellow or white cake mix with pudding in the mix
½ cup (1 stick) butter, melted
1 cup apricot preserves or raspberry jam
1 package (11 ounces) peanut butter and milk chocolate chips

1. Preheat oven to 350°F. Lightly spray 13×9-inch baking pan with nonstick cooking spray.

2. Pour cake mix into large bowl; stir in melted butter until well blended. (Dough will be lumpy.) Remove ½ cup dough and set aside. Press remaining dough evenly into prepared pan. Spread preserves in thin layer over dough in pan.

3. Place chips in medium bowl. Stir in reserved dough until well mixed. (Dough will remain in small lumps evenly distributed throughout chips.) Sprinkle mixture evenly over preserves.

4. Bake 20 minutes or until lightly browned and bubbling at edges. Cool completely in pan on wire rack. *Makes 24 bars*

Almond-Orange Shortbread

1 cup (4 ounces) sliced almonds, divided
2 cups all-purpose flour
1 cup (2 sticks) cold butter, cut into pieces
½ cup sugar
½ cup cornstarch
2 tablespoons grated orange peel
1 teaspoon almond extract

1. Preheat oven to 350°F. To toast almonds, spread ¾ cup almonds in single layer in large baking pan. Bake 6 minutes or until golden brown, stirring frequently. Cool completely in pan. *Reduce oven temperature to 325°F.*

2. Place toasted almonds in food processor. Process using on/off pulses until almonds are coarsely chopped.

3. Add flour, butter, sugar, cornstarch, orange peel and almond extract to food processor. Process using on/off pulses until mixture resembles coarse crumbs.

4. Press dough firmly and evenly into 10×8¾-inch rectangle on large ungreased cookie sheet. Score dough into 1¼-inch squares. Press one slice of remaining almonds into center of each square.

5. Bake 30 to 40 minutes or until shortbread is firm when pressed and lightly browned. Immediately cut into squares along score lines with sharp knife. Remove cookies to wire racks; cool completely. Store loosely covered at room temperature up to 1 week.
Makes about 4½ dozen cookies

Jam Jam Bars

Chunky Caramel Nut Brownies

¾ cup (1½ sticks) butter
4 squares (1 ounce each) unsweetened chocolate
2 cups sugar
4 eggs
1 cup all-purpose flour
1 package (14 ounces) caramels
¼ cup heavy cream
2 cups pecan halves or coarsely chopped pecans, divided
1 package (12 ounces) chocolate chunks or chips

1. Preheat oven to 350°F. Grease 13×9-inch baking pan; set aside.

2. Place butter and chocolate in large microwavable bowl. Microwave on HIGH 1½ to 2 minutes or until chocolate is melted and mixture is smooth when stirred. Stir in sugar until well blended. Beat in eggs, one at a time. Stir in flour until well blended. Spread half of batter into prepared pan. Bake 20 minutes.

3. Meanwhile, combine caramels and cream in medium microwavable bowl. Microwave on HIGH 1½ to 2 minutes or until caramels begin to melt; stir until mixture is smooth. Stir in 1 cup pecan halves.

4. Spread caramel mixture over partially baked brownie base. Sprinkle with half of chocolate chunks. Pour remaining brownie batter over top; sprinkle with remaining 1 cup pecan halves and chocolate chunks. Bake 25 to 30 minutes or until set. Cool completely in pan on wire rack. Cut into squares.

Makes 2 dozen brownies

helpful hint:

Pecans are native to the United Sates, grown in temperate climates, from Georgia to Texas. This nut has a smooth tan shell that's thin but very hard and the flesh is beige with a brown exterior. Pecans are used in a variety of sweet and savory dishes and are also enjoyed eaten out of hand.

Chunky Caramel Nut Brownies

Carrot & Spice Bars

  1 cup milk
¼ cup (½ stick) butter or margarine
  1 cup bran flakes cereal
  2 eggs
  1 jar (2½ ounces) puréed baby food carrots
¾ cup grated carrot
⅓ cup golden raisins, coarsely chopped
  1 teaspoon grated orange peel
  1 teaspoon vanilla
  2 cups all-purpose flour
¾ cup sugar
  1 teaspoon baking soda
  1 teaspoon ground cinnamon
¼ cup orange juice
¼ cup toasted pecans, chopped

1. Preheat oven to 350°F. Lightly coat 13×9-inch baking pan with nonstick cooking spray; set aside.

2. Combine milk and butter in large microwavable bowl. Microwave at HIGH 1 minute or until butter is melted; add cereal. Let stand 5 minutes. Add eggs; whisk to blend. Add puréed carrots, grated carrot, raisins, orange peel and vanilla.

3. Combine flour, sugar, baking soda and cinnamon in medium bowl. Add to carrot mixture, stirring until thoroughly blended. Spread into prepared pan.

4. Bake 25 minutes or until toothpick inserted in center comes out clean. Insert tines of fork into cake at 1-inch intervals. Spoon orange juice over cake. Sprinkle with pecans; press into cake. Cut into 40 bars before serving.   *Makes 40 bars*

Carrot & Spice Bars

Layers of Love
Chocolate Brownies

¾ cup all-purpose flour
¾ cup NESTLÉ® TOLL HOUSE® Baking Cocoa
¼ teaspoon salt
½ cup (1 stick) butter, cut in pieces
½ cup granulated sugar
½ cup packed brown sugar
3 eggs
2 teaspoons vanilla extract
1 cup chopped pecans
¾ cup NESTLÉ® TOLL HOUSE® Premier White Morsels
½ cup caramel ice cream topping
¾ cup NESTLÉ® TOLL HOUSE® Semi-Sweet Chocolate Morsels

PREHEAT oven to 350°F. Grease 8-inch square baking pan.

COMBINE flour, cocoa and salt in small bowl. Beat butter, granulated sugar and brown sugar in large mixer bowl until creamy. Add *2 eggs,* one at a time, beating well after each addition. Add vanilla extract; mix well. Gradually beat in flour mixture. Reserve *¾ cup* batter. Spread *remaining* batter into prepared baking pan. Sprinkle pecans and white morsels over batter. Drizzle caramel topping over top. Beat *remaining* egg and *reserved* batter in same large bowl until light in color. Stir in semi-sweet morsels. Spread evenly over caramel topping.

BAKE for 30 to 35 minutes or until center is set. Cool completely in pan on wire rack. Cut into squares. *Makes 16 brownies*

Layers of Love Chocolate Brownies

Polish Honey Bars
(Piernikowa Krajanka Swiateczna)

8 tablespoons sugar, divided
2 tablespoons boiling water
⅓ cup honey
2 tablespoons butter
1 teaspoon ground allspice
½ teaspoon ground cinnamon
¼ teaspoon *each* ground cloves and ground nutmeg
2 cups all-purpose flour
3 tablespoons cold water
1 egg
1 teaspoon baking soda
   Chocolate Filling (page 193)
1 cup semisweet chocolate chips
32 whole toasted almonds

1. Combine 2 tablespoons sugar and boiling water in small heavy saucepan over medium heat; stir until dissolved and slightly brown. Add remaining sugar, honey, butter, allspice, cinnamon, cloves and nutmeg; bring to a boil over high heat, stirring constantly. Remove saucepan from heat; pour mixture into medium bowl. Cool.

2. Add flour, cold water, egg and baking soda to cooled sugar mixture; stir with spoon until well blended. Cover; let stand 20 minutes.

3. Preheat oven to 350°F. Grease and flour 15×10-inch jelly-roll pan; set aside. Roll out dough on lightly floured surface to almost fit size of pan. Press dough evenly into pan to edges. Bake 10 to 13 minutes or until dough springs back when lightly touched in center. Remove pan to wire rack; cool completely.

4. To remove cookie base from pan, run knife around edges of pan. Place wire rack top side down over pan; flip rack and pan over. Cookie base should drop out of pan onto rack. Cut cookie base in half to form two rectangles.

5. Prepare Chocolate Filling; spread evenly over 1 rectangle. Top with other rectangle, flat side up. Wrap cookie sandwich in plastic wrap. Place baking sheet on top of cookie sandwich; place heavy cans or other weights on baking sheet to press sandwich layers together. Let cookie sandwich stand overnight.

6. When cookie is ready to frost, melt chocolate chips in microwave at MEDIUM (50%) 2 to 3 minutes, stirring occasionally. Dip wide part of each almond into chocolate; place dipped almonds on waxed paper to set.

7. Remove weights and baking sheet from cookie sandwich; unwrap. Spread remaining melted chocolate over top. Before chocolate sets, score top of cookie sandwich into 32 bars. Place 1 dipped almond on each bar. (If chocolate has set, it may be necessary to reheat almonds in microwave for a few seconds.) Let stand at room temperature until set; cut into bars.

Makes 32 bars

Chocolate Filling

¼ cup whipping cream
½ cup semisweet chocolate chips
1 cup natural almonds, toasted and ground
¾ cup powdered sugar, divided
½ teaspoon vanilla

Heat cream and chocolate chips in small saucepan over medium heat until melted and smooth, stirring constantly. Remove from heat; stir in almonds, ½ cup powdered sugar and vanilla. Stir in additional powdered sugar until filling is stiff enough to spread.

Makes about 1 cup filling

Decadent Blonde Brownies

1½ cups all-purpose flour
1 teaspoon baking powder
½ teaspoon salt
¾ cup granulated sugar
¾ cup packed light brown sugar
½ cup (1 stick) butter, softened
2 eggs
2 teaspoons vanilla
1 package (10 ounces) semisweet chocolate chunks*
1 jar (3½ ounces) macadamia nuts, coarsely chopped, to measure ¾ cup

*If chocolate chunks are not available, cut 1 (10-ounce) thick chocolate candy bar into ¼-inch pieces to measure 1½ cups.

1. Preheat oven to 350°F. Grease 13×9-inch baking pan. Combine flour, baking powder and salt in small bowl; set aside.

2. Beat granulated sugar, brown sugar and butter in large bowl with electric mixer at medium speed until light and fluffy. Beat in eggs and vanilla. Add flour mixture. Beat at low speed until well blended. Stir in chocolate chunks and macadamia nuts. Spread batter evenly in prepared pan. Bake 25 to 30 minutes or until golden brown. Remove pan to wire rack; cool completely. Cut into bars. Store in airtight container. *Makes 2 dozen brownies*

Banana Oatmeal Snack Bars

2 packages (18 ounces each) refrigerated oatmeal raisin cookie dough
2 bananas, mashed
3 eggs
½ teaspoon ground cinnamon
1 cup uncooked old-fashioned oats
1 cup dried cranberries
½ cup chopped dried apricots
½ cup chopped pecans
  Powdered sugar

1. Let both packages of dough stand at room temperature about 15 minutes. Preheat oven to 350°F. Lightly grease 13×9-inch baking pan.

2. Combine dough, bananas, eggs and cinnamon in large bowl; beat until well blended. Combine oats, cranberries, apricots and pecans in medium bowl; stir into dough until well blended. Spread into prepared pan; smooth top.

3. Bake 40 to 45 minutes or until top is brown and toothpick inserted into center comes out clean. Cool completely in pan on wire rack. Sprinkle with powdered sugar just before serving. *Makes about 2 dozen bars*

Peanut Butter Candy Bars

1 cup packed brown sugar
¾ cup crunchy peanut butter
½ cup granulated sugar
½ cup (1 stick) butter, softened
2 eggs
1 teaspoon vanilla
¼ cup milk
1¾ cups all-purpose flour
1 teaspoon baking powder
1 package (10 ounces) candy coated peanut butter candies (1⅓ cups), divided
⅓ cup coarsely chopped peanuts
1 container (16 ounces) chocolate frosting

1. Preheat oven to 325°F. Grease 13×9-inch baking pan.

2. Beat brown sugar, peanut butter, granulated sugar and butter in large bowl with electric mixer at medium speed until creamy. Add eggs and vanilla; beat until fluffy. Gradually beat in milk. Gradually add flour and baking powder, beating until well blended. Stir in 1 cup candies and nuts. Spread batter into prepared pan.

3. Bake 40 to 45 minutes or until toothpick inserted in center comes out clean. Cool completely in pan on wire rack. Spread frosting over top of bars. Sprinkle with remaining ⅓ cup candies. Cut into bars. *Makes 2 dozen bars*

Banana Oatmeal Snack Bars

Mexican Brownies

1 box (about 19 ounces) brownie mix, plus ingredients to prepare mix
2 teaspoons ground cinnamon
1 package (8 ounces) cream cheese, softened
½ cup dulce de leche (See Note)
2 tablespoons powdered sugar

1. Prepare and bake brownies according to package directions, adding cinnamon to batter. Cool completely.

2. To prepare frosting, beat cream cheese in medium bowl with electric mixer at medium speed until smooth. Add dulce de leche and powdered sugar; beat until well blended and creamy. Frost brownies with dulce de leche icing. Serve immediately, or, for even richer flavor, refrigerate 8 hours or overnight.

Makes 16 brownies

Note: Dulce de leche is caramelized condensed milk widely used in Mexican desserts. It is sold in cans in most large supermarkets. Or, make dulce de leche by bringing 1 cup whole milk and ½ cup granulated sugar just to a boil; reduce heat to medium-low and cook 30 minutes or until caramel in color, stirring occasionally. Remove from heat; cool completely. Stir in ¼ teaspoon vanilla. If using homemade dulce de leche, omit 2 tablespoons powdered sugar in recipe.

Strawberry Oat Bars

2 cups uncooked quick oats
1 cup all-purpose flour
2 teaspoons baking soda
½ teaspoon ground cinnamon
¼ teaspoon salt
1 cup (2 sticks) butter, softened
1 cup packed light brown sugar
1 can (21 ounces) strawberry pie filling
¾ teaspoon almond extract

1. Preheat oven to 375°F. Combine oats, flour, baking soda, cinnamon and salt in large bowl; mix well.

2. Beat butter in medium bowl with electric mixer at medium speed until smooth. Add brown sugar; beat until well blended. Add flour mixture to butter mixture, beating at low speed until well blended and crumbly.

3. Spread two thirds of crumb mixture on bottom of ungreased 13×9-inch baking pan, pressing firmly. Bake 15 minutes; cool 5 minutes on wire rack.

4. Meanwhile, place strawberry filling in food processor or blender. Cover and process until smooth. Stir in almond extract. Pour strawberry mixture over partially baked crust. Sprinkle remaining crumb mixture evenly over strawberry layer.

5. Return pan to oven; bake 20 to 25 minutes or until topping is golden brown and filling is slightly bubbly. Cool completely in pan on wire rack. Cut into bars.

Makes about 4 dozen bars

Mexican Brownies

Chocolatey Raspberry Crumb Bars

1 cup (2 sticks) butter or margarine, softened
2 cups all-purpose flour
½ cup packed light brown sugar
¼ teaspoon salt
2 cups (12-ounce package) NESTLÉ® TOLL HOUSE® Semi-Sweet Chocolate Morsels, *divided*
1 can (14 ounces) NESTLÉ® CARNATION® Sweetened Condensed Milk
½ cup chopped nuts (optional)
⅓ cup seedless raspberry jam

PREHEAT oven to 350°F. Grease 13×9-inch baking pan.

BEAT butter in large mixer bowl until creamy. Beat in flour, sugar and salt until crumbly. With floured fingers, press *1¾ cups* crumb mixture onto bottom of prepared baking pan; reserve *remaining* mixture.

BAKE for 10 to 12 minutes or until edges are golden brown.

MICROWAVE *1 cup* morsels and sweetened condensed milk in medium, uncovered, microwave-safe bowl on HIGH (100%) power for 1 minute. STIR. Morsels may retain some of their original shape. If necessary, microwave at additional 10- to 15-second intervals, stirring just until morsels are melted. Spread over hot crust.

STIR nuts into *reserved* crumb mixture; sprinkle over chocolate layer. Drop teaspoonfuls of raspberry jam over crumb mixture. Sprinkle with *remaining* morsels.

BAKE for 25 to 30 minutes or until center is set. Cool in pan on wire rack. Cut into bars.

Makes 3 dozen bars

Chocolatey Raspberry Crumb Bars

Cheery Cherry Brownies

¾ cup all-purpose flour
½ cup sugar
½ cup unsweetened cocoa powder
¼ teaspoon baking soda
½ cup evaporated skimmed milk
⅓ cup butter, melted
1 egg *or* ¼ cup egg substitute
¼ cup honey
1 teaspoon vanilla
½ (15½-ounce) can pitted tart red cherries, drained and halved

1. Preheat oven to 350°F. Grease 11×7-inch baking pan; set aside.

2. Stir together flour, sugar, cocoa and baking soda in large bowl. Add milk, butter, egg, honey and vanilla. Stir just until blended.

3. Pour into prepared pan. Sprinkle cherries over top of chocolate mixture. Bake 13 to 15 minutes or until toothpick inserted into center comes out clean. Cool completely in pan on wire rack. Cut into 12 bars. *Makes 12 brownies*

Pecan Pie Bars

¾ cup (1½ sticks) butter, softened
½ cup powdered sugar
1½ cups all-purpose flour
3 eggs
2 cups coarsely chopped pecans
1 cup granulated sugar
1 cup light corn syrup
2 tablespoons butter, melted
1 teaspoon vanilla

1. Preheat oven to 350°F. For crust, beat ¾ cup butter in large bowl with electric mixer at medium speed until smooth. Add powdered sugar; beat at medium speed until well blended. Add flour gradually, beating at low speed after each addition.

2. Press dough evenly into ungreased 13×9-inch baking pan. Press mixture slightly up sides of pan (less than ¼ inch) to form lip to hold filling. Bake 20 to 25 minutes or until golden brown.

3. Meanwhile, for filling, beat eggs lightly in medium bowl with fork. Add pecans, granulated sugar, corn syrup, 2 tablespoons melted butter and vanilla; mix well.

4. Pour filling over partially baked crust. Return to oven; bake 35 to 40 minutes or until filling is set.

5. Loosen edges with knife. Let cool completely on wire rack before cutting into squares. Cover and refrigerate until 10 to 15 minutes before serving. *Do not freeze.*
Makes about 4 dozen bars

Cheery Cherry Brownie

Lemon-Cranberry Bars

½ cup frozen lemonade concentrate, thawed
½ cup sugar
¼ cup (½ stick) butter, softened
1 egg
1½ cups all-purpose flour
2 teaspoons grated lemon peel
½ teaspoon baking soda
½ teaspoon salt
½ cup dried cranberries

1. Preheat oven to 375°F. Lightly coat 8-inch square baking pan with nonstick cooking spray; set aside.

2. Combine lemonade concentrate, sugar, butter and egg in medium bowl; mix well. Add flour, lemon peel, baking soda and salt; stir well. Stir in cranberries; spoon into prepared pan.

3. Bake 20 minutes or until light brown. Cool completely in pan on wire rack. Cut into 16 squares.

Makes 16 bars

Marble Brownies

½ cup plus 2 tablespoons all-purpose flour, divided
½ cup unsweetened cocoa powder
1 teaspoon baking powder
½ teaspoon salt
1¾ cups sugar, divided
2 tablespoons margarine, softened
½ cup MOTT'S® Natural Apple Sauce
3 egg whites, divided
1½ teaspoons vanilla extract, divided
4 ounces low fat cream cheese (Neufchâtel), softened

1. Preheat oven to 350°F. Spray 8-inch square baking pan with nonstick cooking spray.

2. In small bowl, sift together ½ cup flour, cocoa, baking powder and salt.

3. In large bowl, beat 1½ cups sugar and margarine with electric mixer at medium speed until blended. Whisk in apple sauce, 2 egg whites and 1 teaspoon vanilla.

4. Add flour mixture to apple sauce mixture; stir until well blended. Pour batter into prepared pan.

5. In small bowl, beat cream cheese and remaining ¼ cup sugar with electric mixer at medium speed until blended. Stir in remaining egg white, 2 tablespoons flour and ½ teaspoon vanilla. Pour over brownie batter; run knife through batters to marble.

6. Bake 35 to 40 minutes or until firm. Cool on wire rack 15 minutes; cut into 12 bars.

Makes 12 servings

Lemon-Cranberry Bars

Cupcake Creations

Rabbit Power Brownie Cupcakes

1¼ cups sugar
1 cup all-purpose flour
½ cup unsweetened cocoa powder
½ teaspoon baking soda
½ teaspoon baking powder
¼ teaspoon salt
½ cup baby carrots
⅔ cup canola oil
2 eggs
¼ cup milk
1 teaspoon vanilla
1 container (16 ounces) chocolate frosting
Colored sprinkles (optional)

1. Preheat oven to 350°F. Line 20 standard (2½-inch) muffin cups with foil or paper baking cups.

2. Combine sugar, flour, cocoa, baking soda, baking powder and salt in large bowl. Place carrots in food processor; process using on/off pulsing action until finely chopped. Add carrots, oil, eggs, milk and vanilla to flour mixture. Beat with electric mixer at low speed until blended. Increase speed to medium; beat 2 minutes. Spoon batter into muffin cups, filling about two-thirds full. Bake about 15 minutes or until toothpick inserted into centers comes out clean. Cool completely on wire racks.

3. Frost cupcakes with chocolate frosting. Decorate with sprinkles, if desired.

Makes 20 cupcakes

Prep Time: 15 minutes | **Bake Time:** 15 minutes | **Cool Time:** 1 hour

Chocolate-Frosted Peanut Butter Cupcakes

1¾ cups all-purpose flour
1½ teaspoons baking powder
¼ teaspoon salt
⅓ cup butter, softened
⅓ cup creamy or chunky peanut butter
½ cup granulated sugar
¼ cup packed brown sugar
2 eggs
1 teaspoon vanilla
1¼ cups milk
Peanut Butter Chocolate Frosting (recipe follows)

1. Preheat oven to 350°F. Line 18 standard (2½-inch) muffin cups with foil or paper baking cups. Combine flour, baking powder and salt in medium bowl.

2. Beat butter and peanut butter in large bowl with electric mixer at medium speed until smooth; beat in sugars until well mixed. Beat in eggs and vanilla. Add flour mixture alternately with milk, beginning and ending with flour mixture.

3. Spoon batter into prepared muffin cups, filling two-thirds full. Bake 23 to 25 minutes or until cupcakes spring back when touched and toothpick inserted into centers comes out clean. Cool in pans on wire racks 10 minutes. Remove cupcakes to racks; cool completely.

4. Prepare Peanut Butter Chocolate Frosting. Frost cupcakes.   *Makes 18 cupcakes*

Peanut Butter Chocolate Frosting

4 cups powdered sugar
⅓ cup unsweetened cocoa powder
4 to 5 tablespoons milk, divided
3 tablespoons creamy peanut butter

Beat powdered sugar, cocoa, 4 tablespoons milk and peanut butter in large bowl with electric mixer at low speed until smooth. Beat in additional 1 tablespoon milk until desired spreading consistency is reached.   *Makes about 2½ cups frosting*

Chocolate-Frosted Peanut Butter Cupcakes

Toffee-Topped Pineapple Upside-Down Cakes

¼ cup light corn syrup
¼ cup (½ stick) butter or margarine, melted
1 cup HEATH® BITS 'O BRICKLE® Toffee Bits
4 pineapple rings
4 maraschino cherries
¼ cup (½ stick) butter or margarine, softened
⅔ cup sugar
1 egg
1 tablespoon rum *or* 1 teaspoon rum extract
1⅓ cups all-purpose flour
2 teaspoons baking powder
⅔ cup milk

1. Heat oven to 350°F. Lightly coat inside of 4 individual 2-cup baking dishes with vegetable oil spray.

2. Stir together 1 tablespoon corn syrup and 1 tablespoon melted butter in each of 4 baking dishes. Sprinkle each with ¼ cup toffee. Center pineapple rings on toffee and place cherries in centers.

3. Beat softened butter and sugar in small bowl until blended. Add egg and rum, beating well. Stir together flour and baking powder; add alternately with milk to butter-sugar mixture, beating until smooth. Spoon about ¾ cup batter into each prepared dish.

4. Bake 25 to 30 minutes or until wooden pick inserted into centers comes out clean. Immediately invert onto serving dish. Refrigerate leftovers.   *Makes four 4-inch cakes*

helpful hint:

Before measuring corn syrup, lightly coat the measuring cup with nonstick cooking spray. This will help the corn syrup slide out easily instead of clinging to the cup.

Toffee-Topped Pineapple Upside-Down Cake

Angelic Cupcakes

    1 package (16 ounces) angel food cake mix
1¼ cups cold water
    ¼ teaspoon peppermint extract (optional)
        Red food coloring
4½ cups thawed frozen light whipped topping
        Green food coloring

1. Preheat oven to 375°F. Line 36 standard (2½-inch) muffin cups with paper liners; set aside.

2. Beat cake mix, water and peppermint extract, if desired, in large bowl with electric mixer at low speed 30 seconds. Increase speed to medium and beat 1 minute.

3. Pour half of batter into medium bowl; carefully stir in 9 drops red food coloring. In each muffin cup, alternate spoonfuls of white and pink batter, filling baking cups three-fourths full.

4. Bake 11 minutes or until cupcakes are golden with deep cracks on top. Remove to wire rack. Cool completely.

5. Divide whipped topping between three small bowls. Add 2 drops green food coloring to one bowl of whipped topping; stir gently to combine. Add 2 drops red food coloring to one bowl of whipped topping; stir gently to combine. Frost cupcakes with red, green and white whipped topping as desired. Refrigerate leftovers.   *Makes 36 servings*

Toffee Bits Cheesecake Cups

    About 16 to 18 vanilla wafer cookies
    3 packages (8 ounces each) cream cheese, softened
¾ cup sugar
    3 eggs
    1 teaspoon vanilla extract
1⅓ cups (8-ounce package) HEATH® BITS 'O BRICKLE™ Toffee Bits, divided

1. Heat oven to 350°F. Line 2½-inch muffin cups with paper bake cups; place vanilla wafer on bottom of each cup.

2. Beat cream cheese and sugar in large bowl on low speed of mixer until smooth. Beat in eggs and vanilla just until blended. Do not overbeat. Gently stir 1 cup toffee bits into batter; pour into prepared cups to ¼ inch from top.

3. Bake 20 to 25 minutes or until almost set. Remove from oven. Immediately sprinkle about ½ teaspoon toffee bits onto each cup. Cool completely in pan on wire rack. Remove from pan. Cover; refrigerate about 3 hours. Store leftover cups in refrigerator.

Makes about 16 to 18 cups

Angelic Cupcakes

Miss Pinky the Pig Cupcakes

 2 jars (10 ounces each) maraschino cherries, well drained
 1 package (18¼ ounces) white cake mix *without* pudding in the mix
 1 cup sour cream
 ½ cup vegetable oil
 3 egg whites
 ¼ cup water
 ½ teaspoon almond extract
   Red food coloring
 1 container (16 ounces) cream cheese frosting
48 small gum drops
   Mini candy-coated chocolate pieces, mini chocolate chips, white
     decorating icing and colored sugar

1. Preheat oven to 350°F. Line 24 standard (2½-inch) muffin cups with paper baking cups. Spray 24 mini (1¾-inch) muffin cups with nonstick cooking spray. Pat cherries dry with paper towels. Place in food processor; process 4 to 5 seconds or until finely chopped.

2. Beat cake mix, sour cream, oil, egg whites, water and almond extract in large bowl with electric mixer at low speed about 1 minute or until blended. Increase speed to medium; beat 1 to 2 minutes or until smooth. Stir in chopped cherries.

3. Spoon about 2 slightly rounded tablespoons batter into prepared standard muffin cups, filling each about one-half full. (Cups will be slightly less full than normal.) Spoon remaining batter into mini muffin cups, filling each about one-third full.

4. Bake standard cupcakes 14 to 18 minutes and mini cupcakes 7 to 9 minutes or until toothpick inserted into centers comes out clean. Cool cupcakes in pans on wire racks 5 minutes; remove from pans and cool completely on wire racks.

5. Add food coloring to frosting, a few drops at a time, until desired shade of pink is reached. Frost tops of larger cupcakes with pink frosting. Gently press small cupcake onto one side of each larger cupcake top. Frost tops and sides of small cupcakes.

6. Place gumdrops between two layers of waxed paper. Flatten to ⅛-inch thickness with rolling pin; cut out triangles. Arrange gumdrops on cupcakes for ears; complete faces with candy-coated chocolate pieces, chocolate chips, white icing and colored sugar.

Makes 24 cupcakes

Miss Pinky the Pig Cupcakes

Berry Surprise Cupcakes

1 package DUNCAN HINES® Moist Deluxe® White Cake Mix
3 egg whites
1⅓ cups water
2 tablespoons vegetable oil
3 sheets (0.5 ounce each) strawberry chewy fruit snacks
1 container DUNCAN HINES® Vanilla Frosting
2 pouches (0.9 ounce each) chewy fruit snack shapes, for garnish (optional)

1. Preheat oven to 350°F. Place paper liners in 24 (2½-inch) muffin cups.

2. Combine cake mix, egg whites, water and oil in large bowl. Beat at low speed with electric mixer until moistened. Beat at medium speed 2 minutes. Fill each liner half full with batter.

3. Cut three fruit snack sheets into 9 equal pieces. (You will have 3 extra squares.) Place each fruit snack piece on top of batter in each cup. Pour remaining batter equally over each. Bake at 350°F for 18 to 23 minutes or until toothpick inserted in center comes out clean. Cool in pans 5 minutes. Remove to cooling racks. Cool completely. Frost cupcakes with Vanilla frosting. Decorate with fruit snack shapes, if desired.

Makes 12 to 16 servings

Variation: To make a Berry Surprise Cake, prepare cake following package directions. Pour half the batter into prepared 13×9×2-inch pan. Place 4 fruit snack sheets evenly on top. Pour remaining batter over all. Bake and cool as directed on package. Frost and decorate as directed.

Chocolate Cherry Cups

⅓ cup all-purpose flour
⅓ cup sugar
⅓ cup unsweetened cocoa powder
¼ teaspoon baking powder
¼ teaspoon salt
6 ounces vanilla yogurt
3 egg whites
½ teaspoon almond extract
36 no-sugar-added pitted frozen cherries, thawed and drained

1. Preheat oven to 350°F. Line 12 standard (2½-inch) muffin pan cups with foil baking cups. Combine flour, sugar, ground chocolate, cocoa powder, baking powder and salt in large bowl.

2. Beat egg whites in medium bowl with electric mixer at high speed until soft peaks form. Add yogurt to flour mixture; stir well. Fold in beaten egg whites and almond extract.

3. Fill each cup two-thirds full. Place 3 cherries on top of batter, pressing lightly.

4. Bake 20 to 25 minutes, until tops are puffy and edges are set. Centers will be moist.

Makes 12 servings

Berry Surprise Cupcakes

Celebration Chocolate Mini Cupcakes

¾ **cup all-purpose flour**
½ **cup sugar**
2 **tablespoons HERSHEY'S Cocoa**
½ **teaspoon baking soda**
¼ **teaspoon salt**
½ **cup water**
3 **tablespoons vegetable oil**
1½ **teaspoons white vinegar**
½ **teaspoon vanilla extract**
Celebration Chocolate Frosting (recipe follows)

1. Heat oven to 350°F. Line small (1¾-inch) muffin cups with paper liners.

2. Stir together flour, sugar, cocoa, baking soda and salt in medium bowl. Add water, oil, vinegar and vanilla; beat with whisk or mixer on medium speed until well blended. Fill muffin cups ⅔ full with batter.

3. Bake 11 to 13 minutes or until wooden pick inserted in center comes out clean. Remove from pan to wire rack. Cool completely. Frost with Celebration Chocolate Frosting. Garnish as desired. *Makes 28 cupcakes*

Note: Batter can be baked in 8 standard (2½-inch) paper-lined muffin cups. Bake at 350°F for 20 to 25 minutes

Celebration Chocolate Frosting

1 **cup powdered sugar**
3 **tablespoons HERSHEY'S Cocoa**
3 **tablespoons butter or margarine, softened**
2 **tablespoons water or milk**
½ **teaspoon vanilla extract**

Stir together powdered sugar and cocoa. Beat butter and ½ cup cocoa mixture in medium bowl until blended. Add remaining cocoa mixture, water and vanilla; beat to spreading consistency. *Makes about 1 cup frosting*

Celebration Chocolate Mini Cupcakes

White Chocolate Macadamia Cupcakes

1 package (18¼ ounces) white cake mix, plus ingredients to prepare mix
1 package (4-serving size) white chocolate-flavor instant pudding and pie filling mix
¾ cup chopped macadamia nuts
1½ cups toasted flaked coconut*
1 cup white chocolate chips
1 container (16 ounces) white frosting

*To toast coconut, spread evenly on ungreased baking sheet; bake at 350°F for 6 minutes, stirring occasionally, until light golden brown. Cool completely.

1. Preheat oven to 350°F. Line 20 standard (2½-inch) muffin cups with paper baking cups.

2. Prepare cake mix according to package directions, beating in pudding mix with cake mix ingredients. Fold in nuts. Fill muffin cups two-thirds full. Bake 18 to 20 minutes or until toothpick inserted into centers comes out clean. Cool in pans on wire racks 10 minutes. Remove from pans to wire racks; cool completely.

3. Place white chocolate chips in small microwavable bowl; microwave 2 minutes on MEDIUM (50%), stirring every 30 seconds, until melted and smooth. Cool slightly; stir into frosting until smooth.

4. Frost cupcakes; sprinkle with toasted coconut.

Makes 20 cupcakes

helpful hint:

Macadamia nuts are native to Australia, but most of the commercial crop is now grown in Hawaii. This small, round nut has a hard brown shell with cream-colored meat and a buttery rich, slightly sweet flavor. Most are sold shelled, either roasted or raw. They are used for snacking and baking.

White Chocolate Macadamia Cupcakes

"Go Fly a Kite" Cupcakes

1⅔ cups all-purpose flour
½ cup unsweetened cocoa powder
1 teaspoon baking powder
½ teaspoon baking soda
¼ teaspoon salt
1¾ cups granulated sugar
¼ cup firmly packed light brown sugar
½ cup vegetable shortening
1 cup buttermilk
3 large eggs
2 tablespoons vegetable oil
¾ teaspoon vanilla extract
1½ cups "M&M's"® Chocolate Mini Baking Bits, divided
24 graham cracker squares
1 container (16 ounces) white frosting
Assorted food colorings

Preheat oven to 350°F. Lightly grease 24 (2¾-inch) muffin cups or line with foil or paper liners; set aside. In large bowl combine flour, cocoa powder, baking powder, baking soda and salt; stir in sugars. Beat in shortening until well combined. Beat in buttermilk, eggs, oil and vanilla. Divide batter among prepared muffin cups. Sprinkle 1 teaspoon "M&M's"® Chocolate Mini Baking Bits over batter in each muffin cup. Bake 20 to 25 minutes or until toothpick inserted in centers comes out clean. Cool completely on wire racks. Using serrated knife and back and forth sawing motion, gently cut graham crackers into kite shapes. (Do not press down on cracker while cutting.) Reserve 1 cup frosting. Tint remaining frosting desired color. Frost graham crackers and decorate with "M&M's"® Chocolate Mini Baking Bits. Tint reserved frosting sky blue; frost cupcakes. Place small blob frosting at one edge of cupcake; stand kites in frosting on cupcakes. Make kite tails with "M&M's"® Chocolate Mini Baking Bits. Store in tightly covered container.

Makes 24 cupcakes

"Go Fly a Kite" Cupcakes

Honey Chocolate Chip Cupcakes

CUPCAKES
½ cup butter or margarine, softened
⅔ cup honey
1 egg
½ teaspoon vanilla extract
1¼ cups all-purpose flour
½ teaspoon salt
½ teaspoon baking soda

TOPPING
⅓ cup honey
1 egg
½ teaspoon vanilla extract
⅛ teaspoon salt
1 cup semi-sweet chocolate chips
½ cup chopped walnuts

Using electric mixer, beat butter until light; gradually add honey, beating until light and creamy. Beat in egg and vanilla.

In medium bowl, combine flour, salt and baking soda; gradually add to butter mixture, mixing until blended. Spoon batter into 16 paper-lined or greased 2½-inch muffin cups. Bake at 350°F for 10 minutes.

Meanwhile, prepare topping. Using electric mixer, beat honey, egg, vanilla and salt until light; stir in chocolate chips and nuts. Remove cupcakes from oven. Spoon 1 tablespoon topping over each partially-baked cupcake. Return to oven; bake at 350°F for additional 12 to 15 minutes or until topping is set. Cool in pans on wire racks. *Makes 16 cupcakes*

Favorite recipe from **National Honey Board**

Double Chocolate Cocoa Cupcakes

¾ cup shortening
1¼ cups granulated sugar
2 eggs
1 teaspoon vanilla extract
1½ cups all-purpose flour
½ cup HERSHEY¡S Cocoa
1 teaspoon baking soda
½ teaspoon salt
1 cup milk
2 cups (12-ounce package) HERSHEY¡S MINI CHIPS™ Semi-Sweet Chocolate Chips
Powdered sugar

1. Heat oven to 375°F. Line muffin cups (2½ inches in diameter) with paper bake cups.

2. Beat shortening and granulated sugar in large bowl until fluffy. Add eggs and vanilla; beat well. Stir together flour, cocoa, baking soda and salt; add alternately with milk to shortening mixture, beating well after each addition. Stir in small chocolate chips. Fill prepared muffin cups about ¾ full with batter.

3. Bake 20 to 25 minutes or until cupcake springs back when touched lightly in center. Remove from pans to wire racks. Cool completely. Sift powdered sugar over tops of cupcakes.

Makes about 2 dozen cupcakes

helpful hint:

To easily fill muffin cups, place batter in a 4-cup glass measure. Fill each cup three-fourths full, using a plastic spatula to control the flow of the batter. Make sure not to overfill muffin cups or batter will overflow the muffin cups, making it difficult to remove them from the pan.

Red's Rockin'
Rainbow Cupcakes

2¼ cups all-purpose flour
1 tablespoon baking powder
½ teaspoon salt
1⅔ cups granulated sugar
½ cup (1 stick) butter, softened
1 cup milk
2 teaspoons vanilla extract
3 large egg whites
Blue and assorted food colorings
1 container (16 ounces) white frosting
1½ cups "M&M's"® Chocolate Mini Baking Bits, divided

Preheat oven to 350°F. Lightly grease 24 (2¾-inch) muffin cups or line with paper or foil liners; set aside. In large bowl combine flour, baking powder and salt. Blend in sugar, butter, milk and vanilla; beat about 2 minutes. Add egg whites; beat 2 minutes. Divide batter evenly among prepared muffin cups. Place 2 drops desired food coloring into each muffin cup. Swirl gently with knife. Sprinkle evenly with ¾ cup "M&M's"® Chocolate Mini Baking Bits. Bake 20 to 25 minutes or until toothpick inserted in center comes out clean. Cool completely on wire racks. Combine frosting and blue food coloring. Spread frosting over cupcakes; decorate with remaining ¾ cup "M&M's"® Chocolate Mini Baking Bits to make rainbows. Store in tightly covered container. *Makes 24 cupcakes*

Red's Rockin' Rainbow Cupcakes

Fudgy Mocha Cupcakes with Chocolate Coffee Ganache

1 package (18¼ ounces) devil's food cake mix *without* pudding in the mix
1 package (4-serving size) chocolate fudge-flavor instant pudding and pie filling mix
1⅓ cups very strong brewed coffee, cooled to room temperature
3 eggs
½ cup vegetable oil
6 ounces semisweet chocolate, finely chopped
½ cup whipping cream
2 teaspoons instant coffee granules
½ cup buttercream frosting

1. Preheat oven to 350°F. Line 18 standard (2½-inch) muffin cups with paper baking cups.

2. Beat cake mix, pudding mix, coffee, eggs and oil in large bowl with electric mixer at medium speed 2 minutes until well blended. Spoon batter into prepared muffin pan cups, filling two-thirds full. Bake 22 to 24 minutes or until toothpick inserted into centers comes out clean. Cool in pans on wire racks 10 minutes. Remove cupcakes to racks; cool completely.

3. To prepare ganache, place chocolate in small bowl. Heat cream and coffee granules in small saucepan over medium-low heat until bubbles appear around edge of pan. Pour cream mixture over chocolate; let stand about 2 minutes. Stir until mixture is smooth and shiny. Allow ganache to cool completely. (It will be slightly runny.)

4. Dip tops of cupcakes into chocolate ganache; smooth surface. Allow ganache to set about 5 minutes.

5. Place buttercream frosting in pastry bag fitted with small round pastry tip. Pipe letters onto cupcakes. *Makes 18 cupcakes*

Fudgy Mocha Cupcakes with Chocolate Coffee Ganache

Double Malted Cupcakes

CUPCAKES
- **2 cups all-purpose flour**
- **¼ cup malted milk powder**
- **2 teaspoons baking powder**
- **¼ teaspoon salt**
- **1¾ cups granulated sugar**
- **½ cup (1 stick) butter, softened**
- **1 cup milk**
- **1½ teaspoons vanilla**
- **3 egg whites**

FROSTING
- **4 ounces milk chocolate candy bar, broken into chunks**
- **¼ cup (½ stick) butter**
- **¼ cup whipping cream**
- **1 tablespoon malted milk powder**
- **1 teaspoon vanilla**
- **1¾ cups powdered sugar**
- **30 chocolate-covered malt ball candies**

1. Preheat oven to 350°F. Line 30 standard (2½-inch) muffin cups with paper baking cups.

2. For cupcakes, combine flour, ¼ cup malted milk powder, baking powder and salt in medium bowl; set aside. Beat granulated sugar and ½ cup butter in large bowl with electric mixer at medium speed 1 minute. Add milk and 1½ teaspoons vanilla. Beat at low speed 30 seconds. Gradually beat in flour mixture at medium speed 2 minutes. Add egg whites; beat 1 minute.

3. Spoon batter into prepared muffin cups, filling two-thirds full. Bake 20 minutes or until golden brown and toothpick inserted into centers comes out clean. Cool in pans on wire racks 10 minutes. (Centers of cupcakes will sink slightly upon cooling.) Remove cupcakes to wire racks to cool completely. (At this point, cupcakes may be frozen up to 3 months.)

4. For frosting, melt chocolate and ¼ cup butter in heavy medium saucepan over low heat, stirring frequently. Stir in cream, 1 tablespoon malted milk powder and 1 teaspoon vanilla; mix well. Gradually whisk in powdered sugar. Cook 4 to 5 minutes, whisking constantly, until small lumps disappear. Remove from heat. Refrigerate 20 minutes, whisking every 5 minutes or until frosting is spreadable.

5. Spread frosting over cupcakes; decorate with malt ball candies. Store at room temperature up to 24 hours or cover and refrigerate for up to 3 days before serving.

Makes 30 cupcakes

Double Malted Cupcakes

Raspberry Buckle Cupcakes

½ (18-ounce) package refrigerated sugar cookie dough*
½ cup all-purpose flour
¼ cup firmly packed brown sugar
1 teaspoon vanilla
½ cup slivered almonds
1 package (18¼ ounces) lemon cake mix, plus ingredients to prepare mix
1 can (12 ounces) raspberry pie filling

*Save the remaining ½ package of dough for another use.

1. Preheat oven to 350°F. Line 24 standard (2½-inch) muffin cups with paper or foil baking cups.

2. For topping, combine cookie dough, flour, brown sugar and vanilla in large bowl; beat until well blended. Stir in almonds; set aside.

3. Prepare cake mix according to package directions. Divide batter evenly among prepared muffin pan cups; place 1 tablespoon pie filling on batter in each muffin cup. Bake 10 minutes.

4. Sprinkle topping evenly over partially baked cupcakes. Bake 15 minutes or until topping is brown and cupcakes are set. *Makes 2 dozen cupcakes*

helpful hint:

These cupcakes are a fresh take on a traditional fruit buckle, which is a baked dish of fruit topped with simple yellow cake batter. This modern version uses lemon cake batter, raspberry pie filling and a cookie-crumble topping.

Raspberry Buckle Cupcakes

Classy Cakes

Orange Kiss Me Cakes

1 large orange
1 cup raisins
⅔ cup chopped walnuts, divided
2 cups all-purpose flour
1⅓ cups granulated sugar, divided
1 teaspoon baking soda
1 teaspoon salt
1 cup milk, divided
½ cup shortening
2 eggs
1 teaspoon ground cinnamon

1. Preheat oven to 350°F. Lightly grease and flour 6 (1-cup) mini bundt pans or 1 (10-inch) bundt pan.

2. Juice orange; reserve only ⅓ cup juice. Coarsely chop remaining orange pulp and peel. Process pulp, peel, raisins and ⅓ cup walnuts in food processor fitted with metal blade until finely ground.

3. Sift flour, 1 cup sugar, baking soda and salt together in large bowl. Add ¾ cup milk and shortening. Beat 4 minutes with electric mixer at medium speed until well blended. Add eggs and remaining ¼ cup milk; beat 2 minutes. Fold orange mixture into batter; mix well. Pour into prepared pans.

4. Bake 40 to 45 minutes for mini bundt pans or until toothpick inserted near centers comes out clean. Cool in pan 15 minutes. Invert onto serving plate. Poke holes in cakes with wooden skewer or tines of fork.

5. Pour reserved orange juice over cakes. Combine remaining ⅓ cup sugar, ⅓ cup walnuts and cinnamon in small bowl. Sprinkle over cakes. Garnish as desired.   *Makes 12 servings*

Pumpkin Chiffon Cake

CAKE
   1 package DUNCAN HINES® Moist Deluxe® Spice Cake Mix
   3 eggs
   1 cup water
   1 tablespoon vegetable oil plus additional for greasing
1½ cups solid pack pumpkin, divided

FILLING
   2 cups whipping cream, chilled
   ½ cup sugar
   1 cup Sugared Pecans, chopped (recipe follows)
   Sugared Pecan halves for garnish

1. Preheat oven to 350°F. Grease and flour two 8-inch round cake pans.

2. For cake, combine cake mix, eggs, water and oil in large bowl. Beat at low speed with electric mixer until moistened. Beat at medium speed for 2 minutes. Fold in 1 cup pumpkin. Pour batter into pans. Bake and cool cakes following package directions.

3. For filling, place whipping cream and sugar in large bowl. Beat at high speed with electric mixer until stiff peaks form. Fold in remaining ½ cup pumpkin and chopped Sugared Pecans.

4. To assemble, level cake layers. Split each cake layer in half horizontally. Place 1 cake layer on serving plate. Spread with one-fourth filling. Repeat layering 3 more times. Garnish with Sugared Pecan halves.
Makes 12 to 16 servings

Sugared Pecans

   1 cup sugar
   1 tablespoon ground cinnamon
   1 teaspoon salt
   1 egg white
   1 tablespoon water
   1 pound pecan halves

1. Preheat oven to 300°F.

2. Combine sugar, cinnamon and salt in small bowl; set aside.

3. Place egg white and water in medium bowl. Beat with electric mixer at medium speed until frothy but not stiff. Pour pecans into egg white mixture; stir until coated. Add sugar mixture; stir until evenly coated. Spread on cookie sheet. Bake at 300°F for 45 minutes, stirring every 15 minutes. Cool completely.

Pumpkin Chiffon Cake

Blueberry Yogurt Cake

1½ cups cake flour
1 teaspoon baking powder
¼ teaspoon baking soda
1 cup applesauce
½ cup granulated sugar
¼ cup (½ stick) butter, softened
2 eggs
1 teaspoon vanilla
½ cup plain or vanilla-flavored yogurt
1 cup fresh blueberries
1 teaspoon all-purpose flour
1 cup chopped walnuts
½ cup packed brown sugar
1 teaspoon ground cinnamon

1. Preheat oven to 350°F. Line 8-inch square baking pan with foil and spray with nonstick cooking spray. Sift cake flour, baking powder and baking soda into small bowl.

2. Beat applesauce, granulated sugar and butter in medium bowl with electric mixer at medium speed 2 minutes. Beat in eggs and vanilla. Add flour mixture to applesauce mixture with yogurt; beat until smooth. Toss berries with all-purpose flour and gently fold into batter.

3. Combine walnuts, brown sugar and cinnamon in small bowl. Sprinkle half of walnut mixture over bottom of prepared pan. Pour batter over walnut mixture. Sprinkle remaining walnut mixture over top.

4. Bake 30 to 35 minutes or until toothpick inserted into center comes out clean. Cool completely on wire rack.

Makes 9 servings

helpful hint:

Choose firm, plump blueberries with a silvery bloom. Avoid shriveled berries or those with a green or red tint (an indication of an underripe berry). If the berries are packed in a clear plastic container, turn the container over and check for moldy berries. If they are packed in a paperboard container, look for juice stains on the bottom of the container, indicating crushed berries that will mold quickly.

Blueberry Yogurt Cake

Mocha Dream Cake

CAKE
1½ cups hot water
1 tablespoon TASTER'S CHOICE® 100% Pure Instant Coffee
1 cup NESTLÉ® CARNATION® COFFEE-MATE® Powdered Coffee Creamer
2⅓ cups all-purpose flour, *divided*
1½ teaspoons baking soda
1⅓ cups (8 ounces) NESTLÉ® TOLL HOUSE® Premier White Morsels
⅓ cup vegetable oil
1⅔ cups granulated sugar
4 eggs
⅔ cup (5-fluid-ounce can) NESTLÉ® CARNATION® Evaporated Milk
2 tablespoons white vinegar
1 teaspoon vanilla extract
⅔ cup NESTLÉ® TOLL HOUSE® Baking Cocoa

FROSTING
⅔ cup NESTLÉ® TOLL HOUSE® Premier White Morsels
⅓ cup butter or margarine
1 tablespoon TASTER'S CHOICE® 100% Pure Instant Coffee
1½ teaspoons water
2 packages (3 ounces *each*) cream cheese, softened
4 to 4½ cups powdered sugar

PREHEAT oven to 350°F. Grease and flour two 9-inch-round cake pans.

FOR CAKE

COMBINE water and Taster's Choice in medium bowl. Stir in Coffee-Mate with wire whisk. Combine *1⅔ cups* flour and baking soda in another medium bowl.

MICROWAVE 1⅓ cups morsels and vegetable oil in large, uncovered, microwave-safe bowl on MEDIUM-HIGH (70%) power for 1 minute. STIR. Morsels may retain some of their original shape. If necessary, microwave at additional 10- to 15-second intervals, stirring just until melted. Add coffee mixture, granulated sugar, eggs, evaporated milk, vinegar and vanilla extract to melted morsels; mix with wire whisk. Gradually beat in flour mixture until combined. (Batter will be thin.) Pour *3¼ cups* batter into medium bowl; stir in *remaining* flour. Pour into prepared pans.

BLEND cocoa into *remaining* batter with wire whisk until blended. Slowly pour even amounts of cocoa batter into center of each pan. (Cocoa batter will spread evenly outward from center.)

BAKE for 40 to 45 minutes or until wooden pick inserted into centers comes out clean. Cool in pans on wire racks for 10 minutes; remove to wire racks to cool completely. Frost cake with frosting between layers and on top and side of cake.

continued on page 240

Mocha Dream Cake

Mocha Dream Cake, continued

FOR FROSTING

MICROWAVE ⅔ cup morsels and butter in large, uncovered, microwave-safe bowl on MEDIUM-HIGH (70%) power for 1 minute. STIR. Morsels may retain some of their original shape. If necessary, microwave at additional 10- to 15-second intervals, stirring just until melted. Combine Taster's Choice and water in small bowl. Beat cream cheese and coffee mixture into melted morsels. Gradually beat in powdered sugar until mixture reaches spreading consistency. Makes about 2½ cups.

Makes 10 to 12 servings

New-Fashioned Gingerbread Cake

　2 cups cake flour
　1 teaspoon baking powder
　1 teaspoon ground ginger
　½ teaspoon baking soda
　½ teaspoon ground cinnamon
　½ teaspoon ground nutmeg
　¼ teaspoon ground cloves
　¾ cup water
　⅓ cup packed brown sugar
　¼ cup molasses
　3 tablespoons canola oil
　2 tablespoons finely minced crystallized ginger (optional)
　2 tablespoons powdered sugar

1. Preheat oven to 350°F. Coat 8-inch square baking pan with nonstick cooking spray; set aside.

2. Combine flour, baking powder, ginger, baking soda, cinnamon, nutmeg and cloves in large bowl; mix well.

3. Beat water, brown sugar, molasses and oil in small bowl with electric mixer at low speed until well blended. Pour into flour mixture; beat until just blended. Stir in crystallized ginger, if desired.

4. Pour into prepared pan. Bake 30 to 35 minutes or until toothpick inserted into center comes out clean. Let cool 10 minutes. Sprinkle with powdered sugar just before serving.

Makes 9 servings

Sour Cream Pound Cake

   3 cups all-purpose flour
½ teaspoon salt
¼ teaspoon baking soda
   1 cup (2 sticks) butter, softened
2¾ cups sugar
   1 tablespoon vanilla
   2 teaspoons grated orange peel
   6 eggs
   1 cup sour cream
   Citrus Topping (recipe follows)

1. Preheat oven to 325°F. Grease 10-inch tube pan. Combine flour, salt and baking soda in small bowl; set aside.

2. Beat butter in large bowl with electric mixer at medium speed until creamy. Gradually add sugar, beating until light and fluffy. Beat in vanilla and orange peel. Add eggs, 1 at a time, beating 1 minute after each addition.

3. Add flour mixture to butter mixture alternately with sour cream, beginning and ending with flour mixture. Beat well after each addition. Pour into prepared pan.

4. Bake 1 hour 15 minutes or until toothpick inserted near center comes out clean.

5. Meanwhile, prepare Citrus Topping. Spoon over hot cake; cool in pan 15 minutes. Remove from pan to wire rack; cool completely, topping side up.

Makes 10 to 12 servings

Citrus Topping

   2 oranges
   2 teaspoons salt
   Water
½ cup sugar, divided
⅓ cup lemon juice
   1 teaspoon vanilla

1. Grate peel of oranges (not white pith) to measure 2 tablespoons. Cut oranges in half. Squeeze juice from oranges to measure ⅓ cup.

2. Combine orange peel and salt in medium saucepan. Add enough water to cover. Bring to a boil over high heat. Boil 2 minutes. Drain in fine-meshed sieve. Return orange peel to saucepan.

3. Add orange juice and ¼ cup sugar to saucepan. Bring to a boil over high heat. Reduce heat; simmer 10 minutes. Remove from heat. Add remaining ¼ cup sugar, lemon juice and vanilla; stir until smooth.

Makes about ½ cup topping

Jo's Moist and Delicious Chocolate Cake

2 cups all-purpose flour
1 cup sugar
¼ cup unsweetened cocoa powder
1½ teaspoons baking powder
1½ teaspoons baking soda
1 cup mayonnaise
1 cup hot coffee
2 teaspoons vanilla

1. Preheat oven to 350°F. Grease and flour 10-inch bundt pan; set aside.

2. Sift together flour, sugar, cocoa, baking powder and baking soda in large bowl. Stir in mayonnaise, coffee and vanilla until batter is smooth. Pour into prepared pan.

3. Bake 30 minutes or until toothpick inserted near center comes out clean. Cool 10 to 15 minutes on wire rack. Remove from pan to wire rack; cool completely.

Makes 12 servings

Serving Suggestion: Frost this cake with your favorite icing or glaze. It's also delicious sprinkled with powdered sugar!

PB & J Sandwich Cake

1 package (18¼ ounces) white cake mix, plus ingredients to prepare mix
¾ cup powdered sugar
5 tablespoons peanut butter
2 to 3 tablespoons heavy cream or milk
1 tablespoon butter, softened
½ cup strawberry or grape jam

1. Preheat oven to 350°F. Grease two 8-inch square baking pans. Prepare cake mix according to package directions. Spread batter into prepared pans.

2. Bake 30 minutes or until toothpick inserted into centers comes out clean. Cool in pans on wire racks 30 minutes; remove from pans and cool completely on wire racks.

3. Carefully slice off browned tops of both cakes to create flat, even layers. Place 1 layer on serving plate, cut side up.

4. Beat powdered sugar, peanut butter, 2 tablespoons cream and butter with electric mixer at medium speed until light and creamy. Add remaining 1 tablespoon cream if necessary for desired spreading consistency. Gently spread filling over cut side of cake layer on serving plate. Spread jam over peanut butter filling. Top with second cake layer, cut side up.

5. Cut cake in half diagonally to resemble sandwich. To serve, cut into thin slices across the diagonal using serrated knife.

Makes 12 servings

Jo's Moist and Delicious Chocolate Cake

Chocolate Syrup Swirl Cake

1 cup (2 sticks) butter or margarine, softened
2 cups sugar
2 teaspoons vanilla extract
3 eggs
2¾ cups all-purpose flour
1¼ teaspoons baking soda, divided
½ teaspoon salt
1 cup buttermilk or sour milk*
1 cup HERSHEY'S Syrup
1 cup MOUNDS® Sweetened Coconut Flakes (optional)

To sour milk: Use 1 tablespoon white vinegar plus milk to equal 1 cup.

1. Heat oven to 350°F. Grease and flour 12-cup fluted tube pan or 10-inch tube pan.

2. Beat butter, sugar and vanilla in large bowl until fluffy. Add eggs; beat until well blended. Stir together flour, 1 teaspoon baking soda and salt; add alternately with buttermilk to butter mixture, beating until well blended.

3. Measure 2 cups batter in small bowl; stir in syrup and remaining ¼ teaspoon baking soda. Add coconut, if desired, to remaining vanilla batter; pour into prepared pan. Pour chocolate batter over vanilla batter in pan; do not mix.

4. Bake 60 to 70 minutes or until wooden pick inserted near center comes out clean. Cool 15 minutes; remove from pan to wire rack. Cool completely on wire rack; glaze or frost as desired.

Makes 20 servings

helpful hint:

This cake batter would be perfect to make mini bundt cakes or even cupcakes. Try filling six (1-cup) mini bundt pans and baking for 40 to 45 minutes. For cupcakes, line 24 standard (2½-inch) muffin pan cups, fill with batter three-fourths full and bake for 20 to 25 minutes.

Chocolate Syrup Swirl Cake

Chocolate Mint Fluff Roll

⅔ cup cake flour
½ cup unsweetened cocoa powder
1 teaspoon baking powder
½ teaspoon salt
4 eggs, separated
¾ cup granulated sugar, divided
½ cup (1 stick) butter, softened
¼ cup crème de menthe liqueur
2 tablespoons water
1 teaspoon vanilla
  Powdered sugar
  Chocolate Mint Filling (recipe follows)

1. Preheat oven to 375°F. Grease 15×10×1-inch jelly-roll pan. Line with parchment paper; grease paper and dust with flour. Sift flour, cocoa, baking powder and salt into medium bowl; set aside.

2. Beat egg whites in large bowl with electric mixer at high speed until soft peaks form. Gradually add ½ cup granulated sugar, beating until egg whites are stiff and glossy. Set aside.

3. Combine egg yolks, remaining ¼ cup granulated sugar, butter, crème de menthe, water and vanilla in large bowl. Beat about 4 minutes or until mixture becomes thick. Fold flour mixture into egg yolk mixture. Gently fold in egg white mixture until blended.

4. Pour batter into prepared pan. Bake 12 to 15 minutes or until edges begin to pull away from sides of pan and center springs back when lightly touched. Dust clean kitchen towel with powdered sugar. Invert cake onto towel. Peel off parchment paper; starting from long side, gently roll up cake. Cool cake completely. Prepare Chocolate Mint Filling.

5. Unroll cake; spread with filling. Roll up cake and place on serving plate. Sprinkle with additional powdered sugar. Chill before serving. *Makes 8 to 10 servings*

Chocolate Mint Filling

1½ cups whipping cream
 ½ cup sugar
 ¼ cup unsweetened cocoa powder
 ¼ cup crème de menthe liqueur
 ½ teaspoon vanilla
   Pinch salt
1½ cups chopped chocolate mint candies

Combine cream, sugar, cocoa, crème de menthe, vanilla and salt in medium bowl; beat at high speed of electric mixer until stiff peaks form. Gently fold in mints.

Chocolate Mint Fluff Roll

Lazy-Daisy Cake

2 cups all-purpose flour
2 teaspoons baking powder
2 cups granulated sugar
4 eggs
½ cup (1 stick) butter, softened, divided
2 teaspoons vanilla
1 cup warm milk
1 cup flaked coconut
½ cup plus 2 tablespoons packed brown sugar
⅓ cup half-and-half

1. Preheat oven to 350°F. Grease 13×9-inch baking pan. Sift flour and baking powder into medium bowl.

2. Beat granulated sugar, eggs, 2 tablespoons butter and vanilla in large bowl with electric mixer at medium speed 3 minutes until fluffy. Beat flour mixture into egg mixture until well blended. Stir in milk and 2 tablespoons butter. Pour into prepared pan. Bake 30 minutes or until toothpick inserted into center comes out clean.

3. Meanwhile, combine remaining 4 tablespoons butter, coconut, brown sugar and half-and-half in medium saucepan over medium heat. Cook until sugar dissolves and butter melts, stirring constantly.

4. Spread coconut mixture over warm cake. Broil 4 inches from heat source 2 to 3 minutes or until top is light golden brown, being careful not to let topping burn.

Makes 12 to 14 servings

Lemon Crumb Cake

1 package DUNCAN HINES® Moist Deluxe® Lemon Supreme Cake Mix
3 eggs
1⅓ cups water
⅓ cup vegetable oil
1 cup all-purpose flour
½ cup packed light brown sugar
½ teaspoon baking powder
½ cup (1 stick) butter or margarine

1. Preheat oven to 350°F. Grease and flour 13×9-inch pan.

2. Combine cake mix, eggs, water and oil in large mixing bowl. Beat at medium speed with electric mixer for 2 minutes. Pour into prepared pan. Combine flour, sugar and baking powder in small bowl. Cut in butter until crumbly. Sprinkle evenly over batter. Bake at 350°F for 35 to 40 minutes or until toothpick inserted in center comes out clean. Cool completely in pan.

Makes 12 to 16 servings

Tip: Butter or margarine will cut more easily into the flour mixture if it is cold. Use two knives or a pastry cutter to cut the mixture into crumbs.

Lazy-Daisy Cake

Brown-Eyed Susan Sweet Potato Cake

CAKE
2¼ cups all-purpose flour
1 tablespoon baking powder
1 teaspoon baking soda
1 teaspoon salt
1 teaspoon ground cinnamon
½ teaspoon ground ginger
1 can (15 ounces) mashed sweet potatoes or 1 can (15 ounces)
  unsweetened sweet potatoes, rinsed, drained and mashed
1 cup granulated sugar
½ cup packed dark brown sugar
3 eggs
1 cup vegetable oil
1 cup (6 ounces) NESTLÉ® TOLL HOUSE® Semi-Sweet Chocolate Morsels
½ cup chopped pecans
½ cup water

CREAMY PREMIER WHITE ICING
¾ cup NESTLÉ® TOLL HOUSE® Premier White Morsels
1½ tablespoons butter or margarine
½ cup (4 ounces) cream cheese, softened
⅓ cup sour cream
¾ teaspoon vanilla extract
¼ teaspoon almond extract (optional)
3 to 4 cups powdered sugar

FOR CAKE

PREHEAT oven to 350°F. Lightly grease and flour two 9-inch-round cake pans or one 13×9-inch baking pan.

COMBINE flour, baking powder, baking soda, salt, cinnamon and ginger in small bowl. Combine sweet potatoes, granulated sugar and brown sugar in large bowl. Add eggs, one at a time, beating well after each addition. Add oil; beat until well blended. Stir in morsels, pecans and water. Stir in flour mixture; mix until blended. Pour into prepared pans.

BAKE for 35 to 40 minutes or until wooden pick inserted into center comes out clean. Cool completely in pans on wire racks. For layer cakes, remove from pans after 10 minutes. Frost with Creamy Premier White Icing.

FOR CREAMY PREMIER WHITE ICING

MICROWAVE morsels and butter in small, uncovered, microwave-safe bowl on MEDIUM-HIGH (70%) power for 1 minute. STIR. Morsels may retain some of their original shape. If necessary, microwave at additional 10- to 15-second intervals, stirring just until morsels are melted. Cool to room temperature.

BEAT cream cheese and sour cream into morsel mixture until creamy. Add vanilla extract and almond extract. Gradually beat in powdered sugar until mixture reaches spreading consistency. Makes about 3 cups icing.   *Makes 12 servings*

Pumpkin Carrot Cake

    2 cups all-purpose flour
    2 teaspoons baking soda
    2 teaspoons ground cinnamon
    ½ teaspoon salt
    ¾ cup milk
 1½ teaspoons lemon juice
    3 eggs
 1¼ cups LIBBY'S® 100% Pure Pumpkin
 1½ cups granulated sugar
    ½ cup packed brown sugar
    ½ cup vegetable oil
    1 can (8 ounces) crushed pineapple, drained
    1 cup (about 3 medium) grated carrots
    1 cup flaked coconut
 1¼ cups chopped nuts, *divided*
       Cream Cheese Frosting (recipe follows)

PREHEAT oven to 350°F. Grease two 9-inch round baking pans.

COMBINE flour, baking soda, cinnamon and salt in small bowl. Combine milk and lemon juice in liquid measuring cup (mixture will appear curdled).

BEAT eggs, pumpkin, granulated sugar, brown sugar, oil, pineapple, carrots and milk mixture in large mixer bowl; mix well. Gradually add flour mixture; beat until combined. Stir in coconut and *1 cup* nuts. Pour into prepared baking pans.

BAKE for 30 to 35 minutes or until wooden pick inserted into centers comes out clean. Cool in pans for 15 minutes. Remove to wire racks to cool completely.

FROST between layers, on side and top of cake with Cream Cheese Frosting. Garnish with *remaining* nuts. Store in refrigerator.   *Makes 12 servings*

Cream Cheese Frosting: BEAT 11 ounces softened cream cheese, ⅓ cup softened butter and 3½ cups sifted powdered sugar in large mixer bowl until fluffy. Add 1 teaspoon vanilla extract, 2 teaspoons orange juice and 1 teaspoon grated orange peel; beat until combined.

Fudgy Banana Oat Cake

TOPPING
    1 cup QUAKER® Oats (quick or old fashioned, uncooked)
    ½ cup firmly packed brown sugar
    ¼ cup (½ stick) margarine or butter, chilled

FILLING
    1 cup (6 ounces) semisweet chocolate pieces
    ⅔ cup sweetened condensed milk (not evaporated milk)
    1 tablespoon margarine or butter

CAKE
    1 package (18¼ ounces) devil's food cake mix
  1¼ cups mashed ripe bananas (about 3 large)
    ⅓ cup vegetable oil
    3 eggs
      Banana slices (optional)
      Sweetened whipped cream (optional)

Heat oven to 350°F. Lightly grease bottom only of 13×9-inch baking pan. For topping, combine oats and brown sugar. Cut in margarine until mixture is crumbly; set aside.

For filling, in small saucepan, heat chocolate pieces, sweetened condensed milk and margarine over low heat until chocolate is melted, stirring occasionally. Remove from heat; set aside.

For cake, in large mixing bowl, combine cake mix, bananas, oil and eggs. Blend at low speed of electric mixer until dry ingredients are moistened. Beat at medium speed 2 minutes. Spread batter evenly into prepared pan. Drop chocolate filling by teaspoonfuls evenly over batter. Sprinkle with reserved oat topping. Bake 40 to 45 minutes or until cake pulls away from sides of pan and topping is golden brown. Cool cake in pan on wire rack. Cut into squares. Garnish with banana slices and sweetened whipped cream, if desired.

Makes 15 servings

Fudgy Banana Oat Cake

Topsy-Turvy Banana Crunch Cake

⅓ cup uncooked old-fashioned oats
3 tablespoons packed brown sugar
1 tablespoon all-purpose flour
¼ teaspoon ground cinnamon
2 tablespoons butter
2 tablespoons chopped pecans
1 package (9 ounces) yellow cake mix *without* pudding in the mix
½ cup sour cream
½ cup mashed banana (about 1 medium)
1 egg, slightly beaten

1. Preheat oven to 350°F. Lightly grease 8-inch square baking pan.

2. Combine oats, brown sugar, flour and cinnamon in small bowl. Cut in butter with pastry blender or 2 knives until crumbly. Stir in pecans; set aside.

3. Combine cake mix, sour cream, banana and egg in medium bowl. Beat with electric mixer at low speed about 1 minute or until blended. Increase speed to medium; beat 1 to 2 minutes or until smooth. Spoon half of batter into prepared pan; sprinkle with half of oat topping. Top with remaining batter and topping.

4. Bake 25 to 30 minutes or until toothpick inserted into center comes out clean. Cool completely on wire rack.

Makes 9 servings

Taffy Apple Snack Cake

1 package (18¼ ounces) yellow cake mix with pudding in the mix, divided
2 eggs
¼ cup vegetable oil
¼ cup water
4 tablespoons packed brown sugar, divided
2 medium apples, peeled and diced
1 cup chopped nuts (optional)
2 tablespoons butter, melted
¼ teaspoon ground cinnamon
½ cup caramel topping

1. Preheat oven to 350°F. Spray 8-inch square baking pan with nonstick cooking spray. Reserve ¾ cup cake mix; set aside.

2. Pour remaining cake mix into large bowl. Add eggs, oil, water and 2 tablespoons brown sugar; beat with electric mixer at medium speed 2 minutes. Stir in apples; spread in prepared pan.

3. Combine reserved cake mix, remaining 2 tablespoons brown sugar, nuts, butter and cinnamon in medium bowl; mix until well blended. Sprinkle over batter. Bake 40 to 45 minutes or until toothpick inserted into center comes out clean.

4. Cool cake in pan on wire rack. Cut into squares; top each serving with about 2 teaspoons caramel topping.

Makes 9 servings

Topsy-Turvy Banana Crunch Cake

Tropical Bananas Foster Upside-Down Cake

¼ cup (½ stick) butter
2 tablespoons rum *or* 1 teaspoon rum flavoring
½ cup packed brown sugar
2 large bananas, cut diagonally into ¼-inch pieces
1 package (about 18 ounces) banana walnut bread mix, plus ingredients to prepare mix
1 cup flaked coconut
Additional flaked coconut for garnish
Vanilla ice cream (optional)

1. Preheat oven to 350°F. Line baking sheet with foil. Spray bottom and side of 9-inch springform pan with nonstick cooking spray. Place pan on baking sheet.

2. Melt butter in small saucepan over low heat. Add rum; cook and stir 2 minutes. Stir in sugar; remove from heat. Pour sugar mixture into prepared pan; swirl to coat bottom evenly. Arrange banana slices in even layer on sugar mixture.

3. Prepare bread mix according to package directions. Stir in coconut. Pour batter over banana slices.

4. Bake about 45 minutes or until toothpick inserted into center comes out clean. Cool completely in pan on wire rack. Invert cake onto serving plate. Garnish with additional coconut and serve with vanilla ice cream, if desired. *Makes 12 servings*

Cappuccino Cake

½ cup (3 ounces) semisweet chocolate chips
½ cup chopped hazelnuts, walnuts or pecans
1 (18.25-ounce) package yellow cake mix
¼ cup instant espresso coffee powder
2 teaspoons ground cinnamon
1¼ cups water
3 eggs
⅓ cup FILIPPO BERIO® Pure or Extra Light Tasting Olive Oil
Powdered sugar
1 (15-ounce) container ricotta cheese
2 teaspoons granulated sugar
Additional ground cinnamon

Preheat oven to 325°F. Grease 10-inch (12-cup) Bundt pan or 10-inch tube pan with olive oil. Sprinkle lightly with flour.

In small bowl, combine chocolate chips and hazelnuts. Spoon evenly into bottom of prepared pan.

continued on page 258

Tropical Bananas Foster Upside-Down Cake

Cappuccino Cake, continued

In large bowl, combine cake mix, coffee powder and 2 teaspoons cinnamon. Add water, eggs and olive oil. Beat with electric mixer at low speed until dry ingredients are moistened. Beat at medium speed 2 minutes. Pour batter over topping in pan.

Bake 60 minutes or until toothpick inserted near center comes out clean. Cool on wire rack 15 minutes. Remove from pan. Place cake, fluted side up, on serving plate. Cool completely. Sprinkle with powdered sugar.

In medium bowl, combine ricotta cheese and granulated sugar. Sprinkle with cinnamon. Serve cheese mixture alongside slices of cake. Serve cake with cappuccino, espresso or your favorite coffee, if desired.

Makes 12 to 16 servings

Chai Spice Cake

  2¼ cups water
  10 chai tea bags
    1 cup ice cubes
    1 package (18¼ ounces) white cake mix
    3 egg whites
  ⅓ cup vegetable oil
    1 tablespoon cornstarch
  ¼ cup packed dark brown sugar
    6 whole cloves
  ½ teaspoon vanilla

1. Preheat oven to 350°F. Spray bottom only of nonstick tube pan or bundt pan with nonstick cooking spray.

2. Bring water to a boil in medium saucepan over high heat. Remove from heat; add tea bags. Steep 5 minutes. Remove and discard tea bags from saucepan. Add ice cubes to tea; let stand until ice is completely melted. (This should make 2¼ cups tea.)

3. Beat cake mix, 1¼ cups tea, egg whites and oil in large bowl with electric mixer at low speed 30 seconds. Beat at medium speed 2 minutes or until well blended. Pour batter into prepared pan. Bake according to package directions or until toothpick inserted near center comes out almost clean. Invert bundt pan onto wire rack; allow to stand 10 minutes before removing pan. Cool completely.

4. Meanwhile, combine remaining 1 cup tea and cornstarch in medium saucepan; stir until cornstarch is completely dissolved. Add sugar and cloves. Bring to a boil over medium-high heat, stirring constantly; boil 1 minute, stirring constantly. Remove from heat; cool completely. Discard cloves; stir in vanilla. Pour glaze evenly over cake.

Makes about 16 slices

Chai Spice Cake

Chocolate Lava Cakes

6 tablespoons I CAN'T BELIEVE IT'S NOT BUTTER!® Spread
3 squares (1 ounce each) bittersweet or semi-sweet chocolate, cut into pieces
½ cup granulated sugar
6 tablespoons all-purpose flour
   Pinch salt
2 eggs
2 egg yolks
¼ teaspoon vanilla extract
   Confectioners' sugar

Line bottom of four (4-ounce) ramekins* or custard cups with waxed paper, then grease; set aside.

In medium microwave-safe bowl, microwave I Can't Believe It's Not Butter!® Spread and chocolate at HIGH (100% Power) 45 seconds or until chocolate is melted; stir until smooth. With wire whisk, beat in granulated sugar, flour and salt until blended. Beat in eggs, egg yolks and vanilla. Evenly spoon into prepared ramekins. Refrigerate 1 hour or until ready to bake.

Preheat oven to 425°F. Arrange ramekins on baking sheet. Bake 13 minutes or until edges are firm but centers are still slightly soft. (*Do not overbake*). On wire rack, cool 5 minutes. To serve, carefully run sharp knife around cake edges. Unmold onto serving plates, then remove waxed paper. Sprinkle with confectioners' sugar and serve immediately.

Makes 4 servings

*To bake in 12-cup muffin pan, line bottoms of 8 muffin cups with waxed paper, then grease. Evenly spoon in batter. Refrigerate as above. Bake at 425°F for 9 minutes or until edges are firm but centers are still slightly soft. Do not overbake. On wire rack, cool 5 minutes. To serve, carefully run sharp knife around cake edges and gently lift out of pan. (Do not turn pan upside-down to unmold.) Arrange cakes, bottom sides up, on serving plates, 2 cakes per serving. Remove waxed paper and sprinkle as above.

Chocolate Lava Cake

Creamy Cheesecakes

Individual Chocolate Coconut Cheesecakes

  1 cup chocolate cookie crumbs
¼ cup (½ stick) butter or margarine, melted
  2 packages (8 ounces each) cream cheese, softened
⅓ cup sugar
  2 eggs
  1 teaspoon vanilla
¼ teaspoon coconut extract (optional)
½ cup flaked coconut
½ cup semisweet chocolate chips
  1 teaspoon shortening

1. Preheat oven to 325°F. Line 12 standard (2½-inch) muffin cups with foil baking cups.

2. Combine cookie crumbs and butter in small bowl. Press onto bottoms of baking cups.

3. Beat cream cheese and sugar in large bowl with electric mixer at medium speed 2 minutes or until well blended. Add eggs, vanilla and coconut extract, if desired. Beat just until blended. Stir in coconut.

4. Carefully spoon about ¼ cup cream cheese mixture into each baking cup. Bake 18 to 22 minutes or until nearly set. Cool 30 minutes in pan on wire rack. Remove from pan. Peel away foil baking cups.

5. Combine chocolate chips and shortening in small saucepan. Cook and stir over low heat until chocolate chips are melted. Drizzle over tops of cheesecakes. Let stand 20 minutes. Cover and refrigerate until ready to serve.

Makes 12 servings

Triple Chip Cheesecake

CRUST
1¾ cups chocolate graham cracker crumbs
⅓ cup butter or margarine, melted

FILLING
3 packages (8 ounces *each*) cream cheese, softened
¾ cup granulated sugar
½ cup sour cream
3 tablespoons all-purpose flour
1½ teaspoons vanilla extract
3 eggs
1 cup (6 ounces) NESTLÉ® TOLL HOUSE® Butterscotch Flavored Morsels
1 cup (6 ounces) NESTLÉ® TOLL HOUSE® Semi-Sweet Chocolate Morsels
1 cup (6 ounces) NESTLÉ® TOLL HOUSE® Premier White Morsels

TOPPING
1 tablespoon *each* NESTLÉ® TOLL HOUSE® Butterscotch Flavored Morsels, Semi-Sweet Chocolate Morsels and Premier White Morsels

PREHEAT oven to 300°F. Grease 9-inch springform pan.

FOR CRUST

COMBINE crumbs and butter in small bowl. Press onto bottom and 1 inch up side of prepared pan.

FOR FILLING

BEAT cream cheese and granulated sugar in large mixer bowl until smooth. Add sour cream, flour and vanilla extract; mix well. Add eggs; beat on low speed until combined.

MELT butterscotch morsels according to package directions. Stir until smooth. Add 1½ *cups* batter to melted morsels. Pour into crust. Repeat procedure with semi-sweet morsels. Carefully spoon over butterscotch layer. Melt Premier White morsels according to package directions and blend into *remaining* batter in mixer bowl. Carefully pour over semi-sweet layer.

BAKE for 1 hour and 10 to 15 minutes or until center is almost set. Cool in pan on wire rack for 10 minutes. Run knife around edge of cheesecake. Let stand for 1 hour.

FOR TOPPING

PLACE each flavor of morsels separately into three small, *heavy-duty* resealable plastic food storage bags. Microwave on HIGH (100%) power for 20 seconds; knead bags to mix. Microwave at additional 10-second intervals, kneading until smooth. Cut small hole in corner of each bag; squeeze to drizzle over cheesecake. Refrigerate for at least 3 hours or overnight. Remove side of pan.   *Makes 12 to 16 servings*

Triple Chip Cheesecake

Cheesecake Cookie Bars

2 packages (18 ounces each) refrigerated chocolate chip cookie dough
2 packages (8 ounces each) cream cheese
½ cup sugar
2 eggs

1. Let both packages of dough stand at room temperature about 15 minutes. Preheat oven to 350°F. Lightly grease 13×9-inch baking pan.

2. Reserve ¾ of one package of dough. Press remaining 1¼ packages of dough evenly onto bottom of prepared pan.

3. Combine cream cheese, sugar and eggs in large bowl; beat 2 minutes or until well blended and smooth. Spread cream cheese mixture over dough in pan. Break reserved ¾ package of dough into small pieces; sprinkle over cream cheese mixture.

4. Bake 35 minutes or until center is almost set. Cool completely in pan on wire rack. Store leftovers covered in refrigerator. *Makes about 2 dozen bars*

Black Forest Chocolate Cheesecake

1½ cups chocolate wafer cookie crumbs
3 tablespoons butter or margarine, melted
2 (1-ounce) squares unsweetened chocolate
1 (14-ounce) can EAGLE BRAND® Sweetened Condensed Milk (NOT evaporated milk)
2 (8-ounce) packages cream cheese, softened
3 eggs
3 tablespoons cornstarch
1 teaspoon almond extract
1 (21-ounce) can cherry pie filling, chilled

1. Preheat oven to 300°F. In small bowl, combine cookie crumbs and butter; press firmly onto bottom of ungreased 9-inch springform pan.

2. In small saucepan over low heat, melt chocolate with EAGLE BRAND®, stirring constantly. Remove from heat.

3. In large bowl, beat cream cheese until fluffy. Gradually add EAGLE BRAND® mixture until smooth. Add eggs, cornstarch and almond extract; mix well. Pour into prepared crust.

4. Bake 55 minutes or until center is almost set. Cool. Chill. Top with cherry pie filling before serving. Store leftovers covered in refrigerator. *Makes one (9-inch) cheesecake*

Cheesecake Cookie Bars

Fruit-Layered
Cheesecake Squares

1 package (18¼ ounces) yellow cake mix
½ cup (1 stick) butter, softened
2 eggs
3 tablespoons water
2 packages (8 ounces each) cream cheese, softened
1 cup powdered sugar
¼ cup milk
2 teaspoons vanilla
1 can (8 ounces) pineapple tidbits, drained and juice reserved
3 tablespoons orange juice
¾ teaspoon cornstarch
1 medium banana, peeled and thinly sliced
1 cup fresh mango or nectarine pieces
1 pint whole strawberries, quartered

1. Preheat oven to 350°F. Grease 13×9-inch baking pan; set aside.

2. Beat cake mix, butter, eggs and water in large bowl with electric mixer at low speed 2 minutes or until stiff dough forms. Press dough evenly onto bottom of prepared pan.

3. Bake 27 minutes or until toothpick inserted into center comes out clean. Cool completely in pan on wire rack.

4. Meanwhile, beat cream cheese, sugar, milk and vanilla in medium bowl with electric mixer at low speed 30 seconds or until just blended. Beat 1 minute on high speed or until smooth.

5. Combine reserved pineapple juice, orange juice and cornstarch in small saucepan; stir until cornstarch is completely dissolved. Cook and stir over medium heat until mixture comes to a boil; cook and stir 1 minute. Remove from heat; cool completely.

6. Spread cream cheese mixture evenly over crust; alternately arrange pineapple, banana, mango and strawberries on top. Spoon or brush pineapple juice mixture over fruit. Cover with plastic wrap; refrigerate 1 hour or up to 24 hours before serving.

Makes 16 servings

helpful hint:

Mangoes are an exotic fruit with sweet and tart flavors, fragrant flesh and beautiful bright colors. Fresh mangoes are rich in vitamins A, C and D. Their peak season is May through September, but you can find them all year round in specialty markets.

Fruit-Layered Cheesecake Squares

Chocolate Marble & Praline Cheesecake

CRUST
1½ cups vanilla wafer crumbs
½ cup finely chopped toasted pecans*
¼ cup powdered sugar
¼ cup (½ stick) butter, melted

FILLING
1¼ cups packed brown sugar
2 tablespoons all-purpose flour
3 packages (8 ounces each) cream cheese, softened
3 eggs, lightly beaten
1½ teaspoons vanilla
1 square (1 ounce) unsweetened chocolate, melted
20 to 25 pecan halves (½ cup)
Caramel ice cream topping

*To toast nuts, place on a baking sheet. Bake at 350°F for 5 to 7 minutes or until lightly browned.

1. Preheat oven to 350°F.

2. For crust, combine crumbs, pecans, powdered sugar and butter in large bowl; mix well. Press mixture onto bottom and up side of ungreased 9-inch springform pan. Bake 10 to 15 minutes or until lightly browned. Transfer to wire rack.

3. For filling, combine brown sugar and flour in small bowl; mix well. Beat cream cheese in large bowl with electric mixer at low speed until fluffy; gradually add brown sugar mixture. Add eggs and vanilla; beat just until blended. Remove 1 cup batter to small bowl; stir in chocolate. Pour remaining plain batter over warm crust.

4. Drop spoonfuls of chocolate batter over plain batter. Run knife through batters to marbleize. Arrange pecan halves around edge. Bake 45 to 55 minutes or until set. Loosen cake from side of pan. Cool completely on wire rack. Refrigerate 2 hours or until ready to serve.

5. To serve, remove side of pan. Spoon caramel topping over top of cheesecake.

Makes 12 to 16 servings

Premier White Lemony Cheesecake

CRUST

    6 tablespoons butter or margarine, softened
    ¼ cup granulated sugar
 1¼ cups all-purpose flour
    1 egg yolk
    ⅛ teaspoon salt

FILLING

    6 bars (two 6-ounce boxes) NESTLÉ® TOLL HOUSE® Premier White Baking
        Bars, broken into pieces
    ½ cup heavy whipping cream
    2 packages (8 ounces each) cream cheese, softened
    1 tablespoon lemon juice
    2 teaspoons grated lemon peel
    ¼ teaspoon salt
    3 egg whites
    1 egg

PREHEAT oven to 350°F. Lightly grease 9-inch springform pan.

FOR CRUST

BEAT butter and sugar in small mixer bowl until creamy. Beat in flour, egg yolk and salt. Press mixture onto bottom and 1 inch up side of prepared pan.

BAKE for 14 to 16 minutes or until crust is set.

FOR FILLING

MICROWAVE baking bars and whipping cream in medium, uncovered, microwave-safe bowl on MEDIUM-HIGH (70%) power for 1 minute. STIR. Baking bars may retain some of their original shape. If necessary, microwave at additional 10- to 15-second intervals, stirring just until baking bars are melted.

BEAT cream cheese, lemon juice, lemon peel and salt in large mixer bowl until smooth. Gradually beat in melted baking bars. Beat in egg whites and egg. Pour into crust.

BAKE for 35 to 40 minutes or until edge is lightly browned. Run knife around edge of cheesecake. Cool completely in pan on wire rack. Refrigerate for several hours or overnight. Remove side of springform pan. Garnish as desired.   *Makes 12 to 16 servings*

White Chocolate Cheesecake with Raspberry Gelée

CRUST
1½ cups graham cracker crumbs (22 to 23 graham crackers, crushed)
6 tablespoons butter, melted
¼ cup sugar

CHEESECAKE FILLING
8 ounces white chocolate, broken into pieces
¼ cup whipping cream
3 packages (8 ounces each) cream cheese, softened
⅓ cup sugar
½ teaspoon vanilla
3 eggs

GELÉE TOPPING
2 cups sparkling white grape juice or white wine, divided
2 envelopes unflavored gelatin
1 package (12 ounces) frozen raspberries, thawed
½ cup sugar

1. Preheat oven to 350°F. Grease 9-inch springform pan; line side of pan with parchment or waxed paper.

2. For crust, combine graham cracker crumbs, butter and ¼ cup sugar in small bowl. Press onto bottom of prepared pan. Bake 8 to 10 minutes or until golden. Cool crust completely in pan on wire rack. After crust has cooled, wrap bottom and side of springform pan with 2 to 3 layers of foil. *Reduce oven temperature to 325°F.*

3. For filling, place white chocolate and whipping cream in small pan over medium-low heat; stir until chocolate is melted. Cool slightly.

4. Beat cream cheese in large bowl with electric mixer at medium speed just until smooth. Gradually add ⅓ cup sugar and vanilla. Add eggs one at a time. Add chocolate mixture; beat just until blended.

5. Pour batter into prepared crust. Place jelly-roll pan in oven; pour hot tap water into jelly-roll pan. Gently place cheesecake onto jelly-roll pan. Bake 1 hour 20 minutes to 1 hour 30 minutes or until center is almost set. Carefully remove cheesecake from oven; cool completely on wire rack.

6. Meanwhile, to prepare gelée topping, place 1 cup grape juice in small bowl. Stir in gelatin; let stand 10 to 15 minutes.

7. Purée raspberries and ½ cup sugar in blender. Strain mixture into saucepan through fine-mesh strainer to remove seeds. Add remaining 1 cup grape juice; bring to a boil.

continued on page 274

White Chocolate Cheesecake with Raspberry Gelée

White Chocolate Cheesecake with Raspberry Gelée, continued

8. Stir in gelatin mixture; remove from heat. Continue stirring until gelatin has dissolved completely. Transfer to large measuring cup with spout for easy pouring. Cool to room temperature.

9. Skim off foam. Carefully, pour gelée topping onto cheesecake. Pop any air bubbles with toothpick. Refrigerate 6 to 8 hours or until topping has set.

10. To unmold, run small knife around the edge of the cheesecake, then carefully remove side of pan. Transfer cheesecake to serving platter. Decorate with white chocolate curls, if desired.   *Makes 10 to 12 servings*

Creamy Cinnamon Chips Cheesecake

1½ cups graham cracker crumbs
1 cup plus 2 tablespoons sugar, divided
5 tablespoons butter, melted
2 packages (8 ounces each) cream cheese softened
1 teaspoon vanilla extract
3 cartons (8 ounces each) dairy sour cream
3 eggs, slightly beaten
1⅔ cups (10-ounce package) HERSHEY'S Cinnamon Chips, divided
1 teaspoon shortening (do not use butter, margarine, spread or oil)

1. Heat oven to 325°F. Combine graham cracker crumbs, 2 tablespoons sugar and melted butter in medium bowl. Press crumb mixture evenly onto bottom and about 1½ inches up side of 9-inch springform pan. Bake 8 minutes. Remove from oven.

2. Increase oven temperature to 350°F. Beat cream cheese, remaining 1 cup sugar and vanilla on medium speed of mixer until well blended. Add sour cream; beat on low speed until blended. Add eggs; beat on low speed just until blended. Do not overbeat.

3. Pour half of filling into prepared crust. Sprinkle 1⅓ cups chips evenly over filling in pan. Carefully spoon remaining filling over chips. Place on shallow baking pan.

4. Bake about 1 hour or until center is almost set. Remove from oven; cool 10 minutes on wire rack. Using knife or narrow metal spatula, loosen cheesecake from side of pan. Cool on wire rack 30 minutes more. Remove side of pan; cool 1 hour.

5. Combine shortening and remaining ⅓ cup chips in small microwave-safe bowl. Microwave at HIGH (100%) 30 seconds; stir until chips are melted. Drizzle over cheesecake; cover and refrigerate at least 4 hours. Cover and refrigerate leftover cheesecake.   *Makes 12 to 14 servings*

Creamy Cinnamon Chips Cheesecake

Caramel Apple Cheesecake

1¼ cups graham cracker crumbs
¼ cup (½ stick) butter, melted
3 packages (8 ounces each) cream cheese, softened
¾ cup sugar
1½ teaspoons vanilla
3 eggs
1¼ cups apple pie filling
½ cup chopped peanuts
¼ cup caramel ice cream topping

1. Preheat oven to 350°F. Spray 9-inch springform pan with nonstick cooking spray.

2. Combine crumbs and butter in small bowl. Press onto bottom of prepared pan. Bake 9 minutes; cool.

3. Beat cream cheese, sugar and vanilla in large bowl with electric mixer at medium speed 1 minute or until well blended. Add eggs and beat well. Pour cream cheese mixture into crust. Bake 40 to 50 minutes or until center is almost set. Refrigerate at least 3 hours.

4. Before serving, carefully run knife around edge to loosen pan. Remove side of pan. Spread apple pie filling over top of cake. Sprinkle peanuts over apple filling and drizzle with caramel topping. Serve immediately. Refrigerate leftovers.   *Makes 12 servings*

Strawberry Cheesecake

3 packages (8 ounces each) cream cheese, softened
1 cup no-sugar-added strawberry pourable fruit*
3 teaspoons vanilla, divided
¼ teaspoon salt
4 eggs
1 cup sour cream
Fresh strawberry halves

You can substitute ¾ cup no-sugar-added strawberry fruit spread combined with ¼ cup warm water.

1. Preheat oven to 325°F. Grease 9-inch springform pan.

2. Beat cream cheese in large bowl with electric mixer at medium speed 1 minute or until creamy. Beat in pourable fruit, 1 teaspoon vanilla and salt. Add eggs, one at a time, beating after each addition. Pour into prepared pan. Bake 50 minutes.

3. Combine sour cream and remaining 2 teaspoons vanilla; mix well. Carefully spoon over warm cheesecake. Return to oven; continue baking 10 minutes or just until set. Turn oven off; leave cheesecake in oven, with door closed, 30 minutes. Transfer to wire rack; loosen cheesecake from edge of pan. Cool completely before removing rim. Cover and chill at least 6 hours or overnight. Before serving, garnish cheesecake with strawberry halves.

Makes 10 servings

Caramel Apple Cheesecake

Pumpkin Cheesecake with Gingersnap-Pecan Crust

CRUST

1¼ cups gingersnap cookie crumbs (about 24 cookies)
⅓ cup pecans, very finely chopped
¼ cup granulated sugar
¼ cup (½ stick) butter, melted

FILLING

3 packages (8 ounces each) cream cheese, softened
1 cup packed light brown sugar
1 teaspoon cinnamon
½ teaspoon ground ginger
¼ teaspoon ground nutmeg
2 eggs
2 egg yolks
1 cup solid-pack pumpkin

1. Preheat oven to 350°F. For crust, combine cookie crumbs, pecans, granulated sugar and butter in medium bowl; mix well. Press crumb mixture evenly onto bottom of ungreased 9-inch springform pan. Bake 8 to 10 minutes or until golden brown.

2. Meanwhile for filling, beat cream cheese in large bowl with electric mixer at medium speed 1 minute or until fluffy. Add brown sugar, cinnamon, ginger and nutmeg; beat until well blended. Beat in eggs and egg yolks, one at a time, beating well after each addition. Beat in pumpkin.

3. Pour mixture into baked crust. Bake 1 hour or until edges are set but center is still moist. Turn off oven; let cheesecake stand in oven with door ajar 30 minutes. Transfer to wire rack. To prevent cracking, loosen edges of cheesecake from rim of pan with thin metal spatula; cool completely.

4. Cover; refrigerate at least 24 hours before serving. *Makes 10 to 12 servings*

Tip: To help prevent the cheesecake from cracking while baking, place a pan of water in the oven to help create moist heat.

Pumpkin Cheesecake with Gingersnap-Pecan Crust

Frozen Chocolate Cheesecake

1½ cups chocolate or vanilla wafer cookie crumbs
⅓ cup butter, melted
10 ounces (1¼ packages) cream cheese, softened
½ cup sugar
1 cup (6 ounces) semisweet chocolate chips, melted
1 teaspoon vanilla
1⅓ cups thawed frozen nondairy whipped topping
¾ cup chopped pecans
Chocolate Curls (recipe follows)

1. Preheat oven to 325°F.

2. Combine cookie crumbs and butter in small bowl; press onto bottom and side of 9-inch pie plate. Bake 10 minutes. Cool crust completely in pan on wire rack.

3. Beat cream cheese and sugar in large bowl with electric mixer at medium speed 1 minute. Gradually stir melted chocolate chips and vanilla into cheese mixture. Gently fold whipped topping into cheese mixture; fold in pecans. Pour cheese filling into prepared crust; freeze until firm. Garnish with Chocolate Curls. *Makes 8 servings*

Chocolate Curls

¾ cup semisweet chocolate chips

Melt chocolate chips in small saucepan over low heat, stirring constantly. Spread chocolate onto cold baking sheet. Refrigerate about 15 minutes or until firm. Slip tip of straight-sided metal spatula into chocolate. Push spatula firmly along baking sheet, so chocolate curls as it is pushed. Place curls on waxed paper.

Maple Pumpkin Cheesecake

1¼ cups graham cracker crumbs
¼ cup sugar
¼ cup (½ stick) butter or margarine, melted
3 (8-ounce) packages cream cheese, softened
1 (14-ounce) can EAGLE BRAND® Sweetened Condensed Milk (NOT evaporated milk)
1 (15-ounce) can pumpkin (2 cups)
3 eggs
¼ cup maple syrup
1½ teaspoons ground cinnamon
1 teaspoon ground nutmeg
½ teaspoon salt
Maple Pecan Glaze (recipe follows)

Creamy Cheesecakes

1. Preheat oven to 325°F. In small bowl, combine graham cracker crumbs, sugar and butter; press firmly on bottom of ungreased 9-inch springform pan.* In large bowl, beat cream cheese until fluffy. Gradually beat in EAGLE BRAND® until smooth. Add pumpkin, eggs, maple syrup, cinnamon, nutmeg and salt; mix well. Pour into prepared crust. Bake 1 hour 15 minutes or until center appears nearly set when shaken. Cool 1 hour. Cover and chill at least 4 hours.

2. To serve, spoon some Maple Pecan Glaze over cheesecake. Garnish with whipped cream and pecans, if desired. Pass remaining glaze. Store leftovers covered in refrigerator.

Makes one (9-inch) cheesecake

To use 13×9-inch baking pan, press crumb mixture firmly on bottom of pan. Proceed as directed, except bake 50 to 60 minutes or until center appears nearly set when shaken.

Maple Pecan Glaze: In medium saucepan, over medium-high heat, combine 1 cup (½ pint) whipping cream and ¾ cup maple syrup; bring to a boil. Boil rapidly 15 to 20 minutes or until thickened, stirring occasionally. Add ½ cup chopped pecans.

Prep Time: 25 minutes │ **Bake Time:** 1 hour and 15 minutes

Cool Time: 1 hour │ **Chill Time:** 4 hours

Peppermint Cheesecake

CRUST
1¼ cups vanilla wafer crumbs
3 tablespoons melted margarine

FILLING
4 cups (30 ounces) SARGENTO® Light Ricotta Cheese
½ cup sugar
½ cup half-and-half
¼ cup all-purpose flour
1 teaspoon vanilla
¼ teaspoon salt
3 eggs
16 peppermint candies
Fresh mint leaves (optional)

Lightly grease side of 8- or 9-inch springform pan. Combine crumbs and margarine; mix well. Press evenly onto bottom of pan. Refrigerate while preparing filling. Combine Ricotta cheese, sugar, half-and-half, flour, vanilla and salt in large bowl; beat with electric mixer until smooth. Add eggs, one at a time; beat until smooth. Place candies in heavy plastic bag. Crush with meat mallet or hammer. Reserve ¼ cup larger pieces for garnish; stir remaining crushed candies into batter. Pour batter over crust. Bake at 350°F 1 hour or until center is just set. Turn off oven; cool in oven with door ajar 30 minutes. Remove to wire cooling rack; loosen cake from rim of pan with metal spatula. Cool completely; refrigerate at least 4 hours. Immediately before serving, garnish cake around top edge with reserved crushed candies and mint leaves, if desired.   *Makes 8 servings*

Chocolate Sour Cream Cheesecake

    Chocolate Crumb Crust (recipe follows)
    3 packages (8 ounces each) fat-free cream cheese, softened
    1 cup sour cream
    2 eggs
    ¼ cup chocolate syrup
    ⅔ cup sugar
    ⅓ cup unsweetened cocoa powder
    3 tablespoons all-purpose flour
    Whipped topping, chocolate shavings and chocolate curls (optional)

1. Preheat oven to 350°F. Prepare Chocolate Crumb Crust; set aside. Beat cream cheese in large bowl with electric mixer at high speed until fluffy. Beat in sour cream until smooth. Beat in eggs, one at a time. Mix in chocolate syrup, sugar, cocoa and flour until smooth; pour into crust.

2. Bake 50 to 60 minutes or until set in center. Loosen cheesecake from edge of pan with knife. Cool on wire rack. Cover; refrigerate overnight.

3. Remove side of pan. Garnish cheesecake, if desired.   *Makes 12 servings*

Chocolate Crumb Crust

    1¼ cups graham cracker crumbs
    2 tablespoons sugar
    2 tablespoons unsweetened cocoa powder
    ¼ cup (½ stick) butter, melted

Preheat oven to 350°F. Combine graham cracker crumbs, sugar and cocoa in bottom of 9-inch springform pan; stir in butter. Pat mixture evenly onto bottom and 1 inch up side of pan. Bake 8 minutes or until lightly browned. Cool on wire rack.   *Makes 1 (9-inch) crust*

Mocha Marble Cheesecake

    12 ounces cream cheese, softened
    ½ cup sugar
    1 teaspoon vanilla
    2 eggs
    ½ cup white crème de cacao
    1 teaspoon instant coffee granules
    1 (6-ounce) READY CRUST® Graham Cracker Pie Crust

continued on page 284

Chocolate Sour Cream Cheesecake

1. Preheat oven to 325°F. Beat cream cheese in medium bowl until smooth. Add sugar and vanilla. Add eggs, one at a time, beating until well blended.

2. Reserve ½ cup cream cheese mixture; set aside. Pour remaining mixture into crust. Mix crème de cacao and coffee granules with reserved cream cheese mixture.

3. Place crust on baking sheet. Pour coffee mixture over cheesecake filling. Gently cut through coffee layer with knife to create marbled appearance. Bake 30 to 35 minutes or until just set in center. Cool on wire rack. Chill 3 hours. Refrigerate leftovers.

Makes 8 servings

Prep Time: 10 minutes | **Bake Time:** 30 to 35 minutes | **Chill Time:** 3 hours

Reese's® Chocolate Peanut Butter Cheesecake

1¼ cups graham cracker crumbs
⅓ cup plus ¼ cup sugar
⅓ cup HERSHEY'S Cocoa
⅓ cup butter or margarine, melted
3 packages (8 ounces each) cream cheese, softened
1 can (14 ounces) sweetened condensed milk (not evaporated milk)
1⅔ cup (10-ounce package) REESE'S® Peanut Butter Chips, melted
4 eggs
2 teaspoons vanilla extract
Chocolate Drizzle (recipe follows)
Whipped topping
HERSHEY'S MINI KISSES® Brand Milk Chocolates

1. Heat oven to 300°F. Combine graham cracker crumbs, ⅓ cup sugar, cocoa and butter; press onto bottom of 9-inch springform pan.

2. Beat cream cheese and remaining ¼ cup sugar until fluffy. Gradually beat in sweetened condensed milk, then melted chips, until smooth. Add eggs and vanilla; beat well. Pour over crust.

3. Bake 60 to 70 minutes or until center is almost set. Remove from oven. With knife, loosen cake from side of pan. Cool. Remove side of pan. Refrigerate until cold. Garnish with Chocolate Drizzle, whipped topping and chocolate pieces. Store, covered, in refrigerator.

Makes 12 servings

Chocolate Drizzle: Melt 2 tablespoons butter in small saucepan over low heat; add 2 tablespoons HERSHEY'S Cocoa and 2 tablespoons water. Cook and stir until slightly thickened. Do not boil. Cool slightly. Gradually add 1 cup powdered sugar and ½ teaspoon vanilla extract, beating with whisk until smooth. Makes about ¾ cup.

Tip: If desired, spoon drizzle into small heavy seal-top plastic bag. With scissors, make small diagonal cut in bottom corner of bag. Squeeze drizzle over top of cake.

Reese's® Chocolate Peanut Butter Cheesecake

Ganache-Topped Cheesecake

4 packages (8 ounces each) cream cheese, softened
2 cups (1 pint) whipping cream
7 eggs
1½ cups sugar
2 tablespoons all-purpose flour
2 teaspoons vanilla
Chocolate Ganache (recipe follows)

1. Preheat oven to 350°F. Beat cream cheese and cream, a little at a time, in large bowl with electric mixer at medium speed 1 minute until smooth. Add eggs, one at a time, beating well after each addition. Add sugar, flour and vanilla; beat at low speed just until blended.

2. Pour mixture into ungreased 10-inch springform pan. Bake 50 to 60 minutes or until center appears set but still damp. Turn off oven but do not open door; allow to cool completely in oven for at least 4 hours. Prepare Chocolate Ganache.

3. Remove side of springform pan; top with warm Chocolate Ganache, allowing chocolate to run down side of cake. Cover and refrigerate 2 hours or until ready to serve.

Makes 16 servings

Chocolate Ganache

1 cup whipping cream
1 cup semisweet chocolate chips

Heat cream in small saucepan over medium-low heat until bubbles appear around edges of pan. Place chocolate chips in medium bowl. Pour cream over chips, stirring constantly until mixture is smooth and begins to thicken. Keep warm. Mixture thickens and sets as it cools.

Neapolitan Cheesecake

1¼ cups chocolate wafer or graham cracker crumbs
¼ cup (½ stick) butter, melted
3 packages (8 ounces each) cream cheese, softened
¾ cup sugar
1½ teaspoons vanilla
3 eggs
⅓ cup strawberry preserves
6 drops red food coloring
¾ cup white chocolate chips, melted
¾ cup semisweet chocolate chips, melted

continued on page 288

Ganache-Topped Cheesecake

Neapolitan Cheesecake, continued

1. Preheat oven to 350°F. Spray 9-inch springform pan with nonstick cooking spray.

2. Combine crumbs and butter in medium bowl. Press onto bottom of prepared pan. Bake 9 minutes; cool.

3. Beat cream cheese, sugar and vanilla in large bowl with electric mixer at medium speed 2 minutes until well blended. Add eggs; beat until just blended.

4. Divide batter equally among three medium bowls. Stir preserves and food coloring into one, white chocolate chips into second and semisweet chocolate chips into third. Spread semisweet chocolate mixture over crust. Repeat with preserves mixture, then white chocolate mixture.

5. Bake 1 hour or until center is almost set. Cool completely on wire rack. Refrigerate at least 3 hours. Carefully run knife around edge of pan to loosen. Remove side of pan. Serve immediately. Refrigerate leftovers. *Makes 8 to 10 servings*

Decadent Turtle Cheesecake

2 cups crushed chocolate cookies or vanilla wafers (about 8 ounces cookies)
¼ cup (½ stick) butter, melted
2½ packages (8 ounces each) cream cheese, softened
1 cup sugar
1½ tablespoons all-purpose flour
1½ teaspoons vanilla
¼ teaspoon salt
3 eggs
2 tablespoons whipping cream
Caramel and Chocolate Toppings (recipes follow)
¾ cup chopped toasted pecans

1. Preheat oven to 450°F. For crust, combine cookie crumbs and butter; press onto bottom of 9-inch springform pan.

2. For filling, beat cream cheese in large bowl with electric mixer until creamy. Beat in sugar, flour, vanilla and salt; mix well. Add eggs, one at a time, beating well after each addition. Beat in cream. Pour over crust.

3. Bake 10 minutes. *Reduce oven temperature to 300°F.* Continue baking 35 to 40 minutes or until set. Loosen cake from side of pan; cool completely before removing side of pan. Meanwhile, prepare Caramel and Chocolate Toppings.

4. Drizzle cake with toppings. Refrigerate. Sprinkle with pecans before serving.
Makes one 9-inch cheesecake

Caramel Topping: Combine ½ (14-ounce) bag caramels and ¼ cup whipping cream in small saucepan; stir over low heat until smooth.

Chocolate Topping: Combine 4 squares (1 ounce each) semisweet chocolate or 4 ounces semisweet chocolate chips, 1 teaspoon butter and 2 tablespoons whipping cream in small saucepan; stir over low heat until smooth.

Decadent Turtle Cheesecake

Perfect Pies & Tarts

Praline Pumpkin Pie

1½ cups canned solid pack pumpkin
10 packets sugar substitute*
1 teaspoon ground cinnamon
½ teaspoon salt
½ teaspoon ground ginger
½ teaspoon ground cloves
1½ cups whipping cream
2 eggs
2 tablespoons unsweetened flaked coconut, divided
2 tablespoons chopped pecans, divided

*This recipe was tested with sucralose-based sugar substitute.

1. Preheat oven to 425°F.

2. Stir together pumpkin, sugar substitute, cinnamon, salt, ginger and cloves in medium bowl. Stir in cream and eggs until well blended.

3. Sprinkle 1 tablespoon coconut and 1 tablespoon pecans evenly over bottom of 9-inch pie plate. Slowly pour pumpkin mixture into pan and gently spread into even layer. Top with remaining coconut and pecans.

4. Bake 15 minutes. *Reduce temperature to 350°F.* Bake 40 to 50 minutes more or until knife inserted into center comes out clean.   *Makes 8 servings*

Very Cherry Pie

4 cups frozen unsweetened tart cherries
1 cup dried tart cherries
1 cup granulated sugar
2 tablespoons quick-cooking tapioca
½ teaspoon almond extract
   Pastry for double-crust 9-inch pie
¼ teaspoon ground nutmeg
1 tablespoon butter

Combine frozen cherries, dried cherries, sugar, tapioca and almond extract in large mixing bowl; mix well. (It is not necessary to thaw cherries before using.) Let cherry mixture stand 15 minutes.

Line 9-inch pie plate with pastry; fill with cherry mixture. Sprinkle with nutmeg. Dot with butter. Cover with top crust, cutting slits for steam to escape. Or, cut top crust into strips for lattice top.

Bake in preheated 375°F oven about 1 hour or until crust is golden brown and filling is bubbly. If necessary, cover edge of crust with foil to prevent overbrowning.

Makes 8 servings

Note: Two (14½-ounce) cans unsweetened tart cherries, well drained, can be substituted for frozen tart cherries. Dried cherries are available at gourmet and specialty food stores and at selected supermarkets.

Favorite recipe from **Cherry Marketing Institute**

Rhubarb Tart

   Pastry for single-crust 9-inch pie
4 cups sliced (½-inch pieces) fresh rhubarb
1¼ cups sugar
¼ cup all-purpose flour
2 tablespoons butter, cut into chunks
¼ cup uncooked old-fashioned oats

1. Preheat oven to 450°F. Line 9-inch pie plate with pastry; set aside.

2. Combine rhubarb, sugar and flour in medium bowl; place in pie crust. Top with butter. Sprinkle with oats.

3. Bake 10 minutes. *Reduce oven temperature to 350°F.* Bake 40 minutes more or until bubbly and rhubarb is tender.

Makes 8 servings

Very Cherry Pie

Pumpkin Dutch Apple Pie

APPLE LAYER

2 cups (about 2 medium) peeled, cored and thinly sliced green apples
¼ cup granulated sugar
2 teaspoons all-purpose flour
1 teaspoon lemon juice
¼ teaspoon ground cinnamon
1 *unbaked* 9-inch (4-cup volume) deep-dish pie shell with high fluted edge

PUMPKIN LAYER

1½ cups LIBBY'S® 100% Pure Pumpkin
1 cup NESTLÉ® CARNATION® Evaporated Milk
½ cup granulated sugar
2 eggs, lightly beaten
2 tablespoons butter or margarine, melted
¾ teaspoon ground cinnamon
¼ teaspoon salt
⅛ teaspoon ground nutmeg
Crumb Topping (recipe follows)

PREHEAT oven to 375°F.

FOR APPLE LAYER

COMBINE apples with sugar, flour, lemon juice and cinnamon in medium bowl; pour into pie shell.

FOR PUMPKIN LAYER

COMBINE pumpkin, evaporated milk, sugar, eggs, butter, cinnamon, salt and nutmeg in medium bowl; pour over apple mixture.

BAKE for 30 minutes. Remove from oven; sprinkle with Crumb Topping. Return to oven; bake for 20 minutes or until custard is set. Cool completely on wire rack.

Makes 8 servings

Crumb Topping: **COMBINE** ½ cup all-purpose flour, ⅓ cup chopped walnuts and 5 tablespoons granulated sugar in medium bowl. Cut in 3 tablespoons butter with pastry blender or two knives until mixtures resembles coarse crumbs.

Pumpkin Dutch Apple Pie

Strawberry Cheesecake Pie

1 *prepared* 9-inch (6 ounces) graham cracker crumb crust
⅔ cup (5-fluid-ounce can) NESTLÉ® CARNATION® Evaporated Fat Free Milk
1 package (8 ounces) fat-free cream cheese, softened
1 egg
½ cup granulated sugar
2 tablespoons all-purpose flour
1 teaspoon grated lemon peel
1½ to 2 cups halved fresh strawberries
3 tablespoons strawberry jelly, warmed

PREHEAT oven to 325°F.

PLACE evaporated milk, cream cheese, egg, sugar, flour and lemon peel in blender; cover. Blend until smooth. Pour into crust.

BAKE for 35 to 40 minutes or until center is set. Cool completely in pan on wire rack. Arrange strawberries on top of pie; drizzle with jelly. Refrigerate well before serving.

Makes 8 servings

Turtle Pecan Pie

1 (9-inch) frozen deep dish pie crust
1 cup light corn syrup
3 eggs, lightly beaten
½ cup sugar
⅓ cup butter, melted
1 teaspoon vanilla
½ teaspoon salt
1¼ cups toasted pecans, divided*
2 squares (1 ounce each) semisweet chocolate, melted
½ cup caramel ice cream topping
Whipped cream and grated chocolate

To toast nuts, place on ungreased baking sheet. Bake in preheated 350°F oven 5 to 7 minutes or until lightly browned.

1. Preheat oven to 350°F. Place frozen pie crust on baking sheet.

2. Combine corn syrup, eggs, sugar, butter, vanilla and salt in large bowl; mix well. Reserve ½ cup egg mixture. Stir 1 cup pecans and chocolate into remaining egg mixture; pour into pie crust. Stir caramel topping into reserved egg mixture; carefully pour over pecan filling.

3. Bake 50 to 55 minutes or until filling is set about 3 inches from edge. Cool completely on wire rack.

4. Garnish each serving with whipped cream, grated chocolate and remaining pecans.

Makes 8 servings

Strawberry Cheesecake Pie

Apple & Cherry Pie

2 cups all-purpose flour
½ cup plus 2 tablespoons sugar, divided
½ teaspoon salt
3 tablespoons butter or margarine
3 tablespoons shortening
1 tablespoon cider vinegar
5 to 6 tablespoons ice water
½ cup dried cherries
¼ cup apple juice
1 tablespoon cornstarch
2 teaspoons ground cinnamon
6 cups thinly sliced peeled baking apples, preferably Jonagold or
    Golden Delicious
1 teaspoon vanilla

GLAZE
1 egg white, well beaten
1 teaspoon sugar
¼ teaspoon ground cinnamon

1. Combine flour, 2 tablespoons sugar and salt in large bowl. Cut in butter and shortening with pastry blender or two knives until mixture resembles coarse crumbs. Add vinegar and 4 tablespoons water, stirring with fork. Add additional ice water, 1 tablespoon at a time, until mixture forms soft dough. Divide dough into thirds. Shape 1 piece into disk; wrap in plastic wrap. Combine remaining 2 pieces dough, forming larger disk; wrap in plastic wrap. Refrigerate disks 30 minutes.

2. Preheat oven to 375°F. Combine cherries and apple juice in small microwavable bowl; microwave on HIGH 1½ minutes. Let stand 15 minutes to plump cherries. Combine remaining ½ cup sugar, cornstarch and cinnamon in large bowl; mix well. Stir in apples and vanilla.

3. Coat 9-inch pie plate with nonstick cooking spray. Roll larger disk of dough to ⅛-inch thickness on lightly floured surface. Cut into 12-inch circle. Transfer pastry to prepared pie plate. Spoon apple mixture into pastry. Roll smaller disk of dough to ⅛-inch thickness. Cut dough into ½-inch-strips. Place strips over filling and weave into lattice design. Trim ends of lattice strips; fold edge of lower crust over ends of lattice strips. Seal and flute edge.

4. For glaze, brush pastry with egg white; sprinkle with combined sugar and cinnamon, if desired. Bake 45 to 50 minutes or until apples are tender and crust is golden brown. Cool 30 minutes. Serve warm or at room temperature.   *Makes 8 servings*

Tip: If the pie crust is browning too quickly, cover the edges with strips of foil. An alternative is to cut the bottom out of a foil pie pan and invert it over the pie.

Prep Time: 45 minutes | Bake Time: 45 minutes

Sweet 'n' Spicy Pecan Pie

    Prepared pie crust for one 9-inch pie
  3 eggs
  1 cup dark corn syrup
  ½ cup dark brown sugar
  ¼ cup (½ stick) butter or margarine, melted
  1 tablespoon TABASCO® brand Pepper Sauce
1½ cup pecans, coarsely chopped
    Whipped cream (optional)

Preheat oven to 425°F. Place pie crust in 9-inch pie plate; flute edge of crust.

Beat eggs lightly in large bowl. Stir in corn syrup, brown sugar, butter and TABASCO®
Sauce; mix well. Place pecans in prepared pie crust; pour filling over pecans. Bake
15 minutes.

Reduce oven to 350°F. Bake pie 40 minutes or until knife inserted 1 inch from edge comes
out clean. Cool pie on wire rack. Serve with whipped cream, if desired.

Makes 8 servings

Peanut Chocolate Surprise Pie

½ cup (1 stick) butter, melted
 1 cup sugar
 2 eggs
½ cup all-purpose flour
½ cup chopped peanuts
½ cup chopped walnuts
½ cup semisweet chocolate chips
¼ cup bourbon
 1 teaspoon vanilla
 1 (9-inch) unbaked deep-dish pie shell
   Whipped cream for garnish
   Chocolate shavings for garnish

Preheat oven to 350°F. Beat butter and sugar in large bowl with electric mixer at medium
speed until blended. Add eggs; beat until well blended. Gradually add flour. Stir in nuts,
chocolate chips, bourbon and vanilla. Spread mixture evenly in unbaked pie shell. Bake
40 minutes. Cool pie on wire rack. Garnish, if desired.

Makes 8 servings

Mascarpone Cheese Tart with Candied Almonds

CRUST

- ¼ cup slivered almonds
- ¾ cup graham cracker crumbs
- 3 tablespoons melted butter
- 1½ tablespoons sugar

FILLING

- 4 ounces cream cheese, softened
- ¼ cup sugar
- 2 eggs
- ½ teaspoon vanilla
- 16 ounces mascarpone cheese

TOPPING

- ¾ cup strawberry preserves
- Candied Almonds (recipe follows)

1. For crust, preheat oven to 375°F. Place 9-inch tart pan with removable bottom on baking sheet.

2. Place almonds into resealable food storage bag and crush with rolling pin. Combine crushed almonds, graham cracker crumbs, butter and 1½ tablespoons sugar in small bowl. Press onto bottom and side of tart pan. Bake 10 minutes or until golden. Cool completely.

3. For filling, preheat oven to 325°F. Beat cream cheese in large bowl with electric mixer at medium speed until smooth. Add ¼ cup sugar and beat at medium speed 1 minute. Add eggs, one at a time, then vanilla, beating well after each addition. Add mascarpone; beat on high speed 20 seconds until filling is smooth. Do not overmix.

4. Spread filling into crust. Bake 60 to 70 minutes until golden and puffed (filling will settle as cheesecake cools). Cool completely on wire rack.

5. For topping, melt strawberry preserves over low heat. Spread onto tart. Refrigerate until cold. To serve, remove tart from pan. Serve with candied almonds.

Makes 12 servings

Candied Almonds

- 3 tablespoons plus 2 teaspoons sugar
- 3 tablespoons water
- 1⅓ cups whole almonds
- Butter-flavored cooking spray *or* 1 teaspoon clarified butter

continued on page 302

Mascarpone Cheese Tart with Candied Almonds

Mascarpone Cheese Tart with Candied Almonds, continued

1. Cook sugar and water in medium saucepan over medium-low heat until mixture reaches 230°F on candy thermometer. Remove from heat and add almonds. Stir about 2 minutes or until sugar is sandy. Cook over low heat 10 to 15 minutes, stirring constantly, until sugar melts and caramelizes on almonds.

2. Carefully transfer almonds onto nonstick baking sheet; spray with butter-flavored cooking spray. Break almonds apart with spatula. Cool 3 minutes, then use hands to separate almonds, if necessary.　　　　　　　　　　　*Makes 12 servings*

Bourbon-Laced Sweet Potato Pie

1 pound (2 medium) sweet potatoes, peeled, cut into 1-inch chunks
2 tablespoons butter
¾ cup packed brown sugar
1 teaspoon ground cinnamon
¼ teaspoon salt
2 eggs
¾ cup whipping cream
¼ cup bourbon or whiskey
Pastry for 9-inch pie (or half of 15-ounce package refrigerated pastry crusts)
Sweetened whipped cream

1. Preheat oven to 350°F. Place sweet potatoes in saucepan; cover with water. Simmer about 20 minutes or until very tender. Drain well in colander; transfer to large bowl. Add butter; beat with electric mixer at medium speed until smooth. Add brown sugar, cinnamon and salt; beat until smooth. Beat in eggs one at a time. Beat in cream and bourbon.

2. Line 9-inch pie plate (not deep-dish) with pastry; flute edges. Pour sweet potato mixture into crust. Bake 50 minutes or until knife inserted into center comes out clean. Transfer to wire rack; cool at least 1 hour before serving. Serve warm or at room temperature with whipped cream.　　　　　　　　　　　*Makes 8 servings*

Tip: Pie may be cooled completely, covered and chilled up to 24 hours before serving. Let stand at room temperature at least 30 minutes before serving.

helpful hint:

Nothing beats fresh whipped cream with a warm pie. For best results when beating whipping cream, chill the cream, bowl and beaters first—the cold temperature keeps the fat in the cream solid, thus increasing the volume. Add flavorings, such as powdered sugar and vanilla extract, to the cream after it has begun to thicken. Sweetened whipped cream will have a softer texture than unsweetened.

Bourbon-Laced Sweet Potato Pie

Black Forest Tarts

1 package (18 ounces) refrigerated triple chocolate cookie dough
⅓ cup unsweetened cocoa powder
1 can (21 ounces) cherry pie filling
3 squares (1 ounce each) white chocolate, finely chopped

1. Let dough stand at room temperature about 15 minutes. Preheat oven to 350°F. Lightly grease 18 standard (2½-inch) muffin pan cups or line with paper or foil baking cups.

2. Combine dough and cocoa in large bowl; beat until well blended. Shape dough into 18 balls; press onto bottoms and up sides of prepared muffin cups.

3. Bake about 15 minutes or until set. Remove from oven; gently press down center of each cookie cup with back of teaspoon. Cool in pan 10 minutes. Remove cups from pans; cool completely on wire rack.

4. Place 1 tablespoon cherry pie filling in each cookie cup.

5. Place white chocolate in small resealable food storage bag. Microwave on MEDIUM (50%) 1 minute; knead bag lightly. Microwave and knead at additional 30-second intervals until white chocolate is completely melted. Cut off tiny corner of bag. Drizzle white chocolate over tarts. Let stand until set. *Makes 1½ dozen tarts*

Apple-Pear Praline Pie

6 cups peeled, cored and thinly sliced Granny Smith apples
3 cups peeled, cored and thinly sliced pears
¾ cup granulated sugar
¼ cup plus 1 tablespoon all-purpose flour, divided
1 tablespoon ground cinnamon
¼ teaspoon salt
  Pastry for 9-inch double crust pie
½ cup plus 2 tablespoons butter, divided
1 cup packed brown sugar
¼ cup half-and-half
1 cup chopped pecans

1. Preheat oven to 350°F. Combine apples, pears, granulated sugar, ¼ cup flour, cinnamon and salt in large bowl; toss gently. Let stand 15 minutes.

2. Place 1 crust in 9-inch deep dish pie pan; sprinkle lightly with remaining 1 tablespoon flour. Spoon apple and pear mixture into crust; dot with 2 tablespoons butter. Top with second pie crust. Seal and flute as desired; cut slits in crust to vent steam. Bake 50 to 55 minutes.

3. Melt remaining ½ cup butter in small saucepan over low heat. Stir in brown sugar and half-and-half. Bring to a boil, stirring constantly. Remove from heat; stir in pecans. Spread over top of pie.

4. Place pie on baking sheet; bake 5 minutes. Cool on wire rack. Serve warm or at room temperature. *Makes 8 servings*

Black Forest Tarts

Key Lime Tartlets

1 package (18 ounces) refrigerated sugar cookie dough
½ cup finely chopped pecans
1 can (14 ounces) sweetened condensed milk
¼ cup plus 1 tablespoon bottled key lime juice
1 teaspoon freshly grated lime peel
   Whipped cream, additional freshly grated lime peel and lime wedge candies

1. Let dough stand at room temperature about 15 minutes. Preheat oven to 350°F. Lightly grease 18 standard (2½-inch) muffin pan cups or line with paper or foil baking cups.

2. Combine dough and pecans in large bowl; beat until well blended. Shape dough into 18 balls; press onto bottoms and up sides of prepared muffin cups.

3. Bake 12 to 15 minutes or until set. Remove from oven; gently press down center of each cookie cup with back of teaspoon. Cool in pan 10 minutes. Remove cups from pans; cool completely on wire rack.

4. Combine sweetened condensed milk, juice and peel in small bowl; stir until well blended. Divide evenly among cookie cups. Garnish with whipped cream, lime peel and lime candies.

Makes 18 tartlets

Variation: To make lemon tartlets, use lemon juice in place of lime juice and garnish with lemon candies.

helpful hint:

Refrigerated cookie dough is surprisingly versatile. In addition to making cookies with the dozen flavors that are offered, cookie dough makes a great crust for miniature tarts and pies. When baked in muffin pan cups, cookie dough can be a fun base for pudding and ice cream!

Key Lime Tartlets

Walnut Tartlets with Chocolate Ganache Filling

Chocolate Leaves (recipe follows)
½ cup walnut halves, toasted
1 cup all-purpose flour
¼ cup sugar
1 tablespoon grated lemon peel
⅓ cup butter or margarine, cut into pieces
1 egg, lightly beaten
Chocolate Ganache (recipe follows)

1. Prepare Chocolate Leaves. Preheat oven to 350°F. Place walnuts in food processor. Process using on/off pulsing action until walnuts are finely chopped, but not pasty.

2. Reserve 2 tablespoons walnuts. Place remaining walnuts in medium bowl. Add flour, sugar and lemon peel; blend well. Cut in butter with pastry blender or two knives until mixture resembles coarse crumbs. Stir in egg with fork until mixture holds together.

3. Spoon 2 teaspoonfuls dough into *ungreased* mini muffin cups. Press dough onto bottom and up side of each cup with fingers.

4. Bake 16 to 20 minutes or until golden brown. Cool 5 minutes in pan. Remove shells from pans. Cool completely on wire racks.

5. Prepare Chocolate Ganache. Spoon ½ teaspoon ganache into each shell. Sprinkle reserved 2 tablespoons chopped nuts evenly over shells. Gently push chocolate leaf into each shell. Store tightly covered in refrigerator up to 1 week. *Makes 30 tartlets*

Chocolate Leaves

½ cup (2 ounces) chopped semisweet chocolate or semisweet chocolate chips
1 teaspoon shortening
Assorted nontoxic fresh leaves such as rose, lemon or camellia,* cleaned and wiped dry

Nontoxic leaves are available in florist shops.

1. Place large sheet heavy-duty foil on counter.

2. Fill saucepan with 1 inch warm water. Place chocolate and shortening in 1-cup glass measure. Place measure in warm water; stir frequently with rubber spatula until smooth. (Be careful not to get any water into chocolate or chocolate may become lumpy.)

3. Brush melted chocolate onto underside of each leaf with small, clean craft paintbrush or pastry brush, coating leaf thickly and evenly. Carefully wipe off any chocolate that may have run onto front of leaf.

4. Place leaves, chocolate sides up, on foil. Let stand 1 hour or until chocolate is set.

5. Carefully peel leaves away from chocolate beginning at stem ends; refrigerate chocolate leaves until ready to use. *Makes 30 to 40 leaves*

Chocolate Ganache

2 tablespoons whipping cream
1 tablespoon butter
½ cup (2 ounces) chopped semisweet chocolate or semisweet chocolate chips
½ teaspoon vanilla

Heat cream and butter in small saucepan over medium heat until butter melts and mixture boils, stirring frequently with wooden spoon. Remove saucepan from heat. Stir in chocolate and vanilla until mixture is smooth, returning to heat for 20 to 30 second intervals as needed to melt chocolate. Keep warm (ganache is semi-firm at room temperature).

Makes about ⅓ cup

Linzer Tart

¾ cup (1½ sticks) butter or margarine, softened
2 egg yolks
2 tablespoons frozen unsweetened apple juice concentrate, thawed
2 teaspoons vanilla
1 cup all-purpose flour
½ teaspoon baking powder
¼ teaspoon salt
¼ teaspoon ground cinnamon
⅛ teaspoon ground allspice
1½ cups ground blanched almonds *or* hazelnuts (about 8 ounces)
1 jar (10 ounces) raspberry fruit spread (about 1 cup)

1. Beat butter in large bowl with electric mixer at medium speed until light and fluffy. Blend in egg yolks, apple juice concentrate and vanilla. Combine flour, baking powder, salt, cinnamon and allspice; mix well. Stir in almonds. Gradually add flour mixture to butter mixture, beating until well blended.

2. Spread 1½ cups batter evenly onto bottom of 10-inch tart pan with removable bottom or 10-inch springform pan. Spread fruit spread evenly over batter, leaving 1-inch border around edge. Spoon remaining batter into pastry bag fitted with ½-inch plain or star tip. Pipe batter in lattice design over fruit spread. Chill 30 minutes.

3. Preheat oven to 350°F. Bake tart 35 minutes or until crust is golden brown and fruit spread is bubbly. Cool completely on wire rack. Serve at room temperature.

Makes 8 servings

Deep-Dish Peach Custard Pie

1 *unbaked* 9-inch (4-cup volume) deep-dish pie shell
3½ cups (about 7 medium) peeled, pitted and sliced peaches
1 can (14 ounces) NESTLÉ® CARNATION® Sweetened Condensed Milk
2 eggs
¼ cup butter or margarine, melted
1 to 3 teaspoons lemon juice
½ teaspoon ground cinnamon
    Dash ground nutmeg
    Streusel Topping (recipe follows)

PREHEAT oven to 425°F.

ARRANGE peaches in pie shell. Combine sweetened condensed milk, eggs, butter, lemon juice, cinnamon and nutmeg in large mixer bowl; beat until smooth. Pour over peaches.

BAKE for 10 minutes. Sprinkle with Streusel Topping. Reduce oven temperature to 350°F.; bake for additional 55 to 60 minutes or until knife inserted near center comes out clean. Cool on wire rack.

Makes 8 servings

Streusel Topping: COMBINE ⅓ cup all-purpose flour, ⅓ cup packed brown sugar and ⅓ cup chopped walnuts in medium bowl. Cut in 2 tablespoons butter or margarine with pastry blender or two knives until mixture resembles coarse crumbs.

Apple Crunch Pie

1 refrigerated pie crust
1¼ cups all-purpose flour, divided
1 cup granulated sugar
6 tablespoons butter, melted, divided
1½ teaspoons ground cinnamon, divided
¾ teaspoon ground nutmeg, divided
½ teaspoon ground ginger
¼ teaspoon salt
4 cups peeled, cored, diced apples
½ cup packed brown sugar
½ cup chopped walnuts

1. Preheat oven to 350°F. Place crust in 9-inch pie pan; flute edge as desired.

2. Combine ¼ cup flour, granulated sugar, 2 tablespoons butter, 1 teaspoon cinnamon, ½ teaspoon nutmeg, ginger and salt; mix well. Add apples; toss to coat. Place apple mixture in crust.

3. Combine remaining 1 cup flour, 4 tablespoons butter, ½ teaspoon cinnamon, ¼ teaspoon nutmeg, brown sugar and walnuts in small bowl. Sprinkle evenly over apple mixture.

4. Bake 45 to 55 minutes or until apples are tender and topping is golden brown.

Makes 8 servings

Deep-Dish Peach Custard Pie

Reese's® Peanut Butter and Milk Chocolate Chip Cookie Pie

½ cup (1 stick) butter or margarine, softened
2 eggs, beaten
2 teaspoons vanilla extract
1 cup sugar
½ cup all-purpose flour
1¾ cups (11-ounce package) REESE'S ® Peanut Butter and Milk Chocolate Chips
1 cup chopped pecans or walnuts
1 unbaked 9-inch pie crust
Sweetened whipped cream or ice cream (optional)

1. Heat oven to 350°F.

2. Beat butter in medium bowl; add eggs and vanilla. Stir together sugar and flour; add to butter mixture. Stir in chips and nuts; pour into unbaked pie crust.

3. Bake 50 to 55 minutes or until golden brown. Cool about 1 hour on wire rack; serve warm with sweetened whipped cream or ice cream, if desired. To reheat: Microwave one slice at a time at HIGH (100%) 10 to 15 seconds.   *Makes 8 to 10 servings*

Hazelnut Plum Tart

1 cup hazelnuts
¼ cup firmly packed light brown sugar
1 cup all-purpose flour
⅓ cup FILIPPO BERIO® Olive Oil
1 egg, separated
Pinch salt
3 tablespoons granulated sugar
2 teaspoons cornstarch
½ teaspoon grated lime peel
Pinch ground nutmeg
Pinch ground cloves
1¼ pounds plums (about 5 large), cut into halves and pitted
3 tablespoons currant jelly
Sweetened whipped cream (optional)

Preheat oven to 375°F. Grease 9-inch tart pan with removable bottom with olive oil.

Place hazelnuts in food processor; process until coarsely chopped. Remove ¼ cup for garnish; set aside. Add brown sugar to food processor; process until nuts are finely ground. Add flour, olive oil, egg yolk and salt; process until combined. (Mixture will be crumbly.)

continued on page 314

Reese's® Peanut Butter and Milk Chocolate Chip Cookie Pie

Hazelnut Plum Tart, continued

Spoon mixture into prepared pan. Press firmly in even layer on bottom and up side. Brush inside of crust with egg white. Place in freezer 10 minutes.

In large bowl, combine granulated sugar, cornstarch, lime peel, nutmeg and cloves. Cut each plum half into 4 wedges. Add to sugar mixture; toss until combined. Arrange plums in overlapping circles in crust; spoon any remaining sugar mixture over plums. Place tart on baking sheet.

Bake 45 to 50 minutes or until fruit is tender and juices are thickened. Cool 30 minutes on wire rack. Place currant jelly in small saucepan; heat over low heat, stirring frequently, until melted. Brush over plums; sprinkle with reserved hazelnuts. Serve tart warm or at room temperature with whipped cream, if desired. *Makes 6 servings*

Blueberry-Pear Tart

1 refrigerated pie crust
1 medium fully ripened pear, peeled, cored and thinly sliced
8 ounces fresh or thawed frozen blueberries or blackberries
⅓ cup raspberry fruit spread
½ teaspoon grated fresh ginger

1. Preheat oven to 450°F.

2. Spray 9-inch tart pan with removable bottom with nonstick cooking spray. Place dough in pan; press against side of pan to form ½-inch edge. Prick dough with fork. Bake 12 minutes. Remove pan to wire rack; cool completely.

3. Arrange pears on bottom of cooled crust; top with blueberries.

4. Place fruit spread in small microwavable bowl. Cover with plastic wrap; microwave at HIGH 15 seconds; stir. If necessary, microwave additional 10 to 15 seconds or until spread is melted; stir. Add grated ginger; stir until blended. Let stand 30 seconds to thicken slightly. Pour mixture over fruit in crust. Refrigerate 2 hours. (Do not cover.) Cut into 8 slices before serving. *Makes 8 servings*

Prep Time: 10 minutes | **Bake Time:** 12 minutes | **Chill Time:** 2 hours

Blueberry-Pear Tart

Apple-Cheddar Tart

  Cheddar Pastry (recipe follows)
1 egg white
6 cups sliced peeled apples
2 teaspoons ground cinnamon
¼ teaspoon ground nutmeg
½ cup thawed frozen unsweetened apple juice concentrate
2 tablespoons cornstarch
2 tablespoons butter or margarine
  Sharp Cheddar cheese, sliced (optional)

1. Prepare Cheddar Pastry.

2. Preheat oven to 400°F. Roll out pastry dough to 12-inch circle. Place in 10-inch tart pan with removable bottom or 10-inch quiche dish; trim pastry and flute edges, sealing to side of pan. Prick bottom and sides of pastry with fork. Beat egg white until frothy; brush lightly over bottom of pastry. Bake 15 minutes. *Reduce oven temperature to 350°F.*

3. Place apples in large bowl. Add cinnamon and nutmeg; toss lightly to coat. Combine apple juice concentrate and cornstarch; mix well. Add to apple mixture; mix lightly. Spoon into partially baked crust; dot with butter. Bake 35 to 40 minutes or until apples are tender and crust is golden brown. Cool on wire rack. Serve with Cheddar cheese, if desired.

Makes 8 servings

Cheddar Pastry

1½ cups all-purpose flour
⅓ cup (1½ ounces) shredded sharp Cheddar cheese
¼ teaspoon salt
½ cup (1 stick) cold butter or margarine
3 to 4 tablespoons ice water

Combine flour, cheese and salt in medium bowl. Cut in butter with pastry blender or two knives until mixture forms coarse crumbs. Add water, 1 tablespoon at a time, mixing just until mixture forms dough; wrap in plastic wrap. Refrigerate 1 hour.

Apple-Cheddar Tart

Fabulous Fruit Desserts

Winterfruit Cobbler

FILLING
2 cups SUN•MAID® Raisins
2 cups fresh or frozen cranberries
¾ cup sugar
2 teaspoons cornstarch
½ teaspoon ground allspice
1 cup orange juice

TOPPING
1 cup all-purpose flour
2 tablespoons sugar
2 teaspoons baking powder
¼ teaspoon salt
¼ cup butter or margarine
½ cup milk
Sugar
Ground cinnamon

TO PREPARE FILLING
In medium saucepan, combine raisins, cranberries, sugar, cornstarch and allspice. Gradually stir in orange juice. Bring to boil over high heat; reduce heat to low and simmer, stirring until cranberries begin to pop and mixture thickens slightly. Pour into shallow 1½-quart baking dish.

TO PREPARE TOPPING
In small bowl, combine flour, sugar, baking powder and salt. Cut in butter until mixture resembles coarse crumbs. Mix in milk lightly with fork. Drop spoonfuls of batter over filling; sprinkle lightly with additional sugar mixed with a little cinnamon. Bake in preheated 400°F oven about 25 minutes or until golden. Serve warm with ice cream or whipped cream.

Makes 6 servings

Caramel Apple Bread Pudding with Cinnamon Cream

1 package (12 ounces) frozen sliced apples, thawed
8 eggs, lightly beaten
2 cups milk
2 cups half-and-half
1 cup sugar
½ cup (1 stick) unsalted butter, melted
2 teaspoons baking powder
1½ teaspoons ground cinnamon, divided
1 teaspoon vanilla
1 loaf (16 ounces) challah or any sweet bread, cut into ¾-inch cubes
½ cup caramel ice cream topping
2 cups vanilla ice cream
Additional caramel topping and vanilla ice cream (optional)

1. Preheat oven to 350°F. Spray 13×9-inch baking pan with nonstick cooking spray.

2. Combine apples, eggs, milk, half-and-half, sugar, butter, baking powder, 1 teaspoon cinnamon and vanilla in large bowl. Mix well. Gently fold in bread cubes. Pour into prepared pan.

3. Bake 50 minutes or until set. Cool in pan 20 minutes.

4. Drizzle ½ cup caramel topping over bread pudding. Cut into 16 sections.

5. Microwave ice cream in small bowl about 30 seconds or until partially melted. Stir until smooth. Add remaining ½ teaspoon cinnamon and whisk until combined. Place 2 tablespoons ice cream mixture on each serving plate. Top with serving of bread pudding. Drizzle each serving with additional caramel topping and remaining ice cream mixture, if desired.

Makes 16 servings

helpful hint:

For bread pudding, always use the type of bread called for in the recipe. Substituting a different bread can affect the amount of liquid that is absorbed. The pudding is done when a knife inserted in the center comes out clean.

Caramel Apple Bread Pudding with Cinnamon Cream

Pineapple-Rum Napoleons

1 package puff pastry, thawed and cut into 12 (3-inch) rounds
3 egg yolks
½ cup mango nectar*
1 tablespoon granulated sugar
2 teaspoons cornstarch
⅔ cup milk
6 tablespoons butter
1 large pineapple, peeled and cut into 8 (½-inch-thick) slices
⅔ cup packed brown sugar
⅔ cup water
½ cup dark rum
½ teaspoon vanilla
   Powdered sugar, optional

Canned mango nectar is sold in the international or ethnic food section at most supermarkets.

1. Preheat oven to 400°F. Place puff pastry rounds on parchment-lined baking sheet. Bake about 13 minutes or until puffed and golden brown. Remove to wire rack; cool completely.

2. For pastry cream, whisk together egg yolks, nectar, granulated sugar and cornstarch in small bowl. Heat milk in small saucepan over medium-low heat until small bubbles form around edge. Do not boil. Slowly pour hot milk into egg mixture, whisking constantly. Return mixture to saucepan over medium-low heat. Whisk constantly until thick, about 6 minutes. Strain through fine-meshed strainer into medium bowl. Cover with plastic wrap; refrigerate until ready to use.

3. Heat large skillet over medium-high heat. Melt 3 tablespoons butter in skillet. Add half of pineapple slices in single layer and brown lightly on both sides; remove to plate. Repeat with remaining butter and pineapple. Combine brown sugar and water in small bowl. Add reserved pineapple and brown sugar mixture to skillet. Reduce heat to medium-low and simmer 10 minutes or until pineapple is soft.

4. For sauce, remove pineapple from pan leaving sauce in pan. Add rum; carefully light with match or long-handled lighter. Cook about 5 minutes, stirring frequently until sauce reduces and flames go out. Stir in vanilla.

5. Cut out cores of pineapple slices using small cookie cutter. Spoon 3 tablespoons rum sauce onto plate. Place 1 round of puff pastry on sauce and top with 1 tablespoon pastry cream. Top with pineapple slice, followed by another tablespoon of pastry cream and round of puff pastry. Repeat layers. Sprinkle with powdered sugar, if desired.

Makes 4 servings

Pineapple-Rum Napoleon

Double Cherry Crumbles

½ (18-ounce) package refrigerated oatmeal raisin cookie dough*
½ cup uncooked old-fashioned oats
¾ teaspoon ground cinnamon
½ teaspoon ground ginger
2 tablespoons cold butter, cut into small pieces
1 cup chopped pecans, toasted**
1 bag (16 ounces) frozen pitted unsweetened dark sweet cherries, thawed
2 cans (21 ounces each) cherry pie filling

Save remaining ½ package of dough for another use.

**To toast pecans, spread them in single layer on baking sheet. Bake in preheated 350°F oven 5 to 7 minutes or until golden brown, stirring frequently.*

1. Let half package of dough stand at room temperature about 15 minutes. Preheat oven to 350°F. Lightly grease eight ½-cup ramekins; place on baking sheet.

2. For topping, combine dough, oats, cinnamon and ginger in large bowl. Beat with electric mixer at medium speed until well blended. Cut in butter with pastry blender or 2 knives. Stir in pecans; set aside.

3. Combine cherries and pie filling in large bowl; mix well. Divide cherry mixture evenly among prepared ramekins; sprinkle evenly with topping. Bake about 25 minutes or until topping is browned. Serve warm. *Makes 8 servings*

Stuffed Apple Rings

⅓ cup dried cranberries
¼ cup chopped pecans
2 tablespoons butter, softened
1 tablespoon packed dark brown sugar
½ teaspoon ground cinnamon
½ teaspoon vanilla
2 medium apples, such as Gala or Jonathan

1. Preheat oven 425°F. Line baking sheet with foil. Spray with nonstick cooking spray.

2. Combine cranberries, pecans, butter, sugar, cinnamon and vanilla in medium bowl; mix well.

3. Cut ends off apples, then cut each apple into 4 round slices to yield 8 rings total. Core centers, using tip of small spoon.

4. Arrange apple slices on prepared baking sheet. Spoon 1 tablespoon cranberry mixture in center of each apple slice; press down gently. Bake 10 minutes or until apples are just tender. Serve warm or room temperature. *Makes 4 servings*

Variation: Omit sugar and bake according to above directions. When cooked, cool slightly and drizzle 1 tablespoon butterscotch ice cream topping evenly over all.

Double Cherry Crumbles

Apple Puff Pastry

2 cups sliced peeled Michigan Apples
½ cup chopped walnuts
⅓ cup firmly packed brown sugar
¼ cup light corn syrup
2 tablespoons margarine
¼ teaspoon cinnamon
1 package (3 ounces) cream cheese, softened
2 tablespoons granulated sugar
1 egg, separated
¼ teaspoon vanilla
1 teaspoon water
1 sheet (half of 17¼ ounces package) frozen puff pastry, thawed
½ cup powdered sugar
   Vegetable cooking spray

1. Preheat oven to 375°F. Spray baking sheet with nonstick cooking spray; set aside. Place Michigan Apples, walnuts, brown sugar, corn syrup, margarine and cinnamon in 12-inch skillet. Cook over medium heat, stirring frequently, about 5 minutes or until apples are almost tender. Drain Apples, reserving syrup. Cool completely.

2. In small bowl, combine cream cheese, granulated sugar, egg yolk and vanilla; set aside. In separate small bowl, mix egg white and water; set aside.

3. On lightly floured surface, roll pastry into 12×10-inch rectangle. Place on prepared baking sheet. Spread cream cheese mixture vertically down center ⅓ of pastry. Place cooled Apple mixture over cheese. Cut sides of pastry in 1-inch strips to filling. Starting at one end, alternately cross strips at an angle. Brush with egg white mixture.

4. Bake about 35 minutes or until golden brown. Remove to wire rack to cool. In small bowl, mix reserved syrup and powdered sugar; drizzle over pastry. Serve pastry warm or cold.

Makes 8 servings

Suggested Michigan Apple varieties to use: Empire, Gala, Golden Delicious, Ida Red, Jonagold, Jonathan, McIntosh or Rome.

Variations: Substitute 1 can (20 ounces) sliced Michigan Apples, drained, for fresh apples. Cook apples as fresh apples. Continue with above method. OR omit step 1 and substitute 1 can (21 ounces) Michigan Apple pie filling for fresh apples, brown sugar, margarine and corn syrup. Stir walnuts and cinnamon into pie filling. Continue with above method. Stir 1 tablespoon hot water into powdered sugar for glaze.

Favorite recipe from *Michigan Apple Committee*

Peach & Blackberry Shortcakes

¾ cup plain low-fat yogurt
 5 teaspoons sugar, divided
 1 tablespoon blackberry fruit spread
½ cup coarsely chopped peeled peach
½ cup fresh or thawed frozen blackberries
½ cup all-purpose flour
¼ teaspoon baking powder
⅛ teaspoon baking soda
 2 tablespoons butter
½ teaspoon vanilla

1. Place cheesecloth or coffee filter in large sieve or strainer. Spoon yogurt into sieve; place over large bowl. Refrigerate 20 minutes. Remove yogurt from sieve; discard liquid. Reserve ¼ cup yogurt; blend remaining yogurt, 2 teaspoons sugar and fruit spread in small bowl. Refrigerate until ready to serve.

2. Meanwhile, combine peach, blackberries and ½ teaspoon sugar in medium bowl; set aside.

3. Preheat oven to 425°F.

4. Combine flour, baking powder, baking soda and remaining 2½ teaspoons sugar in small bowl. Cut in butter with pastry blender until mixture resembles coarse crumbs. Combine reserved ¼ cup yogurt with vanilla. Stir into flour mixture just until dry ingredients are moistened and dough forms a ball.

5. Place dough on lightly floured surface. Knead gently 8 times. Divide dough in half. Using lightly floured rolling pin, roll each half into 3-inch rounds. Place rounds on ungreased baking sheet.

6. Bake 12 to 15 minutes or until lightly browned. Immediately remove from baking sheet. Cool shortcakes on wire rack 10 minutes or until cool enough to handle.

7. Slice shortcakes horizontally in half. Place bottom half on serving plate. Top with fruit mixture, yogurt mixture and shortcake tops. Serve immediately.   *Makes 2 servings*

helpful hint:

Shortcake in its classic American form consists of a sweet, rich biscuit that is cut in half, filled with fruit and topped with whipped cream. For a modern version, sponge cake, angel food cake and pound cake may also be used.

Cherry-Almond Clafouti

½ cup slivered almonds
½ cup powdered sugar
⅔ cup all-purpose flour
⅔ cup granulated sugar
¼ teaspoon salt
½ cup (1 stick) butter, cut into pieces
⅔ cup milk
2 eggs
½ teaspoon vanilla
1 cup fresh sweet cherries, pitted and quartered

1. Preheat oven to 350°F. Spray 4 (6-ounce) ramekins with nonstick cooking spray and place on baking sheet.

2. Toast almonds in small skillet over medium-high heat 3 minutes, stirring frequently. Remove from heat; cool slightly.

3. Place almonds in work bowl of food processor. Process using on/off pulsing action until almonds are coarsely chopped. Add the powdered sugar and process until blended. Add the flour, granulated sugar and salt. Process to blend. Add the butter gradually, processing until just blended.

4. Combine milk, eggs and vanilla in small bowl. With the food processor running, slowly add milk mixture. Carefully, remove the blade from processor and fold in cherries.

5. Divide batter among the ramekins; bake about 50 minutes or until the tops and sides are puffy and golden. Let cool 5 to 10 minutes. Serve warm in ramekins.

Makes 4 servings

Note: Clafouti is a traditional French dessert made by topping a layer of fresh fruit with a sweet batter. The result is a rich dessert with a cake-like topping and a pudding-like center.

Rustic Cranberry-Pear Galette

4 tablespoons sugar, divided
1 tablespoon plus 1 teaspoon cornstarch
2 teaspoons ground cinnamon or apple pie spice
4 cups thinly sliced peeled Bartlett pears
¼ cup dried cranberries
1 teaspoon vanilla
¼ teaspoon almond extract (optional)
1 refrigerated pie crust, at room temperature
1 egg white
1 tablespoon water

continued on page 330

Cherry-Almond Clafouti

Rustic Cranberry-Pear Galette, continued

1. Preheat oven to 450°F. Coat baking sheet with nonstick cooking spray.

2. Reserve 1 teaspoon sugar. Combine remaining sugar, cornstarch and cinnamon in medium bowl; blend well. Add pears, cranberries, vanilla and almond extract, if desired; toss to coat.

3. Unfold pie crust and place on prepared baking sheet. Spoon pear mixture into center of crust to within 2 inches of edge. Fold edge of crust 2 inches over pear mixture; crimp slightly.

4. Whisk egg white and water in small bowl until well blended. Brush outer edge of pie crust with egg white mixture; sprinkle with reserved 1 teaspoon sugar.

5. Bake 25 minutes or until pears are tender and crust is golden brown. If edge browns too quickly, cover with foil after 15 minutes of baking. Cool on wire rack 30 minutes.

Makes 8 servings

Black Forest Bread Pudding

½ cup dried cherries
¼ cup Kirsch (cherry-flavored liqueur)
5 ounces stale challah, Italian or French bread, cut into 1-inch cubes
2 cups milk
3 ounces bittersweet chocolate
3 egg yolks
1 egg
½ cup sugar
½ teaspoon cornstarch
½ teaspoon vanilla
¼ teaspoon salt
   Whipped topping or vanilla ice cream (optional)

1. Combine dried cherries and Kirsch in small bowl. Cover; let soak 4 hours or until cherries absorb liqueur.

2. Preheat oven to 350°F. Spray 8-inch glass baking dish with nonstick spray. Place bread and cherries with liquid in large bowl.

3. Heat milk and chocolate in medium saucepan over medium-low heat, stirring often, until chocolate is melted. Whisk yolks, egg, sugar, cornstarch, vanilla and salt in medium bowl. Slowly pour the chocolate mixture into egg mixture, whisking constantly. Return to heat about 10 minutes, stirring frequently, until mixture coats the back of metal spoon. Remove from heat.

4. Pour mixture over bread and cherries; let stand 4 minutes. Stir bread and chocolate mixture together and spread into prepared dish. Place dish in large shallow roasting pan; fill with hot tap water until water comes ⅓ of the way up the side of dish.

5. Bake 45 minutes or until set. Serve immediately with whipped topping or ice cream, if desired.

Makes 8 servings

Black Forest Bread Pudding

Banana-Chocolate Bread Pudding with Cream Sauce

BREAD PUDDING
    1 (1-pound) loaf cinnamon-swirl bread, cut into 1-inch cubes
    2 packages (4-serving size) chocolate pudding mix (not instant)
3½ cups milk
    ½ cup (1 stick) unsalted butter, melted
    2 bananas, cut into ½-inch slices

CREAM SAUCE
    1 cup crème fraîche
    ¼ cup whipping cream
    2 tablespoons powdered sugar

GARNISH
    Powdered sugar
    16 strawberries, sliced

1. Preheat oven to 400°F. Spread bread cubes on large baking sheet; toast in oven 5 to 10 minutes or until light brown. Set aside to cool.

2. *Reduce oven temperature to 350°F.* Spray 8 (1-cup) ramekins with nonstick cooking spray.

3. For bread pudding, combine pudding mix and milk in large bowl; mix until smooth. Stir in butter. Add bread cubes and toss gently. Let mixture stand 10 to 15 minutes to allow bread to absorb liquid, stirring gently every few minutes to coat bread completely. Stir in sliced bananas. Divide mixture among prepared ramekins. Transfer to baking sheet; bake 45 to 50 minutes. Remove from oven and let cool slightly.

4. For cream sauce, whisk together crème fraîche, powdered sugar and whipping cream.

5. To serve, dust plate with powdered sugar. Unmold individual pudding and place right side up on each plate. Top with cream sauce and sliced strawberries. *Makes 8 servings*

Note: Crème fraîche is made from heavy cream which is allowed to ferment with a special culture. Crème fraîche is similar to sour cream, but has a unique, slightly sour taste. If you're unable to locate crème fraîche at your supermarket, you can substitute sour cream. To make enough for this recipe, whisk ½ cup of chilled sour cream until it has doubled in volume and thickened slightly.

Banana-Chocolate Bread Pudding with Cream Sauce

Black Cherry and Cheesecake Puff Pastries

2 frozen puff pastry shells
1 cup frozen dark cherries, thawed, juice reserved
2 tablespoons red wine or water
1 tablespoon granulated sugar
1 teaspoon cornstarch
½ teaspoon vanilla, divided
⅛ teaspoon almond extract
1 package (3 ounces) cream cheese, softened
2 tablespoons whole milk
3 tablespoons powdered sugar

1. Preheat oven to 400°F. Spray baking sheet with nonstick cooking spray.

2. Place frozen puff pastry shells on prepared baking sheet. Bake 22 to 27 minutes or until golden brown and puffed. Cool completely. Use fork to remove center of pastry. Reserve round piece to use for garnish, if desired.

3. Meanwhile, combine cherry juice, wine, granulated sugar and cornstarch in small saucepan; whisk until smooth. Bring to boil over medium heat; boil 1 minute, stirring constantly. Add cherries; stir gently to coat cherries. Cook 30 seconds, stirring constantly. Remove from heat; add ¼ teaspoon vanilla and almond extract. Cool completely.

4. Beat cream cheese, milk and powdered sugar in small bowl with electric mixer at low speed until smooth. Add remaining ¼ teaspoon vanilla; beat until well blended.

5. Spoon equal amounts of cream cheese mixture onto bottom of shells and top with black cherries.   *Makes 2 servings*

Black Cherry and Cheesecake Puff Pastry

Mini Strawberry Shortcakes

STRAWBERRY FILLING
    4 cups fresh strawberries, sliced
    1 tablespoon granulated sugar

SHORTCAKES
    1¾ cups all-purpose flour
    2 tablespoons plus 2 teaspoons granulated sugar
    1 tablespoon baking powder
    ½ teaspoon salt
    ⅔ cup fat-free (skim) milk
    ¼ cup vegetable oil

TOPPING
    1 cup vanilla-flavored yogurt
    3 tablespoons packed light brown sugar

1. To prepare filling, combine strawberries and 1 tablespoon granulated sugar in medium bowl. Refrigerate until ready to use.

2. To prepare shortcakes, preheat oven to 425°F.

3. Combine flour, 2 tablespoons plus 2 teaspoons granulated sugar, baking powder and salt in medium bowl. Combine milk and oil in small bowl; add to flour mixture. Stir with fork until mixture forms dough.

4. Turn dough out onto floured work surface; shape into ½-inch-thick disk. Cut out 8 dough circles with floured 2½-inch cookie cutter. Piece together dough scraps, as necessary, to complete circles.

5. Place dough circles on ungreased baking sheet. Bake 10 to 12 minutes or until golden brown. Remove pan from oven; cool completely on wire rack.

6. To prepare topping, combine yogurt and brown sugar in medium bowl. Stir until smooth.

7. Split biscuit in half horizontally. Place about ¼ cup strawberry filling on bottom layer of each biscuit. Cover with biscuit top. Drizzle topping over shortcakes. Garnish with remaining strawberries, if desired.

Makes 8 servings

Fresh Berry Pizza

Ginger Cookie Crust (recipe follows)
1½ cups ricotta cheese
3 tablespoons sugar
1 tablespoon lemon juice
2 teaspoons grated lemon peel
1 pint fresh raspberries
½ pint fresh blueberries

1. Prepare Ginger Cookie Crust; cool completely.

2. Combine cheese, sugar, lemon juice and lemon peel in medium bowl. Stir until smooth. Spread evenly over crust. Arrange raspberries and blueberries on top. Serve immediately or cover and refrigerate up to 6 hours. Remove side of tart pan. Cut into 8 wedges. Garnish as desired.

Makes 8 servings

Ginger Cookie Crust

35 vanilla wafers
20 gingersnaps
1 egg white, lightly beaten

1. Preheat oven to 375°F. Spray 11-inch tart pan with removable bottom with nonstick cooking spray. Combine vanilla wafers and gingersnaps in food processor; process until coarse crumbs form. Transfer to medium bowl. Stir egg white into crumbs until evenly mixed.

2. Press crumb mixture evenly onto bottom and up side of prepared pan. Bake on center rack in oven 8 to 10 minutes or until firm and lightly browned. Cool in pan.

Makes 1 (11-inch) crust

helpful hint:

A tart pan has a shallow fluted side and a removable bottom. Although round is the most common shape, tart pans are also available in square and rectangular shapes. Typically made of black steel, they range in size from 8 to 12 inches in diameter and 1 to 2 inches deep. Tartlet pans, or miniature tart pans, also have fluted sides and are available in a variety of shapes.

Nectarine-Blueberry Crisp

3 cups cubed unpeeled nectarines
2 cups fresh blueberries
2 tablespoons granulated sugar
1 tablespoon cornstarch
½ teaspoon ground cinnamon
¼ cup all-purpose flour
¼ cup uncooked quick oats
¼ cup chopped walnuts
3 tablespoons packed dark brown sugar
2 tablespoons toasted wheat germ
2 tablespoons butter, melted
¼ teaspoon ground nutmeg

1. Preheat oven to 400°F. Spray bottom and side of 9-inch round or square baking pan with nonstick cooking spray.

2. Combine nectarines, blueberries, granulated sugar, cornstarch and cinnamon in medium bowl. Transfer to prepared pan; bake 15 minutes.

3. Meanwhile, combine remaining ingredients in small bowl, stirring with fork until crumbly. Remove fruit mixture from oven; sprinkle with topping. Bake 20 minutes longer or until fruit is bubbly and topping is lightly browned. Serve warm.　　*Makes 6 servings*

Raspberry Napoleons

¼ package (18 ounces) refrigerated sugar cookie dough
1 container (8 ounces) whipped cream cheese
½ cup sifted powdered sugar, divided
2 tablespoons orange-flavored liqueur or brandy, divided
2 cups fresh or frozen blueberries, thawed
2 cups fresh raspberries or sliced strawberries

1. On floured surface, roll cookie dough to ¼-inch-thickness. Cut out 4 (3-inch) cookies using desired shaped cookie cutter; place on nonstick baking sheet. Cut out 1- to 2-inch cookies using desired shaped cookie cutter with remaining dough scraps. Bake according to package directions.

2. Beat cream cheese, ¼ cup sugar and 1 tablespoon liqueur until smooth; set aside.

3. Combine blueberries, remaining ¼ cup sugar and remaining 1 tablespoon liqueur in food processor or blender; process until smooth. Pour mixture through fine-meshed sieve, discarding solids.

4. Place large cookies on serving plates; spoon cream cheese mixture over top. Arrange smaller cookies and raspberries on top. Spoon blueberry sauce around Napoleons.

Makes 4 servings

Prep and Cook Time: 25 minutes

Nectarine-Blueberry Crisp

Rustic Peach-Oat Crumble

4 cups frozen sliced peaches, thawed and juice reserved
¼ cup packed dark brown sugar
1 tablespoon cornstarch
1 to 2 tablespoons water
1 tablespoon lemon juice (optional)
1 teaspoon vanilla
¼ teaspoon almond extract
½ cup uncooked quick oats
2 tablespoons all-purpose flour
2 tablespoons sugar substitute*
½ to ¾ teaspoon ground cinnamon
⅛ teaspoon salt
¼ cup (½ stick) cold butter, cut into small pieces
Whipped topping (optional)

This recipe was tested with sucralose-based sugar substitute.

1. Preheat oven to 375°F. Spray 9-inch pie plate with nonstick cooking spray; set aside.

2. Combine peaches with juice, brown sugar, cornstarch, water, lemon juice, if desired, vanilla and almond extract in medium bowl. Stir until cornstarch is smooth. Transfer to prepared pie plate.

3. Combine oats, flour, sugar substitute, cinnamon and salt in medium bowl. Cut in butter with pastry blender or two knives until mixture resembles coarse crumbs. Sprinkle over peaches.

4. Bake 25 minutes or until bubbly at edges. Cool 20 minutes on wire rack. Top each serving with dollop of whipped topping, if desired.   *Makes 8 servings*

Prep Time: 13 minutes | **Bake Time:** 25 minutes

Rustic Peach-Oat Crumble

Blueberry Streusel Cobbler

1 pint fresh or frozen blueberries
1 (14-ounce) can EAGLE BRAND® Sweetened Condensed Milk (NOT evaporated milk)
2 teaspoons grated lemon peel
¾ cup (1½ sticks) plus 2 tablespoons cold butter or margarine, divided
2 cups biscuit baking mix, divided
½ cup firmly packed light brown sugar
½ cup chopped nuts
 Vanilla ice cream
 Blueberry Sauce (recipe follows)

1. Preheat oven to 325°F. In medium bowl, combine blueberries, EAGLE BRAND® and lemon peel.

2. In large bowl, cut ¾ cup butter into 1½ cups biscuit mix until crumbly; add blueberry mixture. Spread in greased 9-inch square baking pan.

3. In small bowl, combine remaining ½ cup biscuit mix and brown sugar; cut in remaining 2 tablespoons butter until crumbly. Add nuts. Sprinkle over cobbler.

4. Bake 1 hour and 10 minutes or until golden. Serve warm with vanilla ice cream and Blueberry Sauce. Store leftovers covered in refrigerator. *Makes 8 to 12 servings*

Blueberry Sauce: In large saucepan over medium heat, combine ½ cup sugar, 1 tablespoon cornstarch, ½ teaspoon ground cinnamon and ¼ teaspoon ground nutmeg. Gradually add ½ cup water. Cook and stir until thickened. Stir in 1 pint blueberries; cook and stir until hot. Makes about 1⅔ cups sauce.

Prep Time: 15 minutes │ **Bake Time:** 1 hour and 10 minutes

helpful hint:

Cobblers are popular American fruit-based desserts. Baked in a casserole or baking dish, they are similar to deep-dish pies, but have a rich, thick biscuit topping. Fresh fruit filling is placed in a baking dish and a soft biscuit dough is spooned on top of the filling before baking. The dough should not be smoothed but left bumpy and rough, or "cobbled." Cobblers are often served warm with vanilla ice cream or whipped cream.

Blueberry Streusel Cobbler

Year-Round Holiday Treats

Cornucopia Crunchers

5 tablespoons unsalted butter
½ cup packed dark brown sugar
1 egg
¼ cup all-purpose flour
Dash salt
½ teaspoon vanilla
⅓ cup finely chopped dry roasted macadamia nuts
Candy corn or other Halloween candies

1. Preheat oven to 375°F. Grease cookie sheets. Beat butter and sugar with electric mixer on medium-high speed until light and fluffy. Add egg, flour, salt and vanilla. Stir in nuts.

2. Drop batter by rounded tablespoonfuls onto prepared cookie sheets. Arrange no more than 6 cookies per sheet, flattening to 2-inch discs. (Cookies will spread to about 6 inches and become very lacy while baking.)

3. Bake 6 to 9 minutes or until cookies are caramel-colored and firm. *Do not overbake.*

4. Cool 1 minute. Working quickly with spatula, ease 1 cookie at a time from cookie sheet. Keeping top of cookie on the outside, form into cornucopia shape by hand, or by partially wrapping around the handle of wooden spoon. Place cornucopia seam side down on plate to harden. Repeat with remaining cookies. Cookies will firm as they cool, so return them to oven for about 30 seconds to make them more pliable.

5. To serve, arrange on tray. If desired, fill with candy or other treats. Cornucopias may also be used as place cards; insert name tags into each cookie.   *Makes 16 cookies*

Helpful Hints: For best results, use insulated light-colored cookie sheets. Thoroughly cool cookie sheets between batches.

Golden Eggnog Holiday Braid

2 tablespoons warm water (105° to 115°F)
2 tablespoons sugar
1 package (¼ ounce) active dry yeast
2½ cups all-purpose flour
2 tablespoons butter or margarine, cut into 2 pieces
1 teaspoon salt
¼ teaspoon ground nutmeg
½ to ¾ cup dairy eggnog, at room temperature
Vegetable oil
Dairy eggnog
Sliced almonds

1. Combine warm water, sugar and yeast in small bowl. Stir to dissolve yeast and let stand until bubbly, about 5 minutes.

2. Fit food processor with steel blade. Measure flour, butter, salt and nutmeg into work bowl. Process until mixed, about 15 seconds. Add yeast mixture; process until blended, about 10 seconds.

3. Turn on processor and very slowly pour just enough eggnog through feed tube until dough forms a ball that cleans side of bowl. Process until ball turns around bowl about 25 times. Turn off processor and let dough stand 1 to 2 minutes.

4. Turn on processor and gradually pour in enough remaining eggnog to make dough smooth and satiny but not sticky. Process until dough turns around bowl about 15 times.

5. Let dough stand in work bowl 10 minutes. Turn dough onto lightly floured surface and shape into ball. Place in lightly greased bowl, turning to grease top. Cover loosely with plastic wrap and let stand in warm place (85°F) until doubled, about 1 hour.

6. Punch down dough. Let stand 10 minutes. Divide into 3 equal parts. Shape each part into strand 20 inches long. Braid strands together; tuck ends under and pinch to seal. Place on greased baking sheet. Brush top of bread with oil and let stand in warm place until doubled, about 45 minutes.

7. Preheat oven to 375°F. Brush braid with eggnog and sprinkle with almonds. Bake until golden, 25 to 30 minutes. Remove braid from baking sheet. Cool on wire rack.

Makes 1 loaf

Golden Eggnog Holiday Braid

Trick or Treat Ice Cream Sandwiches

2½ cups all-purpose flour
1½ teaspoons baking soda
1 teaspoon ground cinnamon
½ teaspoon salt
½ cup (1 stick) butter or margarine, softened
¾ cup granulated sugar
¾ cup packed light brown sugar
3 egg whites
1 teaspoon vanilla
1 package (6 ounces) semisweet chocolate chips
1½ cups orange sherbet or any flavor frozen yogurt or ice cream, slightly softened

1. Preheat oven to 350°F. Spray cookie sheets with nonstick cooking spray; set aside. Combine flour, baking soda, cinnamon and salt in medium bowl.

2. Beat butter in large bowl with electric mixer at medium speed until creamy. Add sugars; beat until fluffy. Blend in egg whites and vanilla. Add flour mixture; mix until well blended. Stir in chocolate chips.

3. Drop dough by heaping teaspoonfuls onto prepared cookie sheets, making 48 cookies. Bake 10 to 12 minutes or until cookies are lightly browned. Remove to wire racks to cool completely.

4. For each sandwich, place 1 tablespoon sherbet on flat side of 1 cookie; top with second cookie, flat side down. Press cookies together gently to even out sherbet layer. Repeat with remaining cookies and sherbet. Wrap tightly and store in freezer.

Makes 2 dozen sandwich cookies

Goblin Ice Cream Sandwiches: Prepare and freeze cookie sandwiches as directed. Just before serving, decorate 1 side of sandwich with Halloween candies or decorating gel to resemble goblin faces.

Colossal Cookie Sandwich: Prepare dough as directed. Substitute 2 lightly greased foil-lined 12-inch pizza pans for cookie sheets. Substitute 1 quart (4 cups) frozen yogurt or ice cream for 1½ cups orange sherbet. Prepare cookie dough as directed; divide evenly in half. Spread each half evenly onto bottom of prepared pizza pan to within ½ inch of edge. Bake 10 to 15 minutes or until cookies are lightly browned. Cool cookies in pans just until cookies begin to firm; slide off pans onto wire racks to cool completely. Spoon yogurt onto flat side of 1 cookie. Top with remaining cookie, flat side down. Wrap tightly and freeze until yogurt is firm, about 6 hours. Cut into wedges to serve. Makes 24 servings.

Sharing Cookies: Prepare dough as directed. Omit sherbet. Bake cookies on pizza pans as directed for Colossal Cookie Sandwich; cool completely. Serve cookies whole on large platters, allowing each person to break off their own piece. Makes 24 servings.

Trick or Treat Ice Cream Sandwiches

Uncle Sam's Hat

1 package (18 ounces) refrigerated chocolate chip cookie dough
2 cups powdered sugar
2 to 4 tablespoons milk
Red and blue food colorings

1. Let cookie dough stand at room temperature about 15 minutes. Preheat oven to 350°F. Lightly grease 12-inch round pizza pan and one cookie sheet. Remove dough from wrapper. Press dough evenly onto prepared pizza pan. Cut dough into hat shape as shown in photo. Press scraps together and flatten heaping tablespoons of dough onto prepared cookie sheet. Using 1½- to 2-inch star cookie cutter, cut out 3 stars; remove and discard dough scraps.

2. Bake stars 5 to 7 minutes and hat 7 to 9 minutes or until lightly browned at edges. Cool stars on cookie sheet 1 minute. Remove stars to wire rack; cool completely. Cool hat completely in pan on rack.

3. Combine powdered sugar and enough milk, 1 tablespoon at a time, to make medium-thick pourable glaze. Spread small amount of glaze over stars and place on waxed paper; let stand until glaze is set. Using red and blue food colorings, tint half of glaze red, tint one fourth of glaze blue and leave remaining one fourth of glaze white.

4. Decorate hat with red, white and blue glazes as shown in photo; arrange stars on blue band of hat. Let stand until glaze is set.

Makes 1 large cookie

Sweetheart Cheesecake

1¼ cups chocolate cookie crumbs
¼ cup (½ stick) butter, melted
2 packages (8 ounces each) cream cheese, softened
½ cup plus 1 tablespoon sugar, divided
1 teaspoon vanilla, divided
2 eggs
1 cup sour cream
1 can (21 ounces) cherry pie filling

1. Preheat oven to 350°F.

2. For crust, combine cookie crumbs and butter until well blended. Press mixture onto bottom of 9-inch springform pan. Bake 8 minutes; cool.

3. For filling, beat cream cheese, ½ cup sugar and ½ teaspoon vanilla in medium bowl with electric mixer at medium speed until well blended. Beat in eggs. Pour into cooled crust; bake about 40 minutes or until center is almost set. Cool completely.

4. For topping, combine sour cream, remaining 1 teaspoon sugar and remaining ½ teaspoon vanilla in small bowl. Spread evenly over top of cheesecake. Drop teaspoonfuls of sauce from cherry pie filling onto sour cream topping; carefully pull tip of knife or wooden skewer through cherry sauce to form hearts. Cover and refrigerate 3 hours or overnight. Serve remaining cherry pie filling with slices of cheesecake.

Makes 10 servings

Uncle Sam's Hat

Dutch Easter Bread

½ cup milk
¼ cup water
2 tablespoons butter or margarine
1 large egg, beaten
2½ to 2¾ cups all-purpose flour
2 tablespoons sugar
1 package (¼ ounce) active dry yeast
1 teaspoon salt
½ cup dark raisins
½ cup currants
¼ cup chopped citron or mixed candied fruits
Vegetable oil
Sugar Icing (recipe follows)

1. Combine milk, water and butter in small saucepan over low heat until mixture reaches 120° to 130°F. Blend egg into milk mixture.

2. Combine 1 cup flour, sugar, yeast and salt into work bowl of food processor. Process until mixed, about 5 seconds. Turn on processor and add milk mixture through feed tube. Process until smooth, about 30 seconds.

3. Turn on processor and add enough of the remaining flour through feed tube so dough forms a ball that cleans the sides of the bowl. Process until ball turns around bowl about 25 times. Dough should be soft, smooth and satiny but not sticky.

4. Cover processor and let dough stand in work bowl at room temperature until almost doubled, 1 to 1¼ hours. Uncover processor. Sprinkle raisins, currants and citron over dough. Process on/off 3 or 4 times to mix fruit into dough.

5. Shape dough into loaf and place in greased 9×5-inch loaf pan. Brush with oil and let stand in warm place (85°F) until almost doubled, 45 to 50 minutes.

6. Preheat oven to 375°F. Bake 25 to 30 minutes or until golden and loaf sounds hollow when tapped.

7. Prepare Sugar Icing while bread is baking. Remove loaf immediately from pan. Spread Sugar Icing over top crust. Cool on wire rack. *Makes 1 loaf*

Sugar Icing

1 cup powdered sugar
1 tablespoon butter, softened
2 to 3 tablespoons milk

Mix sugar, butter and enough milk to make smooth, spreadable icing.

Candy Cane Biscotti

1 cup sugar
½ cup (1 stick) butter, softened
2 tablespoons water
1 teaspoon peppermint extract
2 eggs
3½ cups all-purpose flour
1 cup finely crushed peppermint candy canes, divided
½ cup slivered almonds, toasted*
1 teaspoon baking powder
½ teaspoon salt
4 squares (1 ounce each) white chocolate, melted

To toast nuts, spread nuts in single layer on baking sheet and toast in preheated 350°F oven 8 to 10 minutes or until very lightly browned.

1. Preheat oven to 350°F. Line 2 cookie sheets with parchment paper.

2. Combine sugar, butter, water, peppermint extract and eggs in large bowl. Beat with electric mixer on medium speed until well blended. Add flour, ½ cup crushed candy canes, almonds, baking powder and salt. Beat on low speed until just blended.

3. Divide dough in half. Shape each half into 10×3-inch log; place each log on separate prepared cookie sheet. Bake 30 minutes or until center is firm to the touch. Let cool 15 to 20 minutes.

4. Using a serrated knife, cut logs diagonally into ½-inch slices. Place slices, cut sides down, on cookie sheets. Bake 15 minutes; turn and bake 12 to 15 minutes longer or until edges are browned. Cool completely on wire racks.

5. Dip each cookie halfway in melted white chocolate. Sprinkle each cookie with remaining ½ cup crushed candy canes. Store in tightly covered container.   *Makes 40 cookies*

Spicy Pumpkin Roll

3 eggs
1 cup granulated sugar
⅔ cup mashed cooked pumpkin or canned pumpkin
1 teaspoon WATKINS® Vanilla
¾ cup all-purpose flour
2 teaspoons WATKINS® Pumpkin Pie Spice
1 teaspoon WATKINS® Baking Powder
¼ teaspoon salt
1 cup chopped pecans
1 cup plus 3 to 4 tablespoons sifted powdered sugar, divided
1 package (8 ounces) cream cheese, softened
2 tablespoons butter or margarine, softened
½ teaspoon WATKINS® Butter Pecan Extract
   Sweetened whipped topping flavored with WATKINS® Vanilla for garnish
   Whole or chopped pecans for garnish

Preheat oven to 375°F. Grease 15×10-inch jelly-roll pan; line with waxed paper. Grease and flour waxed paper. Beat eggs in large bowl with electric mixer at high speed until thick; gradually add granulated sugar and beat for 5 minutes. Stir in pumpkin and vanilla. Combine flour, pumpkin pie spice, baking powder and salt; gradually stir into pumpkin mixture until well blended. Spread batter into prepared pan; sprinkle with pecans. Bake for 12 to 15 minutes or until toothpick inserted into center comes out clean.

Sift 3 to 4 tablespoons powdered sugar into 15×12-inch rectangle on clean cloth or dish towel. Loosen cake from pan; immediately invert hot cake onto towel. Carefully peel off waxed paper and discard. Starting from narrow side, roll up cake with towel jelly-roll fashion. Cool cake completely, seam side down, on wire rack.

Beat cream cheese and butter in large bowl with electric mixer at high speed until fluffy. Gradually add 1 cup powdered sugar and butter pecan extract; beat until well blended. Unroll cake; spread with cream cheese filling and carefully re-roll. Place cake on serving plate, seam side down. Garnish or frost with whipped topping and pecans.

Makes 10 servings

Spicy Pumpkin Roll

Ginger Shortbread Delights

    1 cup (2 sticks) unsalted butter, softened
    ½ cup powdered sugar
    ⅓ cup packed light brown sugar
    ½ teaspoon salt
    2 cups minus 2 tablespoons all-purpose flour
    4 ounces crystallized ginger
       Bittersweet Glaze (recipe follows)

1. Preheat oven to 300°F.

2. Beat butter, sugars and salt in large bowl with electric mixer at medium speed until creamy. Gradually add flour, beating until well blended.

3. Shape dough by tablespoons into balls. Place 1 inch apart on ungreased cookie sheets; flatten to ½-inch thickness. Cut ginger into ¼-inch-thick slices. Place 1 slice ginger on top of each cookie.

4. Bake 15 to 20 minutes or until set and lightly browned. Cool 5 minutes on cookie sheets. Remove to wire racks to cool completely.

5. Prepare Bittersweet Glaze; drizzle over cookies. Let stand until glaze is set.

Makes about 3½ dozen cookies

Bittersweet Glaze

    1 bar (3 to 3½ ounces) bittersweet chocolate, broken into small pieces
    2 tablespoons unsalted butter
    2 tablespoons whipping cream
    1 tablespoon powdered sugar
    ⅛ teaspoon salt

Melt chocolate and butter in top of double boiler over hot, not boiling, water. Remove from heat. Add cream, powdered sugar and salt; stir until smooth.

helpful hint:

Fans of ginger will love the flavor of these cookies. But they're just as flavorful without the crystallized ginger. For another option, before baking, place a pecan or walnut half in the center of each dough ball, or roll them in chopped almonds, hazelnuts or macadamia nuts.

Ginger Shortbread Delights

Citrus Easter Chicks

1 package (18 ounces) refrigerated sugar cookie dough
⅓ cup all-purpose flour
1½ to 2 teaspoons lemon extract
    All-purpose flour
    Lemon Cookie Glaze (recipe follows)
2 cups shredded coconut, tinted yellow*
    Assorted candies and decors

*To tint coconut, combine small amount of food coloring (paste or liquid) with 1 teaspoon water in large bowl. Add coconut and stir until evenly coated. Add more food coloring, if needed.

1. Let dough stand at room temperature about 15 minutes. Preheat oven to 350°F.

2. Place dough, flour and lemon extract in large bowl; beat with electric mixer at medium speed until well blended. Divide dough in half. Wrap each half in plastic wrap; flatten into 2 disks. Refrigerate 30 minutes.

3. Using floured rolling pin, roll one disk of dough on lightly floured surface to ¼-inch thickness. Cut dough with 2- to 3-inch chick cookie cutters. Place cutouts 2 inches apart on ungreased cookie sheets. Repeat with remaining half of dough.

4. Bake 7 to 9 minutes or until firm but not browned. Cool on cookie sheets 5 minutes; remove to wire racks to cool completely.

5. Place wire racks over waxed paper. Prepare Lemon Cookie Glaze; spread over tops of cookies; sprinkle with yellow coconut. Decorate chicks with candies and decors as shown in photo. Let stand about 40 minutes or until completely set.

Makes about 1½ dozen cookies

Lemon Cookie Glaze

4 cups powdered sugar
¾ teaspoon lemon extract
4 to 6 tablespoons milk
    Yellow food coloring

1. Combine powdered sugar, lemon extract and enough milk, one tablespoon at a time, to make medium-thick pourable glaze.

2. Tint glaze yellow with food coloring, a few drops at a time, until desired color is reached.

Citrus Easter Chicks

Pink Peppermint Meringues

  3 egg whites
⅛ teaspoon peppermint extract
  5 drops red food coloring
½ cup superfine sugar*
  6 finely crushed peppermint candies

Or, ½ cup granulated sugar processed in food processor 1 minute until very fine.

1. Preheat oven to 200°F. Line 2 cookie sheets with parchment paper; set aside.

2. Beat egg whites in medium bowl with electric mixer at medium-high speed about 45 seconds or until frothy. Add peppermint extract and food coloring.

3. Add sugar, 1 tablespoon at a time, while mixer is beating. Continue beating until egg whites are stiff and glossy.

4. Use teaspoon to mound 1-inch meringues on prepared cookie sheets. Sprinkle crushed peppermint candies evenly over meringues.

5. Bake 2 hours or until meringues are dry when tapped. Transfer parchment paper with meringues to wire racks to allow meringues to cool completely. When cool, peel meringues off parchment and store in airtight container. *Makes about 74 meringues*

Teeny Tiny Witches' Hats

1½ cups all-purpose flour
  ½ teaspoon baking powder
  ⅛ teaspoon salt
  ½ cup (1 stick) butter, softened
  ⅔ cup powdered sugar
    1 egg
  ½ teaspoon vanilla
    2 squares (1 ounce each) semisweet chocolate, melted
  36 milk chocolate candy kisses

1. Preheat oven to 350°F. Lightly grease cookie sheets.

2. Combine flour, baking powder and salt in medium bowl. Beat butter and powdered sugar in large bowl; beat with electric mixer at medium speed until well blended. Add egg and vanilla; beat until blended. Stir in melted chocolate until blended. Gradually fold in flour mixture until well combined.

3. Shape dough into 36 balls; place 2 inches apart on prepared cookie sheets. Flatten each ball to ¼-inch thickness; press chocolate candy into center. Bake 6 to 7 minutes or until cookies are set. Cool completely on wire rack. *Makes 3 dozen cookies*

Pink Peppermint Meringues

Christmas Cookie Tree

2 packages (18 ounces each) refrigerated sugar cookie dough
2 to 3 tubes (4¼ ounces) green decorator icing with tips
1 tube (4¼ ounces) yellow decorator icing
1 tube (4¼ ounces) red decorator icing

1. Preheat oven to 350°F.

2. Cut parchment baking paper to fit two large cookie sheets. Tape two large sheets of parchment to work surface with masking tape. Unwrap one package of cold dough and roll out to ¼-inch thickness on parchment. Flour rolling pin as necessary to keep dough from sticking. With small sharp knife, cut out one 7-inch circle* and one 6½-inch circle. Untape parchment and transfer circles to cookie sheet. Wrap remaining dough in plastic wrap and return to refrigerator.

3. Unwrap second roll of cold dough and repeat process, cutting out 6-inch circle and 5½-inch circle. Transfer to second cookie sheet and bake both sheets 10 to 14 minutes, checking for doneness after 10 minutes. Cookies should be light golden brown. Remove from oven; cool 2 to 3 minutes until firm, then slide parchment paper and cookies onto racks. Cool completely before removing from parchment.

4. Continue repeating steps, making 8 more circles, each ½ inch smaller in diameter. Reduce baking time as circles get smaller.

5. To assemble tree, secure largest cookie to serving platter with dab of frosting. Using leaf tip and green icing, pipe leaves around outer edge of cookie. Place large dab of frosting in center of cookie. Add next biggest cookie and repeat. Continue adding cookies, largest to smallest.

6. With small plain tip, pipe yellow garlands around tree. Use red frosting to add "ornaments." Pipe additional decorations, if desired.

7. Serve cookies individually by separating layers or cut into pieces using serrated knife.

Makes 6 to 8 servings

*Use a compass to draw 12 circles, each one ½ inch smaller, on parchment paper; cut out and use as patterns to cut dough circles. For a "free-form" look, use various bowls, glasses, and biscuit cutters to trace and cut out 12 graduated circles.

Christmas Cookie Tree

Old-Fashioned Pumpkin Pie

    1 cup sugar
    1 tablespoon all-purpose flour
    1 tablespoon WATKINS® Pumpkin Pie Spice
    ½ teaspoon salt
    3 large eggs
 1½ cups mashed cooked pumpkin or canned pumpkin
    1 cup evaporated milk
    1 unbaked 9-inch pie crust
      Vanilla Whipped Cream (optional)

Preheat oven to 400°F. Combine sugar, flour, pumpkin pie spice and salt in large bowl; beat in eggs until well blended. Stir in pumpkin and milk until smooth. Pour into pie crust. Bake for 50 minutes or until knife inserted into center comes out clean. Serve with Vanilla Whipped Cream, if desired. *Makes 10 servings*

Little Christmas Pizzas

    ⅓ cup olive oil
    1 tablespoon TABASCO® brand Pepper Sauce
    2 large cloves garlic, minced
    1 teaspoon dried rosemary, crushed
    1 (16-ounce) package hot roll mix with yeast packet
 1¼ cups hot water*
      Flour

TOPPINGS
    1 large tomato, diced
    ¼ cup crumbled goat cheese
    2 tablespoons chopped fresh parsley
    ½ cup shredded mozzarella cheese
    ½ cup pitted green olives
    ⅓ cup roasted red pepper strips
    ½ cup chopped artichoke hearts
    ½ cup cherry tomatoes, sliced into wedges
    ⅓ cup sliced green onions

Check hot roll mix package directions for temperature of water.

Combine olive oil, TABASCO® Sauce, garlic and rosemary in small bowl. Combine hot roll mix, yeast packet, hot water and 2 tablespoons TABASCO® Sauce mixture in large bowl; stir until dough pulls away from side of bowl. Turn dough onto lightly floured surface; shape dough into a ball. Knead until smooth, adding additional flour as necessary.

Preheat oven to 425°F. Cut dough into quarters; cut each quarter into 10 equal pieces. Roll each piece into a ball. On large cookie sheet, press each ball into 2-inch round. Brush each with remaining TABASCO® Sauce mixture. Arrange approximately 2 teaspoons toppings on each dough round. Bake 12 minutes or until dough is lightly browned and puffed.

Makes 40 appetizer servings

Passover Chocolate Almond-Orange Cake

½ cup sliced almonds, toasted*
7 eggs, separated
1¼ cups sugar, divided
1 tablespoon water
¼ teaspoon freshly grated orange peel
⅓ cup potato starch
¼ cup matzo cake meal
⅓ cup HERSHEY'S Cocoa
¼ teaspoon salt
Whole blanched almonds and strips of orange peel (optional garnish)
Cocoa-Orange Sauce (optional)

*To toast almonds: Heat oven to 350°F. Place almonds in single layer in shallow baking pan. Bake 7 to 8 minutes, stirring occasionally, until light brown. Cool completely.

1. Heat oven to 300°F. Place toasted almonds in bowl of food processor; process until ground. Set aside.

2. Beat egg yolks in large bowl until lemon-colored. Gradually add 1 cup sugar, beating until thick. Stir in water and orange peel. Stir together potato starch, cake meal and cocoa; fold into yolk mixture. Fold in ground almonds.

3. Beat egg whites and salt in separate large bowl until foamy. Gradually add remaining ¼ cup sugar in small amounts, beating until stiff peaks form. Gently fold about 1 cup egg white mixture into yolk mixture; fold all yolk mixture into remaining whites. Pour into ungreased 10-inch tube pan.

4. Bake 30 minutes. Without opening oven door, *increase oven temperature to 325°F.* Bake 15 minutes or until top springs back when touched lightly. Invert cake on heat-proof funnel or bottle. Cool completely. Carefully run knife along side of pan to loosen cake; remove from pan. Garnish as desired. Serve with Cocoa-Orange Sauce, if desired.

Makes 12 to 16 servings

Cocoa-Orange Sauce: Combine 1 cup sugar and ½ cup HERSHEY'S Cocoa in saucepan. Add ⅔ cup water. Cook over medium heat, stirring constantly, until mixture comes to full boil; boil, stirring occasionally, about 5 minutes. Add ¼ to ¾ teaspoon freshly grated orange peel; cook 1 minute. Cool to room temperature. Makes about 1 cup sauce.

Delectable Chocolate Wreath

½ cup milk
¼ cup water (70° to 80°F)
3 tablespoons butter or margarine, cut up
1 large egg
⅓ cup sugar
¼ cup unsweetened cocoa powder
¾ teaspoon salt
2½ cups bread or all-purpose flour
2 teaspoons FLEISCHMANN'S® Bread Machine Yeast
    White Chocolate, Raspberry and Pecan Filling (recipe follows)
    Frosting (recipe follows)

BREAD MACHINE DIRECTIONS

Add all ingredients except filling and frosting to bread machine pan in the order suggested by manufacturer. Select dough/manual cycle. When cycle is complete, remove dough to lightly floured surface. If necessary, knead in enough flour to make dough easy to handle.

Roll dough to 22×6-inch rectangle. With sharp knife, cut in half lengthwise to make two 22×3-inch strips. Spread half of White Chocolate, Raspberry and Pecan Filling down center length of each strip. Fold long sides of dough over filling; pinch seams and ends to seal. Place ropes, seam sides down, on greased large baking sheet. Twist ropes together. Form into wreath; pinch ends to seal. Cover and let rise in warm, draft-free place until risen slightly, about 1 hour.

Bake at 350°F for 35 to 40 minutes or until done. Remove from baking sheet; cool on wire rack. Drizzle with frosting. Garnish with candied fruit, if desired.   *Makes 1 wreath*

White Chocolate, Raspberry and Pecan Filling: Combine ¾ cup white chocolate morsels, ½ cup chopped toasted pecans, and 2 tablespoons seedless red raspberry jam.

Frosting: Combine 1 cup sifted powdered sugar, 1 to 2 tablespoons milk and 1 teaspoon Spice Islands® Pure Vanilla Extract. Stir until smooth.

Delectable Chocolate Wreath

Star-Of-The-East Fruit Bread

½ cup (1 stick) butter or margarine, softened
1 cup sugar
2 eggs
1 teaspoon vanilla extract
2 cups all-purpose flour
1 teaspoon baking soda
¼ teaspoon salt
1 cup mashed ripe bananas (about 3 medium)
1 can (11 ounces) mandarin orange segments, well-drained
1 cup HERSHEY'S Semi-Sweet Chocolate Chips
½ cup chopped dates or Calimyrna figs
½ cup chopped maraschino cherries, well-drained
Chocolate Drizzle (recipe follows)

1. Heat oven to 350°F. Grease two 8½×4½×2⅝-inch loaf pans.

2. Beat butter and sugar in large bowl until fluffy. Add eggs and vanilla; beat well. Stir together flour, baking soda and salt; add alternately with mashed bananas to butter mixture, blending well. Stir in orange segments, chocolate chips, dates and cherries. Divide batter evenly between prepared pans.

3. Bake 40 to 50 minutes or until golden brown. Cool; remove from pans. Drizzle tops of loaves with Chocolate Drizzle. Store tightly wrapped.   *Makes 2 loaves*

Chocolate Drizzle: Combine ½ cup HERSHEY'S Semi-Sweet Chocolate Chips and 2 tablespoons whipping cream in small microwave-safe bowl. Microwave at HIGH (100%) 30 seconds; stir. If necessary, microwave at HIGH an additional 15 seconds; stir until chips are melted and mixture is smooth when stirred. Makes about ½ cup.

Luck o' the Irish Cupcakes

1 package (18¼ ounces) cake mix (any flavor), plus ingredients
    to prepare mix
1 container (16 ounces) white frosting
1 tube (4¼ ounces) green decorating icing with tip
Green and orange sprinkles, decors and sugars

1. Preheat oven to 350°F. Line 24 standard (2½-inch) muffin pan cups with decorative paper baking cups. Prepare cake mix according to package directions. Spoon batter into prepared muffin cups, filling two-thirds full.

2. Bake 15 to 20 minutes or until toothpick inserted into centers comes out clean. Cool in pans on wire racks 10 minutes. Remove cupcakes to racks; cool completely.

3. Frost cupcakes. Use icing to pipe Irish words (Sláinte, Blarney, etc.) or shamrock designs onto cupcakes as desired. Decorate with sprinkles, decors and sugars as desired.

Makes 24 cupcakes

Star-Of-The-East Fruit Bread

Pumpkin Pecan Pie

1 can (15 ounces) solid-pack pumpkin
1 can (14 ounces) sweetened condensed milk
¼ cup (½ stick) butter, softened
2 eggs, divided
1 teaspoon ground cinnamon
1 teaspoon vanilla
½ teaspoon ground nutmeg
¼ teaspoon salt
1 (9-inch) graham cracker crust
2 tablespoons packed brown sugar
2 tablespoons dark corn syrup
1 tablespoon butter, melted
½ teaspoon maple flavoring
1 cup chopped pecans

1. Preheat oven to 400°F.

2. Combine pumpkin, condensed milk, softened butter, 1 egg, cinnamon, vanilla, nutmeg and salt in large bowl. Pour into pie crust. Bake 20 minutes.

3. Beat remaining egg, brown sugar, corn syrup, melted butter and maple flavoring in medium bowl with electric mixer at medium speed until well blended. Stir in pecans.

4. Remove pie from oven; top with pecan mixture. *Reduce oven temperature to 350°F.* Bake 25 minutes more or until toothpick inserted in center comes out clean.

Makes 8 to 10 servings

helpful hint:

Sweetened condensed milk is a canned product that is the result of evaporating about half of the water from whole milk and adding cane sugar or corn syrup to sweeten and preserve the milk. The thick milk is used for desserts and candy. It should not be confused with evaporated milk.

Pumpkin Pecan Pie

Mardi Gras King Cake

4 packages (3 ounces each) cream cheese, softened
½ cup powdered sugar
¾ teaspoon vanilla
3 tablespoons granulated sugar
1½ teaspoons ground cinnamon
¼ teaspoon ground nutmeg
   Nonstick cooking spray
2 packages (11 ounces each) refrigerated French bread dough
   Small plastic baby
1½ cups powdered sugar
3 tablespoons whole milk
   Green, yellow and purple sugar

1. Preheat oven to 350°F. Coat large baking sheet with nonstick cooking spray.

2. For filling, beat cream cheese, powdered sugar and vanilla in medium bowl with electric mixer at low speed until smooth.

3. Combine sugar, cinnamon and nutmeg in small bowl.

4. Lightly coat plastic cutting board or work surface with nonstick cooking spray. Unroll 1 package refrigerated dough onto work surface. Unroll second package alongside first, overlapping slightly to make one long piece. Press along seam to seal well. Sprinkle dough evenly with cinnamon mixture. Spread cream cheese mixture lengthwise on dough, leaving 1 inch along edge uncovered. Roll up dough lengthwise, starting with cream cheese side, pinching along seam to seal in filling. Place dough on prepared baking sheet and gently twist. Attach ends of dough pieces to form large twisted circle (to resemble crown); pinch tightly to seal ends together. Insert plastic baby* inside dough.

5. Bake 25 to 35 minutes or until golden. Do not overbake. Remove from oven, place baking sheet on cooling rack and cool completely. If filling has leaked, trim away excess while still warm.

6. For icing, combine powdered sugar and milk in small bowl; stir until smooth. Drizzle icing evenly onto coffeecake. Sprinkle with colored sugars, alternating colors to make 3 sections of 3 colors each. Let coffeecake stand at least 1 hour to allow icing to set. Cut into 2- to 3-inch pieces to serve. *Makes 16 servings*

Be sure everyone knows there's a plastic baby in the cake. Mardi Gras tradition says the person who finds the baby is king for the day. However, that person also has to provide the next king cake.

Acknowledgments

The publisher would like to thank the companies listed below for the use of their recipes and photographs in this publication.

ACH Food Companies, Inc.

Bob Evans®

California Olive Industry

Cherry Marketing Institute

Dole Food Company, Inc.

Duncan Hines® and Moist Deluxe® are registered trademarks of Pinnacle Foods Corp.

EAGLE BRAND®

Filippo Berio® Olive Oil

The Hershey Company

Keebler® Company

© Mars, Incorporated 2006

McIlhenny Company (TABASCO® brand Pepper Sauce)

Michigan Apple Committee

Minnesota Cultivated Wild Rice Council

Mott's® is a registered trademark of Mott's, LLP

National Honey Board

Nestlé USA

The Quaker® Oatmeal Kitchens

Reckitt Benckiser Inc.

RED STAR® Yeast, a product of Lasaffre Yeast Corporation

Sargento® Foods Inc.

The Sugar Association, Inc.

Sun•Maid® Growers of California

Unilever

USA Rice Federation

Watkins Incorporated

Wisconsin Milk Marketing Board

Index

Index

METRIC CONVERSION CHART

VOLUME MEASUREMENTS (dry)

$1/8$ teaspoon = 0.5 mL
$1/4$ teaspoon = 1 mL
$1/2$ teaspoon = 2 mL
$3/4$ teaspoon = 4 mL
1 teaspoon = 5 mL
1 tablespoon = 15 mL
2 tablespoons = 30 mL
$1/4$ cup = 60 mL
$1/3$ cup = 75 mL
$1/2$ cup = 125 mL
$2/3$ cup = 150 mL
$3/4$ cup = 175 mL
1 cup = 250 mL
2 cups = 1 pint = 500 mL
3 cups = 750 mL
4 cups = 1 quart = 1 L

VOLUME MEASUREMENTS (fluid)

1 fluid ounce (2 tablespoons) = 30 mL
4 fluid ounces ($1/2$ cup) = 125 mL
8 fluid ounces (1 cup) = 250 mL
12 fluid ounces ($1 1/2$ cups) = 375 mL
16 fluid ounces (2 cups) = 500 mL

WEIGHTS (mass)

$1/2$ ounce = 15 g
1 ounce = 30 g
3 ounces = 90 g
4 ounces = 120 g
8 ounces = 225 g
10 ounces = 285 g
12 ounces = 360 g
16 ounces = 1 pound = 450 g

DIMENSIONS

$1/16$ inch = 2 mm
$1/8$ inch = 3 mm
$1/4$ inch = 6 mm
$1/2$ inch = 1.5 cm
$3/4$ inch = 2 cm
1 inch = 2.5 cm

OVEN TEMPERATURES

250°F = 120°C
275°F = 140°C
300°F = 150°C
325°F = 160°C
350°F = 180°C
375°F = 190°C
400°F = 200°C
425°F = 220°C
450°F = 230°C

BAKING PAN SIZES

Utensil	Size in Inches/Quarts	Metric Volume	Size in Centimeters
Baking or Cake Pan (square or rectangular)	8×8×2	2 L	20×20×5
	9×9×2	2.5 L	23×23×5
	12×8×2	3 L	30×20×5
	13×9×2	3.5 L	33×23×5
Loaf Pan	8×4×3	1.5 L	20×10×7
	9×5×3	2 L	23×13×7
Round Layer Cake Pan	8×1½	1.2 L	20×4
	9×1½	1.5 L	23×4
Pie Plate	8×1¼	750 mL	20×3
	9×1¼	1 L	23×3
Baking Dish or Casserole	1 quart	1 L	—
	1½ quart	1.5 L	—
	2 quart	2 L	—